USES OF
EMOTION

USES OF
EMOTION

Nature's
Vital Gift

Kenneth S. Isaacs

Foreword by Matthew Enos

Westport, Connecticut
London

Library of Congress Cataloging-in-Publication Data

Isaacs, Kenneth S.
    Uses of emotion : nature's vital gift / Kenneth S. Isaacs ;
foreword by Matthew Enos.
        p.   cm.
    Includes bibliographical references and index.
    ISBN 0–275–96236–9 (alk. paper)
    1. Emotions. 2. Affect (Psychology) I. Title.
BF531.I83 1998
152.4—dc21   97–32999

British Library Cataloguing in Publication Data is available.

Library of Congress Catalog Card Number: 97–32999
ISBN: 0–275–96236–9

First published in 1998

Praeger Publishers, 88 Post Road West, Westport, CT 06881
An imprint of Greenwood Publishing Group, Inc.

Printed in the United States of America

(∞)™

The paper used in this book complies with the
Permanent Paper Standard issued by the National
Information Standards Organization (Z39.48–1984).

10 9 8 7 6 5 4 3 2 1

Copyright Acknowledgments

Grateful acknowledgment is given for permission to quote from the
following sources:

Robert C. Solomon, "The Philosophy of Emotions," in *The Handbook
of Emotions*, ed. Michael Lewis and Jeannette M. Haviland (New
York: Guilford Press, 1993), p. 3. Reprinted with permission.

Kenneth S. Isaacs, "Affect and the Fundamental Nature of Neurosis:
Logic and Reality," *Psychoanalytic Psychology* 7:2 (1990): 270. Reprinted with permission from Lawrence Erlbaum Associates, Inc.

NOTHING IS MORE PERSISTENT THAN REALITY

ANY TRUTHS WE FIND
ARE APPROXIMATIONS OF REALITY

Contents

PART III: THE BIOGRAPHY OF AN IDEA

Foreword

No chapter in the typical introductory psychology textbook bedevils my college students as much as the one carrying the seductively plain title, "Emotion." The bear that caused a frightened William James to run through the woods continues to terrorize undergraduate students to this day, at least those serious students who work at trying to make sense of this chapter. Many give up in despair, which is a shame because young adults have a deep longing to come to grips with the complexities of emotion. Almost all of them experience their own ursine worries and long for some understanding of the mysteries of their emotion lives.

The textbook offers many theories. Do we become frightened because we run? That clearly is counterintuitive. Or do we run because the autonomic nervous system activates our fight-or-flight response? That makes sense, but it does not begin to explain the richness of our emotion experience. Perhaps we feel frightened because we cognitively label our physiological arousal as "fear," logical enough with a bear at our heels but not so clear in other situations. Or does the feeling of terror come from an even more surprising source—the muscles in our face? In the facial feedback theory, as a response to the ideational recognition of danger, the face contorts into a universally recognized expression of fear, which informs us that we are afraid. This is provocative, since the face does mirror feelings for at least a few fundamental emotions, yet the face hardly seems logical as the origin of the many subtle feelings that daily bombard our consciousness. And why should it? Why would evolution have created an emotion system that seems inside-out? It seems more logical that facial muscles originally evolved to facilitate functions like chewing, breathing, and even hearing, but not to communicate feelings. That the same muscles also came to be used for communicating emotion states does not mean the feelings originated there.

By this point student readers are well into the textbook chapter on emotion, but have not yet found a plausible explanation of the psychology of emotion. Next comes a bewildering assortment of further questions with answers that are interesting, but which do not speak to what these readers really want to know. Do we think first, then feel, or the other way around? Does the fact that certain emotion expressions are recognized in all cultures show that there are "universal" emotions? And if so, how many? Each of the several theories offers a somewhat different list, which itself weakens the basic idea. Do we work more efficiently when our emotion arousal is higher or lower? Or does it vary with the task? Why doesn't happiness last? How do cultures differ in the ways they rate the intensity of different emotions? Why are "lie detectors" unreliable? Are emotions purely products of the brain, with the ultimate answers about emotion to be found in neuroscience? And so the diligent among my students reach the end of the chapter—and have scarcely caught a glimpse of themselves anywhere in it. Something seems to be missing. None of the classic theories of emotion has triumphed in psychology, and none seems either compelling or potentially helpful to a species increasingly troubled by emotion. The research findings on emotion are in themselves intriguing, but disjointed and unsatisfying to our larger questions.

When one of my students giving a talk about stress asked for a show of hands as she went down a list of everyday experiences of anxiety and tension, I was surprised at how many hands went up for the various psychosomatic symptoms, but when she got to the common symptoms of anxiety there was a forest of hands. The same thing happened when I presented the list included in a recent advertisement for a new "anti-anxiety" medication. I am beginning to think that, at least for students, trouble with emotions could be the modal state. Maybe for faculty, too, judging from the talk among my colleagues when they let their hair down.

When I lecture on the ideas offered in this book, the room becomes quiet and the students more attentive. There is nothing like immediate acceptance, however, because these ideas are too much at variance with everything else a serious psychology student "knows" about feelings. It is more an inaudible wish, "If only that were true . . . , If only I wouldn't have to be uncomfortable with my feelings. . . . " When I go on to suggest the greater richness life could offer when emotions are used, instead of feared and fought, the hunger is almost palpable. Nothing in contemporary psychology speaks clearly and convincingly to these most human needs that I see in my students, and that I am sure therapists, counselors, pastoral workers, and other health professionals sense in the people they are struggling to help. But it is exactly that knowledge that is now available.

With the book you hold in your hands, for the first time we have a radically different view of emotion, devised by theorist, psychotherapist, and writer Kenneth Isaacs. In a nearly lifelong project, Isaacs has worked out a view of emotion that to my mind is more logical, more natural, and far more helpful than any theory offered so far. Isaacs' ideas have had the same effect on many other people, colleagues who have studied his scholarly papers and heard him speak at professional meetings, psychology buffs who have met him or read articles about him, and patients in therapy who have benefited from his ideas. Their common experience is an almost immediate and appropriately visceral realization that Isaacs' approach to understanding emotion seems very right and true. And yet, in the absence of a major theoretical publication, Isaacs' influence has grown only slowly. When this remarkable book finds the audience it deserves—every mental health worker, every graduate student in psychology—that will change.

Dr. Isaacs has practiced psychotherapy in the Chicago area for forty-five years. After earning a B.A. in psychology and economics from the University of Minnesota (conferred while he was serving in the U.S. Army in Europe), he earned a Ph.D. from the University of Chicago. Still searching for a better understanding of psychology, he became the first psychologist to complete psychoanalytic education at the Institute for Psychoanalysis in Chicago. While still a graduate student, he worked as the first administrative chief of psychology for the agency that became the Illinois Department of Mental Health. As Chief Psychologist of its outpatient clinic system, he helped organize psychology departments across the state. Early in his career, Isaacs served as the administrator of several NIH funded research projects in psychoanalysis at the University of Illinois Medical School, taught clinical psychology, and supervised residents in psychiatry. He has been a psychology consultant to school systems and private business, helping develop prevention programs concerned with stress issues, child development, and interpersonal relations. He has been a teacher and a supervisor in psychiatry residency programs at Evanston Hospital and Northwestern Memorial Hospital and a staff member of St. Therese Medical Center.

Kenneth Isaacs developed an early interest in emotion and has written extensively about theoretical issues concerning emotion. In the final two chapters of this book, he tells the fascinating (and at times painful) story of his struggle to obtain a hearing for his new thinking on emotion. Over the years he has written technical journal articles on emotion. He wrote a popular syndicated newspaper column of educational essays in psychology titled "A Psychologist's Notebook," and a sampling of those columns were collected in his book *Again With Feeling*. He has several works in progress, each expanding on themes presented in the present volume.

Finally, and somewhat ironically, in view of his candid aim of transforming the official orthodoxies of emotion and health, Isaacs is a well-respected member of his profession. He has served in leadership positions in a long list of professional associations and has achieved a gratifying degree of professional recognition. He was instrumental in the founding of several psychological organizations and has participated in the continuing governance of those organizations variously as board member, secretary, president, or chairman. Most recently, he has been a founder, secretary, and chairman of the American Board of Psychoanalysis in Psychology, which established the board certification process in psychoanalysis and became a specialty board within the American Board of Professional Psychology (ABPP). He is a member of the board of trustees of that organization.

But it is not his honorable curriculum vitae that explains the remarkable ideas you will encounter in this book. The breathtakingly fresh point of view Isaacs offers springs from a unique blend of the humanist's empathy for all people who are suffering and the scientist's refusal to be content with any theory that cannot withstand the test of falsifiability. (There is a separate chapter on science in this book that I believe you will come to appreciate as both essential to Isaacs' theory and valuable as a framework for judging other theories.) The theory arose from a foundation of thorough understanding of human psychology in all its facets.

All his life Kenneth Isaacs has been a pursuer of truth, never comfortable with a well-established theory or an accepted system of thought when he encountered facts it could not adequately explain. An indefatigable and voracious reader from his childhood, Isaacs devoured home and school libraries in search of understanding. After exhausting his parents' collection, he literally read his way, shelf by shelf, around the room in his grade school library, and has continued to read assiduously ever since. His relentless acquisition of knowledge typically ran well ahead of his formal training. In college he was an outstanding student who always roamed far beyond the "required" material. When the war ended and he came to The University of Chicago to study psychology, he had already read most of the work required in the courses he took. On a national examination of knowledge in clinical psychology, all psychology graduate students in all the major universities took the test. Isaacs achieved the highest score nationally. It is typical of his thirst for comprehension of the field, rather than formal degrees or recognitions, that by the time he took his degree he had accumulated half-again the required number of course credit hours. I tell this history not to make the point that his is a formidable intellect, although I believe it is, but to suggest that Kenneth Isaacs' ideas about emotion are not casual speculation based on scanty knowledge, nor were they easily or superficially arrived at. I think some appreciation of Isaacs' long endeavor to understand emotion may fortify us in our own efforts to grasp his theory.

After graduating with a doctoral dissertation (summarized in Appendix A) that has been widely cited and that some colleagues still refer to as seminal in their own thinking about object-relations differentiation, Isaacs embarked on a career as a psychotherapist and psychoanalyst, authorship of professional papers, leadership positions in psychoanalytic organizations, and an enviable reputation for effectiveness as a practicing therapist. Today Isaacs enjoys an esteem that is less important to him than his satisfaction in solving some of the puzzle. I suspect that Isaacs would prefer his work to be used to benefit humanity by causing us to rethink everything we ever thought we know about psychology, while he personally remains in the background.

And here we come to two problems that interfere with ready acceptance of Kenneth Isaacs' theory of the uses of emotion. The first is that the theory is comprehensive and necessarily complex. An unfortunate but unavoidable defect of this book is that it overwhelms the reader with more ideas, more theory, more ramifications and interconnections than most can bear. There is too much. Readers typically absorb one or another of its parts but not the whole. It touches on and contains too many important implications for many areas of psychology and health and illness. Readers of this book will often have the experience of pausing over a paragraph because in it they discover the germs of a whole new line of investigation. Among his interested following, Isaacs has yet to find anyone who has understood the full range of the theory in a single reading. Nor has he found a way to present his theory in a simple, linear manner. That is because the parts interconnect as a network, and therefore each new insight enriches the ideas the reader encounters both before and after. Many readers, in their second and third reading of the book, will find themselves realizing, "Now I see why. . . ."

The second problem is that Isaacs' new theory won't slip neatly into the interstices between traditional ideas about emotion, psychology, and psychotherapy. If this book is kept on the desktop or bedside table to study again and again and if its ideas are taken seriously and followed to their logical conclusions—here I take a deep breath before I say it—*everything* in psychology must be reexamined. Everything about the functions of emotion and cognition and their interrelation must be reworked. All of our ideas about personality, psychopathology, diagnosis, and psychotherapy must be rethought and reorganized. That is why these new ideas must become a part of every psychology course.

As a lifelong psychoanalyst, Isaacs' goal was to improve his understanding of psychology, not to invent a "briefer" psychotherapy. Yet his more valid theory, combined with the affect tutoring approach he uses, offers the hope of effectively curing, not just treating, and doing so more efficiently than has been thought possible. In addition, Isaacs' theory holds a wondrous potential not only for the prevention of many of the disorders that hamper so many people, but also for the further and even more valuable result of helping multitudes of people experience Nature's gift of emotion vitality in everyday life and the consequent freeing of their creativity.

Paradoxically, so Isaacs has learned from hard experience, the more knowledge one has of past theories, the more difficult it may be to grasp new ideas. Everything in the training of many knowledgeable readers will militate against serious consideration of these ideas. Their past training brings little expectation that the fundamentals of that training may be in error. Therefore they read the new theories as if they should fit on the foundation of their old theory, and that makes the new theory sound preposterous to them. Isaacs' theories are not modifications of what we "know" now, but often wholesale replacements of portions of traditional knowledge. To make matters worse, Isaacs does not hesitate to criticize, and sometimes to criticize harshly, what he views as a received false wisdom that blinds workers and retards progress in psychology. Hardly a way to win friends and influence people in an alien congregation.

This is a book readers will be fascinated by and find hard to put down and to which many will want to return from time to time for further readings. But it's not an easy book and not a simple theory. Will psychology be able to tolerate the idea that much of what has gone before is of only minor importance and sometimes just plain wrong, even harmfully wrong? Isaacs' compelling logic, the internal coherence of the whole theory, and the remarkable results of therapeutic applications tell us that eventually it will win. When psychology begins to consider these ideas seriously, there will be a whole new world to explore and an exciting new maturity to gain. After psychology's torturous history of many diverse investigations into the processes and functions of emotion, Kenneth Isaacs now offers a concept of emotion and its uses upon which an entire new psychology of personality can be constructed. This new psychology would suggest a more logical understanding of the basis of both health and illness, not just a hodgepodge of disorders based on description of symptoms.

Psychology's long and largely fruitless struggle for a valid theory of emotion is remindful of a notorious fictional struggle for maturity, a struggle more humorous but equally fruitless. To paraphrase the famous question with which the novel ends, put by an untiring analyst to a finally spent Portnoy, "Shall we begin?" To the exciting possibilities presented in this book, let us hope increasing numbers of readers of this seminal work will respond, "Let us begin."

MATTHEW ENOS

Preface

It is logical. It is simple. Any genetically built-in process passes from generation to generation and continues to exist if it is either neutral to or supports functions that increase chances of reproduction. The harsh obverse of that rule is that any gene that hampers life in ways that reduce the chances of reproduction is less likely to be passed on and gradually drops from the gene pool. It and the processes it supports disappear. Unfortunately, this simple rule of evolution appears to have been set aside by psychological theorists.

It seems strange that such elegantly simple rules of evolution have been disregarded in so important a matter as the fundamental elements of mind. Of the two major built-in functions of mind—emotion and cognition—cognition has been viewed as always valuable. In contrast, emotion often has been regarded as being of doubtful value and has been repeatedly deprecated as a burden. It is sometimes disparaged as a human defect or a damaging illness that requires treatment. Such low regard for emotion has unfortunately been a common theme in psychological theories. That view of emotion is highly illogical. It is theory based upon erroneous premises. Derivatives of false premises are errors. Such are the various psychological theories that create the theoretic chaos that has confronted us.

By starting from the simple, more realistic premise that because emotion is a built-in process that has continued over the ages, it is useful, we take a divergent path to explore the wonderful implications of its uses. The consequences are profound. Everything in psychology is beneficially changed at least a little bit. Step-by-step new ideas unfold as we follow that path. Views of psychological processes in development, health, and illness are transformed in valuable ways and many old questions are now more satisfactorily answered. More important, new questions are asked and answered. Sixty years of thought, study, exploration, and experimentation have yielded the theory in this volume.

In the past, great efforts had been made in applying understandings, beliefs, and practices of the mental health professions. The accomplishments from those efforts have been so limited it becomes obvious that the theories on which they were based are insufficient. The fact that applications of past theories so often prolong or even worsen conditions shows that they are error-laden.

Other theorists have also formed the same conclusion as I, that anxiety theory is not sufficient as an emotion theory. Some have also suggested that all emotions, not only anxiety, have signal function. They too have noted that each can inform us about what is going on in and around us, that each can initiate ego processes. However, none of those theorists has yet taken the next logical step of inference that theory of neurosis derived from anxiety theory is a mistake.

Had we been aware of need for improvement, we would have eagerly welcomed promising alternatives. That has not happened. Why it has not happened is explained, in large part, by the startling and difficult to accept discovery that perhaps most people are limited in capacity for self-observation. The discovery means that self-observation may be regarded as a talent, and like all talents it is unevenly distributed among people. It is this fact of individual differences in self-observation that may partly explain the continuing common diffidence about some mental processes. Whatever the basis, that omission excludes some wonderfully helpful explanations about psychological function. To those people (perhaps most) who are blind to some parts of the mind, those parts are, of course, nonexistent. Ironically, if self-observation had been a more broadly distributed attribute, the remainder of this book would have been written and understood decades (or centuries) ago.

New sets of descriptions and explanations of the fundamental nature of neurosis, including mental processes transparent or invisible to many people, offer valuable understanding of human mental functioning. These descriptions and explanations assert a new taxonomy of psychological disorders, change definitions and paradigms of treatment, and improve effectiveness of treatment. The discoveries enable both cure (instead of amelioration) and prevention (instead of early intervention) for many previously refractory illnesses. *In order to follow the discussion of theory, readers must tenaciously stay aware of the concept that both emotion and cognition are built-in processes that continue as a part of the human race because they are always useful.* Those who stray from that fundamental concept may find the theory difficult to comprehend.

Acknowledgments

It is not possible to include all who participated in some way during the several decades taken to develop and formulate the theory that I describe in the following pages.

A significant portion of my perseverance in working to discover processes of emotion is attributable to having crossed paths with James Alexander after World War II. In our comfortable bond of friendship over decades we discussed psychological matters that seemed irrelevant to others. With our minds open to take seriously what each other thought, we willingly puzzled about mental process and many other subject matters over whatever time it took to bring some solution, to state a question properly, or to return to the same issue decades later with new ideas to modify it. He contributed much from his greater knowledge of philosophy and logic that augmented my greater knowledge of science. His interests centered on specific emotions. My interests focused on general mental process. We discussed all at great length before they became published articles. That combination of interests with their overlapping focuses was helpful to each. We gave ourselves the luxury of examining issues from points of view of the many schools of thought and when those were unconvincing to us, from fresh looks at what could be. Both of us had the tendency to review each question in relation to fundamental concepts as we understood them. Each offered whatever he could bring to bear on the questions. We both knew and spoke of the fact that for each of us the other made the world seem a bit more logical, a bit more understandable, a bit more sane.

Leslie Phillips played a role in awakening me to the intricacies of the interplay between free association and fantasy. It was his lively intellect that provided my education about the interworking of unconscious, preconscious, and conscious mental content as necessary steps to utilize primary process in attaining comprehension, and how these become of value only after applying a secondary process of careful logical critiquing to search for reality. His were lessons in full usage of all mental processes and avoidance of both wild inductive reasoning and its alternative of such constriction of thought that we exclude all new ideas.

Edoardo Weiss guided me to increased freedom to sense—as well as think—things in my personal way.

Arthur Miller and I combined knowledge to formulate phenomena related to self-observation that he and I had discovered independently along our separate paths, I with Relatability and he in analytic listening to patients. My current views on self-observation developed from that foundation.

Gerhart Piers encouraged my following a path of study of emotion from the point at which psychoanalysis became a drive theory even though that did not seem to have a goal, only an aim.

Lucia Tower seemed to understand that Alexander and I were on the path of something of sure interest and possible worth and encouraged that path.

Donald Fiske was of positive influence supporting the pursuit of what had seemed a questionable path to many others.

John Friedman's sensive awareness of his own emotion process immediately enabled him to understand concepts of uses of emotion. He was helpful and supportive in many ways over decades.

Louis Gross very quickly understood the basic concepts and used new theory in his practice and teaching. His reports of successful use and continuing encouragement has been important to me.

Matthew Enos read and reread my manuscript and offered quantity and quality of help in various ways of value beyond easy description. His support ranged from removing unclarities and redundancies or syntactic folly, to suggested paths to follow in organization, exposition, styles of writing, elaborations and inclusions, offerings of sentences and paragraphs, and in the preparation of camera-ready copy. His many valuable questions and suggestions in discussion of theory and writing, make this book better than it would otherwise be.

It is also important to acknowledge that so many of my patients over decades were contributors by sharing their subjectivity, graciously tolerating my "digressive" pursuits, and endlessly restating what they noticed so that I could finally understand. Even those whose exasperation made them chide and berate me for my stupidity and incompetent interferences were often helpful by doing that.

As all writers and long-term searchers for truths acknowledge, their wives, children, sibs, and colleagues are invaluable in many small ways that get lost in memory but sum to mountainous contributions. Adele tolerated years of my late night, early morning, and weekends of time spent honing ideas, sculpting paragraphs, and in quiet (unsocial) thinking when I might have been a more constant companion. James aided by critiquing and extending ideas to add clarity, offerings from his font of knowledge about computers, and being always supportive. Jonathan offered suggestions for improvements in presentation to make the whole project more palatable to editors in the path to reach readers and more communicative to those readers. Curtis quickly adopted my ideas and when he spoke to others met the same resistance I did. Ted helped with questions, computer operations, editing, and many tasks. Peter repeatedly repaired my grammatical improprieties. Charles was ever supportive of the whole project and helped to keep things in perspective. Reginald was always supportive for many years, though he did not live to see the fruition. All of these and others encouraged my keeping at it despite blank looks from colleagues and discouraging rebuffs from editors and program committees.

Finally, a debt of gratitude is owed to those who performed the many services in the final stages of moving a manuscript to a book. These activities are invisible to readers but crucial in producing a volume that says what it is meant to say and does not distract the reader with poor grammar, spelling, syntax, poor organization, etc. George Zimmar was able to understand the theory presented and find it worthy of dissemination when others had not, and he generously aimed it toward publication. It was a crucial step. James Sabin was able to comprehend the worth of the ideas, accept the quality of the writing, and of vital importance, arranged for publication. Arlene Belzer took the editing process in hand, healed many ailments including footnotes, bibliography, pagination, found redundancies, and repaired other defects beyond my understanding and skills. Megan Hull, with an inch by inch examination, corrected a surprising amount of punctuation, grammatical, and syntactical errors that had passed me by. Other unnamed behind-the-scenes workers performed the many preparations that transformed this manuscript to a bound book on the shelves of bookstores. To all these I express my gratitude.

Introduction: "I Hate Being Angry"

I can still conjure an image of him, although it is so many years ago that I no longer remember his name—I will call him Sean. Burly build, medium height, blonde, pink skinned, pleasant Irish face—together they gave an impression of intense physical energy rippling under a restrained surface. His face was usually expressionless, but occasionally a stern look would surface, only to be immediately covered with an ingratiating smile. He had above average intelligence, which he used in his well-paying, self-taught vocation. The impression he gave was of serious concern about rebuilding a good relationship with his wife.

Sean was in my office because his wife had insisted that she would leave him if he did not do so. Most of the time he was kind, considerate, gentle, concerned, and loving to her—a wonderful companion. But she was terrified (as was he) that he would hurt her in one of his frequent rages. To him, rage appeared suddenly from nowhere. Then he had yelled, pushed, and slapped her, but never bruised her or broke her bones. Those episodes were sufficiently disturbing that she lived in fear of his instant rages that were always unexpected because they were out of keeping with anything going on between them. She knew she could not continue being with him without it breaking her spirit for even her constant caution did not protect her.

He told me that he loved his wife, that she had delighted him in many ways since he first met her. He liked the way her mind worked, her sense of humor, her free expression of emotion, the beauty of her body, and her intensity of involvement in any project she undertook whether it was cooking, decorating, or taking care of their children. I had no question of the sincerity of his love.

It was striking that with his professed intense love and admiration for his wife that what his wife experienced as dreaded hostility erupted from time to time. Of course his rage episodes had not started at age thirty-one; they started in early adolescence. Fresh out of my training, I expected to find some trace of an unconscious pattern of hostility. From theory, it should stem from his early childhood and now be displaced to his wife from that "whomever" and "whenever." I asked him to tell me about the rage that threatened to blast his marriage apart. My naive expectation was that I could help him find that early pattern and, by using knowledge of it, help him to change or disconnect it from his wife.

I listened carefully to discern the pattern I was sure would emerge. Instead, in response to my request to tell me about his rage, I heard his complaint about the terrible (human) burden of emotion. I heard him declare how unpleasant anger was to him. His statement, indelible over decades was, "I hate being angry. I can't stand being angry!" Translation: *Being angry angered him*. Clearly he did not accept emotion experience as the useful, functioning part of him it always is. Instead, he regarded emotion, and especially anger, as a destructive, awesome enemy. He had adopted unfortunate common wisdom about emotion (taken into psychology without examination) that urges the impossible—ejecting, regulating, tolerating, transcending, or somehow managing emotion experience. It was apparent that when he was angry the anger became more important to him than whatever had evoked the anger. Like millions of others, he struggled with the messenger while ignoring the message.

Perhaps it was his great sincerity. Perhaps his story resonated with my awareness since childhood that I and others often had feeling reactions to feelings. Until hearing Sean's words, I had not considered feelings *against* feelings. Perhaps I heard because I had been more involved than most with the study of emotion dynamics. I had assumed that my awareness of emotion process was commonplace and did not have much implication. Only much later did I recognize that the literal emotion processes I knew, which some of us directly observe, are merely hypothetical to many people because they do not, or perhaps cannot, observe them. For whatever reason, from his words, *I heard something new, something more meaningful*.

His statement with its message of contending with emotion, took me away from the standard quest for a singular "cause" in childhood patterns and launched me into decades of considering two causes of problems and disorders instead of one. The long familiar residual conflict resolution pattern search was now paired with thinking about and exploring dynamics of emotion process.

It seems likely that I may very well have started on that same journey from some other genesis at some other time, for my work was heading in that direction. Nevertheless, Sean was the one who triggered the thoughts that moved me along a path. From that start over decades of study, exploration, tests, and in discussions—especially with my friend and collaborator, James Alexander, over the remainder of his life—an alternative psychoanalytic theory of neurosis unfolded.[1]

While I had not yet understood enough to help Sean come to acceptance of his emotion experiences as uncontrollable automatic functions that are always useful, transient, and benign, and because they are, I was able to help him separate the *experience* that is emotion from *actions* that emotions may urge. That understanding was enough to make his home situation far better.

Over the years I have gradually learned that much (if not most) of spouse abuse comes from two major types of abusers. While their behavior is similar, for both types bruise, maim, and kill, what goes on within their minds is different. Thus one basis is in the personality of cruel, callous, insensitive, controlling, unevolved personalities who are relatively free of awareness of their own subjectivity. Their rages often develop visibly, starting from what they see as an affront to their requirements for obedience. Theirs is an insistence on "correcting" or punishing in which they often enjoy cruelty. The desired civilizing in such persons could come only from further maturation in Relatability (see Appendix A) to become considerate of others in a mutual relationship. They can, however, be taught to refrain from abuse by using conscious self-restraint. Some of them respond slowly to psychoanalysis, but most are inaccessible. In contrast, what goes on in the minds of those with more developed personalities, like Sean, occurs with rage storms starting invisibly as contention with emotions—to them it is as if emotions, rather than conditions that evoke emotions, are a problem. Usually such people become rapidly free of storm tendencies when they understand enough about their emotion phobia.

When Sean's statement started me thinking about emotion in a new way, I had been on a path, but moving slowly along it. What evolved has freed people of psychological illness because we now cure instead of treat psychological disorders and may do much more over the years ahead. Many other persons with psychological illnesses have learned from therapists who have read my work to become free of emotion phobia and various psychological disorders and change their lives. It is clear, as I think back to the genesis of the evolving theory, that Sean triggered a sequence of questions, answers, and elaborations resulting in corrections to existing theories of psychological health and illness.

Probably because I was ready to hear about emotion process, the same sequence of questions and answers might have been spawned by others' somewhat similar messages, such as Marilyn Monroe's delightfully perceptive observation that, "It's exciting to be excited." But as a patient who allowed me access to his mind, Sean deserves the credit for nudging me along the path by saying the right words in the right context. What he gained from that was a better marriage with greater comfort with self and others. I gained a lifetime chore and the satisfaction of developing and demonstrating new understanding of personality. Although I have no knowledge of what happened to him in the decades since, I believe that if he had encountered further trouble he would have returned to me.

Our experiences with patients enlighten us, but only when something strikes through the filter of preconceptions built by our hard-won education. Otherwise, we congratulate ourselves for "open-mindedly listening to everything," but in truth only *think* about what we hear after first translating it to the explanatory terms of our indoctrination. That translation marshals whatever understanding exists in current knowledge while imposing constraints limiting us to past concepts and definitions.

NOTE

1. Alexander and I had long before realized that emotion never could store inside us. He originated the concept of affective reaction to affective reaction as potentiation. I conceptualized the consequences of increasing degrees of potentiation and the move from potentiation to self-sustaining emotion storms and their consequences. I suggested the issue of affect phobia, an unease with emotion, as a universal human trouble that led either to (1) emotion muting, bringing unsatisfying lives, distanced and isolated, without vitality and suffering grayed off and limited human emotion experience, or (2) potentiation of emotion and storm leading to many psychological problems, including all the distraught states and psychological symptom disorders.

PART I

A NEW UNDERSTANDING
OF EMOTION

Thinking about Emotion

Fundamental theories are usually simple. It should not be surprising, therefore, that three simple facts that controvert previously held beliefs bring revolutionary advances in understanding and enable psychologists to cure instead of merely treat many psychological disorders. The reasons the facts remained unrecognized are important parts of the story. Crucial, previously unappreciated basic facts about emotion as experience and as process became evident to me during decades of observation, inductive reasoning, thought, questioning, exploration, and study. Their seminal importance becomes discernible when you study the logic of the resulting theory, the astonishing results of applications to a broad array of psychological disorders, and the many implications for psychological health.

The clear finding worth reiterating until it registers indelibly is that *the nature of psychological disorder is different from what has been offered by any past theory*. The benefits from use of these discoveries give far more hope for better lives for multitudes of people.

EMOTIONS ARE FRIENDS NOT ENEMIES

We start with three simple fundamental concepts that are now available as premises for psychology:

1. *Emotion events are always briefly transient, existing only for microseconds, although they often rapidly repeat over lengthy periods*[1]

2. *Emotion functions are always benign and never a danger*[2]
3. *Each emotion always provides constructive function*[3]

These premises and the consequent new theoretical formulations derived from them and elucidated in the next chapter describe many implications of transient, benign, constructive emotion. This new knowledge about fundamentals in the psychology of emotion corrects errors and omissions in the affect underpinnings of theory for all schools of psychology. These three premises launch a cascade of consequent implications that inform us of psychological truths. Each school of psychology eventually will modify its theory by adopting the fact of affect as always transient, benign, and useful. Until that change occurs, psychological theories remain incompetent. Worse, some theories, including mainstream theories, promote applications that are not only wasteful, but are often irrevocably damaging to patients.

MYTHS AND ACTUALITIES ABOUT AFFECT

The following five statements are explicit or implicit universal beliefs. They describe how most people view emotion. Because they are ego syntonic, they are usually unrecognized, autonomous, preconscious ego content—and therefore rarely verbalized. Because they are universal beliefs, they have become (without examination) implicitly premisal to all psychological theory.[4]

1. *Affects can be dangerous*
2. *Affects have no constructive function*
3. *Affects, once evoked, remain in a kind of pressured storage until discharged, and therefore accrue increments to a point of maximal containment*
4. *Affects, while in storage, become a source of damage to the person*
5. *The necessary affect discharge must be accomplished very carefully to cause the least possible damage*

All these beliefs are error. It is our misfortune that psychological theories have incorporated these errors as a part of their underlying premises, although no convincing explanation has been formulated about how affect stores or where it stores (in either psychological or physiological space) nor how it discharges.

Contrast the set of beliefs in the myths with what I believe are the actualities of human emotions:

1. *Affects are vital aspects of human functioning operating as automatic subjective responses to internal and external events*
2. *Affects serve the function of informing us of qualities of internal and external events*

3. *Affects are briefly transient and in their initial reactive form are impossible to store or accrue*

4. *Because affects are transient, their discharge is not mandatory and their expression is optional*

5. *The residual effects of affect experiences are the memories of those affective experiences stored as quiescent affective attitudinal sets; these secondarily autonomous affective attitudes in turn are psychologically vital aspects of personality as they become building blocks of personality and character*

The two lists present a sharp contrast. The myths declare a whole series of dangers and problems that are widely believed to stem from affect. The actualities declare affect a benign, natural, automatic, healthy, transient, useful mental event. The views I hold fit more adequately with facts of careful observation of affect phenomena and accord more adequately with rules of logic. They have a pleasing simplicity of internal concordance, which is a first requirement for a theory, and have proved remarkably useful in application to human matters, which is a second and absolute requirement for acceptability of any psychological theory.

The three fundamental concepts and the lists of myths and actualities of affect form the general backdrop against which we can begin to lay out more carefully the several groups of theoretical underpinnings for a new understanding of emotion and its uses.

Our Dual Mental System

We are born with the advantage of a dual set of mental processes. These two interconnected systems operate concomitantly and relatively independently to perform separate tasks. Their coordination enables us to understand the world and ourselves. One system provides our valuable set of cognitive processes. The other system provides our valuable set of emotion processes.

Cognition and affect are two modalities of mental function, each providing information about evaluations of the events discerned within and around us. These are essentially autonomous processes, even though we may voluntarily work at tampering with their manifestations. Those processes are usually preconscious or unconscious, although their products are consistently conscious. Cognition and affect each appears to include its own underlying system of cataloging and indexing of experience (memory) with separate lines of associative connections. That makes a dual system of indexing of memory of experience available to pursue content and meaning of earlier experience analytically. Thus associative process may be pursued through either a cognitive path or an affective path. The affective path brings information of meaning and significance with it that is not available in the cognitive path, and thus a closer tie to relevance of mental content.

This line of thought has not been pursued seriously in psychological studies, although such investigation would be fruitful.

Being endowed with a marvelous dual mental system gives us great advantage in comprehension of our world—if we use both parts of the system. Attempting to function with only affect or only cognition is to function as crippled. With the former we comprehend feeling without ideational content. With the latter we comprehend thought content without knowing significance.

The most apt description of the pathway used by both interoceptive and exteroceptive raw sensory data is of a passage first to a cortical staging area, and next being routed from there concomitantly to independent cognitive and affective processing systems, each of which provides its own kind of evaluation of the same data for further ego processing. We begin to see in this that there are advantages to the dual processing.

There is a vast literature of studies of cognitive processing. In comparison, studies of affective processing are fewer, and those that exist include many that appear to be fumbling, cloudy, and quite imprecise in what they work with. Many are self-contradictory. This may be a result of our being more accustomed to feeling about what we think than thinking about what we feel.

Cognitive evaluation provides information in the form of ideation. That material includes information such as who, what, where, when, how, and how much. It also includes what has traditionally been thought of as rational, including logic and computation.

Affective evaluation provides equally important information for ego processing. That information includes evaluations of the significance and meaning of events and is presented to us in experiential form (a sense of or a feeling of). These latter evaluations also have a clear, systematic rationality, meaning, and connotation that have not ordinarily been given deserved credence. Affect as discharge has usually been considered a disruptive interference that distracts from more important matters. Affect as signal has been considered a bit of information about conflict (rather than about sensory data in general). Issues of these mental processes and products have been studied in the past without due consideration for other possibilities and important distinctions suggested in what follows here.

If either of these two vital evaluative functions is distorted or diminished, we are deprived of our optimal awareness and comprehension of self and world. Such deprivations may occur from either psychological or physiological dysfunction. It may surprise those who have not previously considered the issues of affect muting and affect storming that the vast majority of the population of the world has suffered such hampering psychologically, and apparently has suffered that over the ages. An important part of the story of psychopathologies is a description of various sorts of diminished psychological function and the implications of each kind and degree of diminution.

Storms always start with impairments placed in the path of access to one's own emotions. Most people make the mistake of trying to "deal with" their emotions. They mistakenly work at trying to manage them, control them, tolerate them, suppress them, or get them out. Instead, we are better off noticing our emotions and using the information they bring because acting on them is optional.

All attempts to "deal with" feelings are unfortunate. For instance, moderate degrees of muting of emotion cause problems such as doubt, indecision, weakened judgment, and an over- or underestimation of the significance of events or actions. Extremes of muting can cause severe disorders.

In other instances, which will be described in detail in chapters 5 and 6, storms can lead to mayhem or murder. When we structure patterns of response to such storms, we develop neurotic phobias, compulsions, physical symptoms, depressions, and paranoias. Newspaper reports of estimates of spousal (and other family) abuse incidents point to thousands of occurrences per day. Understanding of storms could cut that number significantly. Understanding of my concept of Relatability (described in Appendix A) would cut those instances even further.

As mental health professionals learn more about emotion, they cease the futile and sometimes destructive medication of these conditions and turn away from interminable treatments to the simple and (comparatively) rapid cure of the disorders. That is better for all than costly, long-term extension of painful, disabling disorder for only amelioration or palliation.

Our view of affect also places phobia, compulsion, obsession, conversion, multiple personality, and several other troubles as varieties of manifestations of occurrences of the same underlying simple, preventable, curable disorder—affect storm. With this understanding, these disorders usually become simple treatment problems despite the pain and serious disablement they typically involve. The new understanding may eventually remove these and some other disorders from the category of illness. Without proper treatment, however, patients can retain such disorders as chronic incapacity for decades.

Many puzzles about the processes of affect are yet to be solved. That so many issues remain may be due in considerable part to the language of affect and descriptions about affect process often being euphemistic, unclear, imprecise, obscure, and poorly defined. It will take a continuing effort to clarify various aspects of affect so that we can better study and eventually understand its processes and interactions with other mental functions.

Troubled Taxonomy

Perhaps one of the reasons the new principles had not previously been formulated is that our language about emotion has been unclear. With clear definitions as a foundation, we have clearer theories. Many have tried to do this. Strongman,[5] for instance, points to the various views of emotion as conscious experience, psychological states, inadequate adaptation, motivation, as behavior, but reasonably uses the trichotomy of cognitive, physiological, and experiential for his discussions.

The concept that every emotion is always useful, benign function often perplexes those who have not carefully distinguished specific emotion experience as different from *para emotions*—mental events that are not truly emotions but are commonly thought of as emotions. Those who have made only a coarse classification, by grouping all emotion-tinged conditions, states, actions, and feelings, even including some purely cognitive elements as if emotion, have deprived themselves of valuable distinctions. Such looseness of definitions has been apparent in biological psychiatry approaches, behaviorism, cognitivism, all the popular psychologies, and in psychoanalytic theory.[6] Certainly it is common in novels, legal terminology, and other nonpsychological usage. Academic studies of emotion have also been seriously hampered by the assumption that we can group all emotion-tinged mental, physical, and action events together as having the same processes, functions, and sources. Further, all these have been presumed to have the same processes, functions, and sources as pure emotion. It is small wonder that the utility of studies and explanations of emotion has been so limited.

Why the taxonomic confusions among emotions and para emotions have persisted, despite the clear and rather easy to make distinctions we could have made years ago, is a puzzle. Attributing that failure to careless thinking is not a persuasive argument, for we are talking about centuries in which billions of people have lived without seriously questioning the muddled definitions.

Could that have happened if the human race as a whole were not affect phobic enough to avert their minds from issues of affect? Could the general populace have accepted the anxiety-centered affect theory proposed by Freud if they were not averting their minds from serious thought about emotion? Would they not have seen through the superficiality of the single emotion theory if they had noticed affect dynamic processes of each of the large variety of emotions that were operating within themselves?

Para emotions have processes and functions different from those of pure emotion. They are unlike what we may call real or pure emotions in that they are not necessarily transient, benign, or useful. We may categorize the varieties of para emotions as those mental processes that may include emotion plus other elements, those that evoke emotion, and those personality elements we often mistakenly consider emotion but that are not emotions. Recognizing the following varieties of para emotion gives the psychology of emotion greater precision.

Complex states that include emotion along with other components are often mistaken for emotion.

- Healthy states such as *love* and *hate* are examples of para emotions that include emotions, but being affective attitudes, also include expectations, beliefs, aims, etc. That is why they do not (cannot) function as pure emotion evaluations, despite their poetic usage in literature and psychology and their great importance in our lives.

  Pathological states can be para emotions. The word *depression* is often taken to mean "a lot of sadness." That is why people commonly say they "feel depressed about . . . " when they are "sad, grieving, or mourning about . . . . " A *phobia* is often taken to be a lot of fear. People say they "feel phobic about . . . " when they mean "afraid about." The term *paranoia* is often used to convey a lot of suspiciousness. People say they are "paranoid about so-and-so" when they mean they "don't trust so-and-so." When any of these para emotions is taken to be a pure emotion, it brings mistakes that have taken theories and therapies on wild-goose chases or into blind alleys that have impeded healing.

- Internal and external conditions that evoke emotion, such as frustration, inadequacy, superiority, or inferiority, are all too often loosely spoken of as emotion, although they are not. People commonly say, "I feel frustrated!" They intend the phrase to convey a feelingful experience of some sort. However, "frustration" is not a feeling, but is a situation in which one is blocked or balked, a situation that usually evokes emotion. The feeling response that is evoked is a response to the condition of frustration, of being balked. That feeling response may be any of several emotions (anger, sadness, resentment, joy), depending on the person and the meaning of the situation for that person. Confusing a situation with a feeling about the situation impedes understanding people and their life situations. Comparable confusions exist with conditions and attributes mistakenly expressed as feeling inferior, superior, esteem, confused, lost, bewildered, etc.

- Ego processes as patterns that direct one's constraint or release of actions are often considered emotions, although they are not. These processes often are derivative of superego function and are patterns of style of personality and character.

- *Temper* is an example of a para emotion that can be understood better as a personality attribute related to degree of control over actions. (The common phrase used is of a person "having a temper" to describe what would be more accurately conveyed by the opposite phrase, a "loss of temper," as being "untempered," or "without temper.")

- *Obsequiousness* is an example of a characteristic attitudinal stance that is not an emotion, but is a derivative of emotion experience.

- *Hostility* is a para emotion that belongs in the category of affective attitude. It often includes components of anger or other emotions such as scorn, disgust, and contempt. It has often been confused with emotion.

- *Competitiveness* is a para emotion that belongs in the category of affective attitude. It can have emotion components of envy, jealousy, greed, false pride, covetousness, and attitudes of vengeance or emulation.

- *Controllingness* is a para emotion in the category of attitudinal stance, a pseudo-emotion that is tightly bonded to the Delta level stage of development.[7] It is important, especially to those who have not yet evolved to the emotion of trust in self or others, and is urgently vital to those who are insecure about their ego boundaries. Popular language looseness brings another type of para emotion in which the introductory phrase "I feel that . . . " is foggily joined with opinions, ideas, judgments, or beliefs. It is often used in an attempt to make those dissemble as emotions. These latter sorts of statements belong in the category of pseudo-emotions within the category of para emotions. The economists' statement, "I feel that interest rates will go up" is not a feeling statement. Instead, it is an intellective opinion or a prediction about which the speaker wishes to declare only a moderate level of confidence. This erroneous usage debases emotion by using the term "feeling" to describe imprecise thought. Feeling, however, is not second-class thought.

- Emotion is neither a thought process nor imprecise. Such distortion of terms and concepts also stems from and promotes foggy comprehension of mind and mental processes.

- Voluntary and involuntary *physical reactions,* such as *laughing, crying, weeping, increased pulse rate, sexual arousal, rapid breathing,* etc., may typically have close connections with emotion, but are not in themselves emotions.

The confused mixture of emotions and para emotions has bemused the field of mental health and not merely stopped progress, but, unnoticed, also has stultified the field for many decades in its corruption of rationality despite pretensions of building a serious science. Hundreds of thousands of therapists sincerely engage in the daily activity of faithful pursuit of health and comfort for their patients, while working with a hodgepodge of definitions that cloud their theories, confuse their thinking, and obstruct their aims. But the therapeutic and preventive usefulness of understanding the internal coherence and meaningfulness of the categories of each mental element described here follows logically. These distinctions of categories are valuable aids in clarifying mental processes in health and illness.

One of the several minimal requirements for a therapist should be a capacity to distinguish between observations of feeling and thought. Nothing like this is taught or required in clinical training programs. Elusiveness of solutions for psychological problems in the past is directly correlated to amount of reliance on euphemistic descriptions.

Muddled Language. A current popular psychology theme relates to level of self-esteem. Proponents imply that the basic psychological issue for healthy functioning is the building of a "feeling of self-esteem" to make one's life good. It may be an unfortunate offshoot of Kohutian[8] self-psychology declaring self-esteem to be fundamental rather than the underlying issue it is. One now regularly hears that theme on radio and television talk shows and in various media presentations. The notion that one should have esteem for oneself, regardless of one's conduct, achievements, failures, or character, is an excellent example of how affect phobia has led to the degradation of language and from that to a degradation of thought in psychological theory.

Confusing the concepts of feeling and cognition confuses more than the words, it confuses the issues involved. Working with intellective processes and mistaking them for affective processes decreases our likelihood of solving problems in either cognition or affect. We judge esteem as we judge inferiority or superiority. The original dictionary meanings of the word esteem are "estimate, evaluation, estimation, judgment, favorable opinion, regard, respect, account, worth, reputation, estimate value, to deem to think [of] the number, quantity, magnitude of anything, to think, be of opinion." Thus the dictionary correctly defines esteem with cognitive meanings, although at the end the list begins to wander from these into the error of a few feeling meanings. The lexicographer finally strays into the general trap of fusing the processes of emotion and cognition and ignoring the roots of words. The problem arises from generations of speaking (and thinking) carelessly, as when the definition migrates from recognition of a *feeling about* one's perceived inferiority to become a *feeling of* inferiority.

It is the mark of popular psychologies to degrade words, concepts, thought, and theory, aiming to offer a simplified understanding the public can easily absorb. Because of that simplification, the information usually becomes distorted. It would be a travesty if our universities and even our specialized professional training institutes produced graduates who readily settle for euphemisms with increasing indifference to meaning.

Anxiety as the All-Purpose Emotion. Besides the importance of recognizing that para emotions are different from emotions, we can abandon the limiting concept that anxiety is the paradigm and the only important emotion. By making that shift, we recast the entire metapsychological structure based on that paradigm. That is a formidable, unwelcome task for most in the field of mental health. *But that highly esteemed, entrenched theory, offered as an affect theory, has itself been a formidable barrier to advancement of knowledge instead of being the enlightening concept it has been held out to be.*

Anxiety does not serve well as a multiuse concept. The concept of anxiety is not sturdy enough to carry the entire burden of complex affect process. That is one reason the effectiveness of applications of anxiety theory has been so limited. We can profit from narrowing, rather than generalizing, the meanings of each specific emotion. In particular, we can stop confusing anxiety with eagerness, apprehension, fretfulness, worry, tension, uneasiness, and fear. Drawing conclusions about the meaning and process of anxiety from such a melange of meaning is a futile activity. We can move on from the belief that anxiety is the singular generative factor for energizing symptom formation to reach understanding of how any emotion, when potentiated by an emotion evoking more emotion, can create symptoms.[9] We can understand how the processes in emotion storms are very different from the processes in anxiety, and how a variety of other emotion dynamics function to create health and illness. Once we absorb all that, the regularity of the processes of pure emotion and the different regular processes of para emotions can be more easily recognized as each being in a separate class, following its own roots and rules and having singular effects. Along with this we can abandon the growing use of the unfortunate wandering euphemism "anxiety disorder," which has confused thought about health, illness, and treatment in recent years.

Several other writers have also noticed that anxiety is no longer sufficient to carry the weight of a theory of emotion. Despite that they have not suggested the obvious implicit consequent that the theory of neurosis depending on anxiety theory must change.[10] The beneficial move away from the single affect theory is now underway. But once it is generally acknowledged that anxiety theory is not sufficient as emotion theory, the psychoanalytic theory of neurosis, insofar as it is founded on anxiety theory, is revealed as incompetent and must fall away to be replaced by new theory. That involves a "sea change."

A New Understanding of Simple Emotion

All these ideas together create a new understanding of simple emotion. It is separate from complex states (depression, phobia, temper, love, hate) and from emotion-evoking circumstances (frustration, inadequacy, inferiority). It is different from attitude, opinion, and judgment used foggily as in "I feel that interest rates will go up . . . " (as if feeling is a kind of imprecise thought process). Most important, when we give up the obsolete idea that anxiety is the paradigm and only important emotion, then the regularity of the processes of emotion may be seen as scientifically lawful aspects of personality, so their therapeutic and preventive usefulness become apparent.

Beyond making the distinction between affect and cognition, it aids theoretical clarity to recognize the specificity and precision of emotions. At an earlier time I described it as follows:

> If we are not affect blind, we have feeling awareness. We know very clearly what each emotion is. We know quite distinctly and precisely without confusion that we are frightened, angry, ashamed, sad, surprised, lonely, joyful, guilty, hopeful, irritated, annoyed, furious, enraged, apprehensive, remorseful, anxious, thrilled, lonesome, eager, grieving, vengeful, awed, disgusted, bitter, trustful, compassionate, despairing, delighted, suspicious, resentful, indignant, indifferent, regretful, loathing, fond, displeased, satisfied, calm, sorry, overwhelmed, ecstatic, uneasy, admiring, zestful, playful, gleeful, etc. Rarely are we likely to be unsure of which feeling we are experiencing. Rarely are we likely to be indefinite about the feeling. To look upon

emotion as imprecise is to misconstrue the nature of emotion experience in all its distinctive variation. Each emotion is a precise, clear message telling us quantitatively and qualitatively something about what is going on in and around us. The message is not merely proximal. It is a very exact message. This exactness is comparable to the exactness of color sense in those who are not color blind. (For instance, each person knows instantly and without question whether they are seeing red or blue.) The intellective sphere on the other hand is susceptible to error, vagueness, generality, and imprecision (in such matters as memory, conceptualization, calculation, or estimation), but receives undeserved credit for precision, clarity, and relevance compared with emotion. If one seriously considers the reality of multifarious distinct feelings that humans experience, it becomes absurd to consider that feelings represent the general, imprecise, or uncertain. It becomes even more absurd to omit this major vital aspect of mind from centrality in psychological theories as has been done in fatal flaws of behavioral and cognitive theories. The consistent implication is that an emotional human being is a defective human being; that a freely emotional human is pathological.[11]

The total work described in this book comprises an extensive, complicated alternative theory of emotion markedly divergent in fundamental assumptions from past theories of affect. In many ways, these revisions are significantly more useful for theoretic explanations and sometimes astonishingly more useful clinically. The revisions touch on issues of development of personality and character and suggest an alternative explanation of some psychological disorders, particularly the classic neuroses. Consequently, therapeutic approaches to these disorders are implied that are somewhat at variance with traditional approaches.

I present a simple alternative set of hypotheses for consideration. These explanations applied to psychopathology provide important clues to treatment—particularly of symptom disorders—and the psychogenic bases of character pattern disorders.

A clinical emotion theory based on transient rather than stored (or accumulated) emotion provides a very different set of explanations of clinical phenomena. This alternative set of explanations has proved very useful in understanding, ameliorating, and finally achieving permanent cure of several psychological disorders.

If we adopt the view that emotion is a mental event produced as evaluative response to each mental focus and fades immediately, we are relieved of many sorts of tasks that are central to so many therapies—ejection, control, management, modulation, regulation, release, or tolerance of emotion. Instead, when we understand emotion as a benign momentary bit of information, we stop fighting emotion; we stop fearing emotion. Each emotion then becomes neither ignored as trivial nor focused upon as an awesome event. It becomes a mental process useful to us instead of an unfortunate mental pathology needing treatment or some sort of "dealing with."

NOTES

1. Current neurophysiological knowledge supports this premise even though our subjective experiencing usually reads emotions as if they were enduring and storable states.

2. Activities aiming to tame, modulate, control, regulate, tolerate, deny, express, release, repress, or fight emotion are wasted effort. Even worse, any such contending with and dealing with emotion is itself a pathology.

3. If emotions were destructive, or even if they were merely useless, evolutionary forces would have dropped them from the human repertoire of response a few million years ago. Aristotle observed that "Nature does nothing uselessly" (*Politics*, Book 1, Chapter 2). Usefulness of emotions becomes evident to us once we carefully apply logic in first defining and then studying them.

4. In this book, the terminology will closely follow that used by many psychoanalysts. The term *affect* refers to felt experience subsuming both the physical and mental feeling experiences. *Emotion* will be used to refer to mental feeling experience such as sad, mad, frightened, joyful, and admiring. The term *appetite* will be used as the closest term to denote highly motivating physical feeling experiences such as hunger, thirst, and lust, even though other physical experience fall into a category of less intensely motivating drives, such as chilled, nauseous, fatigued, or sated require a different term. In many instances, the distinctions between affect and emotion or emotion and appetite are immaterial so that affect and emotion are synonymous. In other instances, the difference is important enough to be distinguished. Such matters are followed as carefully as possible in this book.

5. K. T. Strongman, *The Psychology of Emotion*, 2d ed. (Chichester, Eng.: John Wiley and Sons, 1978).

6. Patients frequently tell their physicians that they have pain (or other sensation) in their stomachs. Listening to that, most physicians have consistently considered the possibility that the pain might be in the stomach or in some other organ of the abdominal cavity. They generally accept that the public may use terms with less precision than professionals and allow for that. Mental health professionals have moved from the specific to the general by adopting the common parlance of the public. The damage from use of such murkiness of definition has been that theory, diagnosis, and treatment lack specificity and therefore are too filled with error to be as useful as they could be.

7. Throughout this book there are references to "Delta level," "Gamma level," etc., in discussions of personality and character. These terms are described in Appendix A, in which the reader will find a concise description of this object relations differentiation concept.

8. H. Kohut, *The Analysis of the Self* (New York: International Universities Press, 1971).

9. Again an issue here is how theories have gone wrong apparently because the theorists depended upon insufficient awareness of the full span of affective experience. If theorists consciously experienced only the powerful emotions, only those would be deemed worth theorizing about, for the less intense emotions would be known only as intellectual abstractions, not as feeling experience, and therefore of trivial importance.

10. See M. Kissen, *Affect, Object, and Character Structure* (Madison, Conn.: International Universities Press, 1995).

11. K. S. Isaacs, "Crisis Intervention and Affect Theory." Paper presented at the midwinter meeting of the American Psychological Association, Division 29, San Antonio, Texas, February 1981. This passage was later included in Kenneth S. Isaacs, "Affect and the Fundamental Nature of Neurosis: Logic and Reality," *Psychoanalytic Psychology* 7:2 (1990): 270 and thus accessible as a published paper.

2

Elements of a New Theory

By adopting more valid basic facts about emotion, we can contrive a more valid personality theory. Those better basic facts derive from the fundamental concepts about affect, the actualities of emotion, and an improved taxonomy of emotion, all described in the previous chapter, and the several new discoveries to be presented in this chapter. The theory of health and illness becomes increasingly informative and useful as we add and interweave the discovered principles.

PRINCIPLES OF EMOTION: BASIC DISCOVERIES

We have available a cluster of new ideas. Each of them is singly of some importance, but when interwoven, can support complex explanations of psychological process.

Emotion and Cognition Are Equally Useful Mental Functions

By recognizing that emotion and cognition are each natural mental functions operating as independent, interconnected systems that concomitantly evaluate the same sensory data, we recognize that each emotion, as well as each idea, brings us information about what is going on in and around us. Affect offers its information in the form of feeling experience. Cognition offers its information in the form of idea. From following the ramifications of benign, useful affect, we gain comprehension of how each emotion participates in our personalities and in our moment-by-moment living.

Both emotion and cognition function to evaluate and tell us, each in its own way, something about what goes on in and around us. These are not duplicative for each kind of information is distinctive and supplements what the other provides. Thus sensory data is cognitively evaluated, bringing a yield of factual, logical, ideational comprehension. That includes who, what, when, where, how, and how much. Simultaneously, independent emotion evaluation of that same sensory data brings a yield of feeling experience, giving meaning and vitality to our comprehension of what goes on in and around us.

While ideation orders, measures, and counts the sensory data of current focus, we need emotion to "move" us in relation to the significance and meaning of the content of that data. From this point of view, both may be considered rational. The emotion system (from our current knowledge) is seemingly the simpler of the two, which may be why it is the more accurate and precise in accomplishing its task. The intellective appears to be more complex. That may be one of the reasons why, contrary to popular belief, it is often the more error prone and imprecise in performing its task.

Emotion plays its particular valuable role by informing us about the significance of those inner and outer events. Each emotion serves by providing the type of feeling experience message that by its quality informs us of the meaning of the event evoking it and by its intensity informs us how important the event is to us. No emotion, whether pleasurable or painful, has a more important function in this evaluation system than any other among the roster of emotions. Despite a series of misguided (sometimes elaborate) theories attempting to declare a primacy of anxiety, anger, guilt, shame, or fear in the processes of psychological development, health, and illness, each of these emotions takes its place as merely equal in importance to all other emotions, such as hope, loneliness, pride, or surprise.[1] Each emotion has its own important special function.

Psychology has a serious and growing problem of taxonomy. Particularly, emotion theory has cloudy, rambling sets of definitions of what we mean by "emotion." If we accept that we have two major mental functions—cognition and affect—that are debatably left and right brain hemisphere activity, it seems likely that parsimonious Nature has made those brain functions parallel. My studies are corroborative of that view.

It is clear that with theory of intellective matters we do not burden our concept of the mental event "idea" with a variety of mental and physical elements, even if they are often closely associated with thinking, and then study the whole concoction as if all are essentially idea. Why should we lumber the concept of the mental event *affect* with associated actions, physiological processes and states, etc., and then study that admixture as if it is all an integral mental event? I believe that such fusing of mental events with other sorts of functions is one of the reasons we have a chaotic current theory of affect. To me, what we have in the current state of affairs compares with mistaking a glomerate for an indivisible molecule of some entity. In order to understand human emotion, we should be working with the simpler equivalent of atoms or, better yet, of subatomic particles.

With the advantage of the purity of such an unencumbered definition, affect is recognized as one of the two built-in autonomous mental processes that serve to evaluate sensory data. It provides its information in the form of specific feeling experience. By the quality and intensity of experience evoked, such emotion events tell us the significance and meaning to us of whatever is in the focus of our minds, whether conscious or unconscious. *Because it is completely autonomous it is unamenable to regulation, modification, management, control, or "dealing with." Such activities are possible with related elements, not affect itself.*

Working from that definition, we begin to clear away some of the mystery and confusion that surrounds much of the study of mind. For instance, neurosis can be viewed helpfully as significantly different from what it has been thought to be. One enters a whole new world of understanding psychological development, physical as well as mental health and illness, treatment, longevity, the freeing of energies for social interactions, creativity, comfort in everyday life, qualities of experiencing life, use of intellect, drug use, etc.

Various elements of mind, physiology, and action that are so often associated with affect are real and important. Nevertheless they do not fit within a differentiated specification of affect. Their past inclusion, as if affect, has interfered with, rather than enhanced, scientific advance.

We need to start over with a more logical, more scientific approach. We need to revise Freudian theory of neurosis and treatment, forget Tomkins' (and his sequaces') ideas about storage, regulation, and discharge, ignore the pop psychologies with their ideas of affect excretion, and put behavioral and cognitive theories in perspective as partial theories. The resulting platform for understanding minds and their processes can be better coordinated with understanding of physiology and brain. Of more importance, the usefulness of applications of psychology will be greater.

All Emotion Is New Emotion (Affect Does Not Store)

Affect is a nerve-mediated mental process. As with all nerve-mediated processes, the sensory data transmitted to the central nervous system and the message of response speedily move as electrical impulses along nerve fiber in pulsing action and then subside. That process (and its speed) means the duration of each affect event can only be microseconds. The *objective* rapidity of the repetition overrides the interruptions and gives the *subjective* impression of a much longer continuous state. In that, it is comparable to our subjective impression in the visual processes.

We evoke affect as an evaluation of whatever mental data is within a conscious or unconscious focus at any moment. The particular affect repeatedly appears and vanishes during whatever time we hold a focus on a particular mental content. A different affect appears in relation to each new mental focus. As with all such processes, there is no storage of the specific electrical energy used; instead, there may be a memory of the evocative event and a memory of the affect evoked by it. Without the existence of storage of affect as some kind of substance or potential, the affect that appears in response to recall of a memory of some affect-evocative occasion can be only new replications of the original affect in response to a mental focus on that memory of the original occasion. That is not re-presenting a "piece" of the original affect (as energy or substance). Although the new affect event is very often similar in kind and intensity, that happens because it is the same person with the same personality reacting anew in the same way to the similar sensory data.

Thus the evoked emotion does not move into some kind of storage with the prospect of causing trouble while waiting to be expelled, as common belief has had it. Instead we have new affect evoked either by new data or by old (remembered) data. Because it is a new affect event, the processes in emotion response are quite different from what they would be if there were a reappearance of a "chunk" of the old affect that is retrieved and then perhaps returned to storage. The ejective "discharge" of affects (so-called catharsis or abreaction) rarely gives even the appearance of relieving the pressure of some stored stuff, despite the claims of the affect ejective schools of therapy. Indeed, the term "discharge" is a poor description of the process involved, just as it would be for the visual process.[2]

Affect residuals are of a different form. Emotion appears and vanishes in rapid pulsations, giving us information of its evaluation and then vanishing. Because there is neither place nor system of storage, it leaves only a memory of its occurrence. After that memory is sufficiently supported by emotion repeatedly evoked in response to similar events, it structures into a residual, prepared reaction pattern in the form of an affective attitude. That may be the common basis of internally generated individual attitudes.[3]

By moving to this more valid view of microsecond transient affect, rather than affect enduring for hours, minutes, or even seconds, we gain more understanding about emotion in health and illness. We have a new basis for comprehending the deviant paths of a variety of illnesses (such as phobia, compulsion, multiple personality, anorexia, some homosexualities, reactive depression, and conversion) that have been the object of impotent psychotherapy efforts for so many years. The simple new explanations usually make those illnesses minor treatment problems.

Affect Phobia, Potentiation, and Storms Are the Root Causes of Symptom Disorders

The belief that after we evoke an emotion we hold it in storage in some undefined way until we eject it is a creed that has caused great mischief for the human race. It has created an attempt to accomplish an unnecessary and impossible task—the task of trying to eject or in some way "deal with" the danger of emotions that have already automatically vanished.[4]

The belief that emotion stores typically brings a concern to people that their accruing affect content may exceed their available capacity for storage and discharge. This concern generates an unfortunate belief in a necessity for emotion ejection.

Most schools of psychology that consider affects as a part of their theory have, in various ways, adopted the unexamined common wisdom error that storage and discharge are appropriate descriptions of affect process as a central fact at the core of both healthy functioning and symptom creation.

The concern with storage generalizes to a concern about both affect and its storage. Because of the universal concern that problems result from the storage of emotions, extreme discomfiture and unease about one or another emotion or appetite is universal. I believe the most suitable term for that state of mind is "affect phobia." It is an important basis of psychological pathology through two derivative processes.

First, as increasing intensity of affect phobia promotes increasing repression of emotion awareness, the result may be the proportionally increasing degrees of emotion muting. Affect phobia at even moderate intensity thus can impair access to feeling, resulting in uncertainty, indecision, and judgmental deficiencies. With a greater intensity of affect phobia, a decrease in emotion awareness results in emotion muting to the point of depersonalization. It is easy to understand why that disorder has occurred in almost everyone at some time in their lives and is especially likely during adolescent turbulence.

When emotion phobia at great intensity engenders potentiation instead of repression, a different set of issues and disorders ensues. In this second type of response to emotion phobia, the unease with emotion creates a tendency to be further excited about emotion and to respond to an emotion response with a further emotion response. That in turn creates increasingly powerful emotion responses. This sequencing can potentiate emotion to such a point as to create a temporarily self-sustaining emotion storm. These storms are described at considerable length in chapter 6.

Freedom from affect phobia speeds the associative and observing processes, and that makes character analysis far swifter because it allows increased awareness of the breadth of patients' associations. This enhancement occurs because our dual mental processes are freely operating and freely noticed. Many patients have fought hard against my efforts to pursue the emotion issues first, before moving to the classic analytic pattern they had learned was the "right" way to go about things. However, many more patients, after having freed themselves of affect phobia, have even engaged effectively in self-analysis because they can consider a broader panorama of associative material with a reduced tendency to fight off or reject that mental content.[5]

In the past, various theoretic formulations had been devised and became popular by proposing that either emotion or cognition is crucial and the other process is not important. Either type of those partial theories are alternatives that deny and therefore omit the value of the natural dual processes of the dual mind with which we have been endowed. Those partial theories do not encompass a sufficient grasp of mind to be explanatory, thus their dismal treatment outcome record. For full mental function we need to use both ideation and emotion. The dysfunction or absence of either cognition or emotion is mentally crippling. That is why any competent psychological theory has to encompass and integrate both.

Universally we have taught people that emotions, or at least some of them, are big events that unfortunately are disruptive, interfering, and destructively dangerous. Therefore most people seem to believe that at least some emotions must be contended with, ejected, controlled, managed, tolerated, modulated, or suppressed. One of the common illogical treatments are represented by "anger clinics" and "anger therapies" that intensify affect phobia by teaching people to fight, control, or resist anger. When we come across an anger therapist we can be sure we have found a therapist who does not understand emotion. Many ways of "dealing with emotion" have been suggested in the various schools of psychology. Those schools that try to foster such "dealings with" fail to recognize that because emotions are built-in automatic experience processes, they cannot be regulated, prevented, controlled, managed, or "dealt with."[6] They can only be noticed, used, responded to, or ignored. At risk to psychological health, they are ignored as trivial, overresponded to as if irresistible, or fought as if dangerous.

Specific Symptom Disorders Result from the Conflation of Storm with Character and Personality Patterns

Emotion storms turn normal, idiosyncratic mental processes into symptoms. This happens because the individual's characteristic psychodynamic patterns, which determine and enable a consistent pattern of response to moment-by-moment everyday life events, become exaggerated by storm process. This is not, as had previously been thought, because the psychodynamic patterns involved are pathological. It is because the healthy psychodynamic patterns are drawn into distorted misuse by virtue of the excitement of emotion response to emotion response consuming an unusual amount of mental energy. To supply this, mental energy seems to be diverted from cognitive function to affect process, thus depriving intellectual processes of required energy. Capacity for intellective activity during a storm is reduced so the imbalance momentarily makes any of us intellectually incompetent, incapable of sufficient judgment for critiquing whatever goes on in or around us.

It is during such mental conditions that the flow of sensory and other data continues at its usual pace while the capacity for intellective critiquing of that data is so diminished that ability to discern or judge becomes quite defective. Errors of judgment of all sorts may ensue. The subjective experience during storms is sometimes reported by patients as if the imbalance occurs from an extraordinary overabundance of ideas rather than a temporary inundation of the momentarily underpowered intellective system. The intellective processes, in their energy deprivation, are reduced to habit or rote patterns of operation or to happenstance acceptance or rejection of ideas. The limited remaining capacity is overwhelmed by what seems to be a flood to the processes of recognition, processing, and critiquing—but it is that now this processing of the ordinary flow of data for critiquing is more than the underenergized system can handle—it cannot keep up with the ordinary flow.[7]

At such moments we may appear to others to be psychotic although the mental condition is more nearly that of idiocy. The problem is insufficiency of available intellect rather than disarrangement or derangement of thought process.[8] Also, in storm states the ego's integrative capacities are weakened, allowing what have been called dissociative illnesses.

The fourth theory gives us new ways to understand the human difficulties that have been called neuroses. Although all the symptom neuroses turn out to be the same disorder at base, from a surface view the usual manifestations have made each disorder appear to be very different from the others. In psychoanalysis, it had been thought that individual faulty psychodynamic patterns built from resolution of conflicts creates the basis of each neurosis. Many other schools have adopted that view. Compromise formations have been searched for in personal analyses to rebuild newer and better resolutions. With each better resolution of conflict, there is one less psychodynamic trigger for anathematized emotions, and therefore the frequency of triggering of symptom episodes is reduced. Through psychoanalytic treatment the patient becomes healthier in this sense of reduced number of triggers. That has been the typical, protracted path undertaken by analysts. They have diligently sought real, relevant issues that, lamentably, despite their conviction, happen to have trivial importance in cause and cure of symptom disorders.

With recognition of storm disorders and their processes we reach elements of symptom disorders that are not only relevant, but more significant. This repositions psychodynamics as only a minor factor in those illnesses. Psychodynamics play a role in determining what sorts of events will trigger a storm in a person susceptible to storming. But we now understand that emotion dynamic (not psychodynamic) processes are the determining factors in storms and therefore are the determining factors in neurotic episodes. That is why there is considerable advantage in removing the susceptibility to storming. It means that regardless of how many psychodynamic triggers continue to exist in a person they no longer have anything to activate. Sufficient conditions for symptom disorder no longer exist. The disorders cannot occur. *Because these latter processes, the emotion dynamics, are complicit in the formation of a whole series of symptom disorders, they are ultimately more important than specific psychodynamics in working to cure or prevent the whole category of storm disorders.* Freedom from storms makes one free of all such neuroses. Freedom from psychodynamics is not possible, of course, for these constitute our personalities.

Because psychologists have not worked with a competent unifying concept of the fundamentals of psychological disorder, they have resorted to classifying disorders by specificity of symptom manifestations. Erroneous approaches to diagnosis have involved making distinctions where the differences were superficial, and failing to consider important distinctions that were present. Compulsive disorders have been separated from phobic disorders as if they are basically (instead of superficially) different illnesses. Further, a general category of phobia subsumes several subcategories as if they were intrinsically distinct disorders according to the object of the phobia. Thus, agoraphobia has been distinguished from bug phobia, and phobias related to specific bugs (spider or cockroach phobias) are each considered as if they are very different problems. Such a distinction, in which the differences are peripheral to the disorders, has unfortunately brought different diagnoses and treatments for differing manifest symptoms of the same illness instead of direct treatment of the underlying affect phobia. Because the attention of therapists was diverted in this way to superficial, idiosyncratic, or irrelevant symptoms without recognition of the identity of underlying processes, it is natural that we have had more than a century of treatment focus on triggers and symptoms rather than the underlying bases of the disorders.

With our new understanding of emotion process, we find that we can treat and cure all symptom disorders (phobias such as agoraphobia, bug phobia, claustrophobia, heterophobia, and varieties of conversion, panic, multiple personality, compulsion, and anorexia) as a single disorder. Treatment of the underlying major factor is so straightforward and comparatively rapid that cure of these disorders long held to be difficult, refractory illness is no longer a large or long-term challenge to the field of psychology. The new and more important challenge becomes that of eradicating these illnesses by preventing them, so that future generations will be free of the burden of symptom disorders.

Because Symptoms Are the Result of Storms, Cure and Prevention Ensue with Freedom from Storms: Knowledge of Affect Sets One Free

In the absence of knowledge, we can resort only to some sort of technique that has been devised to help with some other problems, hopeful that it will also take care of mysterious processes and bridge our ignorance. Perhaps worse, we create a fictional theory, make a superficial test of it, and sell to the public technique appropriate to that fiction, with claims that it is a scientifically based approach for psychological disorders. The mental health field has spawned many such technical approaches. But test of process and results are always necessary so that efficaciousness can be established for each approach.

As the actual processes of emotion become understood by therapists, their enlightenment about affect phobia, emotion muting, potentiation, and storm helps patients include emotion in guiding their lives. A marvelous change occurs with this insight. The swift "going away" of the illnesses that so frequently happens is only a small part of that change. The change in the details of the everyday lives of patients is far greater and, in the end, far more consequential to the person than the urgently necessary pursuit of freedom from a disabling disorder. For these people, emotion becomes a natural, useful part of their mental processes and they develop an ease with themselves, including their personal symphony of emotions, that is beyond comparison with their previous experiencing of life. Their lives become more vital; they are far better able to understand themselves and others.

The fifth theory presents a new way of understanding what happens during successful treatment: Emotion storm theory describes disassembling a symptom disorder by first teaching patients to halt and reverse storm process and finally to prevent its occurrence, as an advantageous alternative to the traditional concept of "working through." The result of this is cure rather than amelioration.

In working at following emotion to comprehend the inner experience of a patient, the task can be simplified by our recognition of the varieties of emotion experience that can be evoked within people. Most psychologists seem to have devised some kind of categoric approach to the quality of particular emotions. Most are comfortable about naming an emotion experience they perceive even though others might disagree about which emotion it is. Knowing the emotions helps us understand the evocation. However, few analysts or psychologists of any school seem to have given much attention to or recognized meanings of variation in emotion intensity. Significantly, the implications of the varieties of processes of intense emotion experience have been ignored.

Each Emotion Has Its Unique Meaning

Each kind of emotion experience can be understood as participating in mental function in its own way with each having distinctly different implications. Cognizance of these important qualitative distinctions gives the advantage of a considerable increase in analytic effectiveness. Ignoring them creates problems, as the following story suggests.

Years ago a fellow student in psychoanalytic training created an analytic impasse when his patient spoke of her love (an affective attitude) for him, and for weeks he repeatedly responded with a supervisor approved reference to her "sexual interest" (an appetite—lust) for him.[9] Doing that was a biologizing effort to get her to transform the concept of emotion into the concept of physical (appetite) drive. She denied she felt that; he insisted that meant she was repressing feelings. The impasse evaporated instantaneously only when after six weeks (thirty sessions later) he responded by inadvertently adopting her word "love." The affective attitude had, up to that time, been instantly (automatically) translated by him to the sexual. From his trained illusion of knowledge, he believed he was helping the patient understand better what was going on within herself. To him (and to his supervisor), love equaled lust. The error was beyond mere inexactness, it diverted the patient from her reality and lessened her confidence in him. The complex affective attitudinal state of love and the simpler appetite of lust are different in meaning, process, and implications. The student analyst and his supervisor apparently had no cognizance of the distinction. To them the two words were synonymous. They believed the biological was the more direct or honest of the words. They did not perceive that the complexity of interpersonal meaning of "love" does not boil down to something as simple and vagrant as sexual interest. Attempting to communicate by substituting one for the other, as though they are equivalent, is an error that diverts people (patients and analysts) from meaningfulness. How many treatment impasses are created by comparable misunderstandings from comparable failed translations? In therapy it is destructive. In everyday life it adds damaging confusion to relationships.

This student's inability to understand the meaning, function, and use of emotion was even more apparent months later when it became my turn to make a presentation. He was critical of my "intellectualizing of affects" with the patient. He was referring to my speaking with the patient of her emotion experience and its sequential relations as intellectualizing that emotion. "Patients should be allowed to experience affects without thinking or talking about them," he insisted. The reciprocal that "patients should be allowed to experience sexual feelings without talking or thinking about them" was not a concept he could accept, for such an acceptance would point to the silliness of bypassing either. A proper definition of intellectualizing of affect would be "the transforming of and substituting of idea for affect." That would have a distancing and cooling effect in any relationship, including therapy.

A better understanding of psychology would suggest, "Patients should be encouraged to feel about thoughts and think about feelings to integrate their minds but not to substitute one for the other in either direction." Certainly, intellectualizing and biologizing are both psychic dangers.

Intensity of Affect Conveys the Significance of an Event

While the quality of affect experience tells us something of the meaning of an affect evocative event, it is the intensity of that affect that tells us of the significance of that event for us. For instance, crossing a busy highway on foot produces important cognitive information about the distance across several lanes, the number of vehicles, the consistent high speed of those vehicles, estimates of where those vehicles will be in one, two, or three seconds, knowledge of the effects of vehicles colliding with people, the speed we can jog, and our experiences in similar situations.

The facts of the situation, but not the meaningfulness of that information, are conveyed by these cognitive evaluations. It is our accompanying mild apprehension that points out the perceived danger. The mildness of the intensity conveys to us that the perceived danger is of modest consequence to us. Our experience assures us that we are quick enough of foot, and on a bright day, with a dry highway, we can do what we have done many times before. Our apprehension helpfully keeps us alert. A greater intensity of apprehension, or perhaps terror, would guide us not to attempt the crossing under current conditions.

Terror involves extreme feeling experience within the same fear spectrum. That intensity tells us that there is some perceived danger affectively evaluated as being of very considerable consequence to us. Anticipation of jogging across a roadway filled with vehicles moving at sixty to eighty miles per hour *should* bring terror if our minds are working properly. Usually there are many other simultaneous affect messages related to such matters as, for instance, our aims, wishes, and expectations about being on the other side of the street.

The qualities of affect in the two examples are similar in that both are within the fear spectrum of affects, but they convey different messages. With modest intensity (apprehension), we are alert. It is the greater intensity that moves us across that spectrum from apprehension to terror and provides the urgent and impelling force necessary to activate us to deal vigorously and appropriately with any situation—such as to fight, avoid, flee, hide, give up our possessions.

UNDERSTANDING INTENSE EMOTION

The failure to notice distinctions among different processes of emotion may be a consequence of preference for surface manifestations. Inner process sheds far more light on issues of mind. Perhaps because these normal informational emotion functions can become disturbed, distorted, or even disrupted for a variety of reasons, the normal emotion functions have sometimes been disregarded as if unreliable. Among the disturbances of these helpful functions is that a crisis intensity of emotion may be produced by psychodynamic processes distorting perceptions and *bringing healthy responses appropriate to the distorted perceptions.* The intensity may be perfectly *appropriate* to a misperception, although *inappropriate* to the reality. Because the validity of the emotion information is always in relation to the perceived data to which it responds, wise guidance from our emotion system is not possible under such circumstances.

Healthy guidance from our emotion system may be either optimized or overthrown by the presence of intense emotion experiences. We can discern and describe the effects of four types of intense emotion experience:

1. *Exigent emotion*—intense single emotion response evoked by an extreme situation

2. Emotion chords—a combination of multiple simultaneous appropriate emotion responses, evoked by a single situation, that in sum provide an intense, complex emotion experience

3. *Overreaction*—a single supercharged emotion response to a current situation due to combining the responses to several different remembered events that had occurred over a time, because they had yielded similar emotion responses

4. *Emotion storms*—a sequential series of escalating emotion responses to emotion responses building to create an intense emotion state that becomes self-sustaining

The first two types of intense emotion responses usually lead to healthy appropriate intensity of activity to respond to the situation that evokes the emotion. These are the natural emotion response processes of health from infancy on through our lives. Whether mild or intense, emotion serves to move us to activity appropriate to our perception of the internal or external life situation. Mild emotion may suggest or gently nudge toward either continuation or easing away from a situation. Intense emotion powerfully presses us to perform either enabling or protective functions.

Emotion chords are very common emotion responses that too frequently go unnoticed by therapists as well as others. These are syntonic mixtures of emotions appropriate to the evocative situation. We feel admiration, pride, sadness, longing, hope, and lonesomeness, for example, when our children go away to school or to a new life separate from ours. In this experience we can accept the various coexisting emotions as part of our need to adapt to the situation. These chords do not interfere with one another. Dystonic emotion chords, however, may temporarily disrupt our tranquility in their guiding of us to attempt to integrate the disparate events. For instance, if anger or resentment toward the children accompanied the several emotions listed above, we would have a dystonic emotion chord needing some resolution.

One unnoticed factor in the storm process is the possibility of multiple storms arising from contending with more than one emotion within dystonic emotion chords. The simultaneous storms arising from more than one emotion in a chord is just as destructive to the functioning of a person as a single emotion storm.

Recognition of chords requires healthy, free acceptance of emotion as a useful part of ourselves. Thus emotion chords are more often noticed by healthy people or by persons who are healthily accepting of emotion as a useful part of themselves.

Intense appropriate emotion serves to move us to activity appropriate to a life situation. These are the natural emotion responses from infancy on throughout our lives. They are automatic, healthy, benign signal-information functions.

In urgent situations we have intense feeling responses. Not to have vigorous emotion response in such situations is a mark of dysfunction. For instance, to be held at gun point, in an auto accident, or unexpectedly fired from a job exigently calls for activity. Intense emotion urges that.

The second two types of intense responses, overreaction and emotion storms, are usually pathological and often create serious problems.

Overreaction can occur in anyone at times, but is most likely to occur among persons who do not easily process their experiences to bring resolution to their conflicts, or who for any reason do not easily bring decision to their quandaries. Such persons tend to have more interpersonal disruptions than most. In my experience, these occur more commonly in persons with severe character pattern disorders.

We commonly understand the pattern of overreaction as a reaction of intensity seemingly disproportionate to the triggering event. Analysis of overreaction usually reveals that separate events evocative of the same emotion have come together in one's mind. In overreaction, that bringing together does not create a summing of the emotion intensity of the several events, but instead results in multiplicative intensity. We can describe this in the trite pattern of a man who had been bullied by his father in childhood and by his boss at work. In neither situation has he dared to respond, despite his resentment. After an unpleasant day on the job, his wife is mildly urging about some small task to which he responds with a "screaming fit" far out of proportion to her mild request. It is comparatively safe to scream at his wife. He is "set" to be indignant when triggered by anything that remotely resembles "bullying." He also is set to resent his own indignation. The rest follows naturally.

The importance for psychological understanding of mental conditions through knowledge and recognition of these different processes is that we can notice the crucial distinction between benign versus malignant process. It is of no small consequence that storms and overreaction create physiological reactions that strain the capacities of the individual and lead to physical as well as psychological disorders. The pure (or simple) emotions, regardless of intensity, do not appear to have those deleterious effects. Many highly touted biological studies establishing emotion as harmful to one's heart or gut have fallen into the trap of confusing emotion with para emotion. Thus, for those researchers, anger, storm, competitiveness, and hostility are the same. Such failures to make distinctions where there are important differences have made hundreds of study results questionable enough to require review.

Resistance to a New Understanding of Emotion

The several new principles introduced in the earlier pages are sets of simple ideas, but they have been more difficult for sophisticated mental health workers to absorb because these new ideas conflict sharply with long-accepted notions of mental processes, health, symptom formation, and illness. They are also troublesome for professionals who do not observe emotion dynamics within themselves. Typically, mental health professionals sincerely aim to help their patients. They ordinarily want to help by using whatever system they already know, for they believe it to be as near to valid reality as one can attain. Even though among themselves they may acknowledge their theory's weaknesses, making a change calls for expenditure of a great deal of intellectual energy and a loyalty to scientific principles that seems to them to be a disloyalty to what they have believed are truths.

The simplicity of the new concepts conforms with the simplicity of most fundamental truths. Yet in any theory, fundamental truths connect in very complex arrangements to everything in the field of study. Such complexity is so difficult to absorb that, for most professionals, it is an overwhelming task. The shift in fundamental premises forces us to look anew at everything. Those persons with the flexibility of mind to consider myriad connections of these new premises gain the advantage of perceiving everything in their field of study as a little different from what, in the past, they believed it to be. This brings the advantage of enabling them to answer old questions in new ways, raise new questions, and use the answers to understand mental health and its deviations better.

These advances in knowledge were made only after first confronting a most formidable barrier to understanding emotion. That barrier was composed of several parts, some of which are usual in scientific development, as described in chapter 12. *Perhaps the most important related discovery is that of the rarity of self-observational capacity among people, including professionals.* This limitation resulted in some processes intrinsic to this theory seeming to be invisible to many people. If not for that limitation, the remainder of the discoveries would have arrived in common wisdom millennia earlier. The relatively insensive can only view emotion processes as mere constructs to be easily rejected. Other problems existed because the most fundamental step in any field of study—construction of a consistent and useable taxonomy—had never been taken. This omission may be merely derivative of affect blindness in the insensive majority of the population.

Problems of Taxonomy and Language

The taxonomy in each field of study is what allows ideas to be shared, issues to be commonly understood and communicated, and studies to fit with and build upon one another. Without that step, there would be no reasonable communication among workers within a field of study. Because true communication never actually existed, but had only seemed to exist among those working in the study of emotion, that inadequacy prolonged the chaotic condition of the field.

Serious study in any field begins with calling attention to some phenomena that appear to be important. When enough people become interested in the phenomena, they begin to study the processes, causes, and implications of these phenomena. That requires clarifying the definitions of terms and descriptions of processes, which brings a better comprehension of cause, effect, and meaning of the phenomena. With each advance in taxonomy, there are resulting increases in usefulness of applications of the knowledge gained. Without agreement on taxonomy, various workers study different problems and produce findings that cannot be put together to build on each other's work.

For a variety of reasons, the study of emotion has not had the series of clarifying steps necessary for advances in understanding. Instead there has been something worse than a Tower of Babel. In that biblical story no one maintained the misconception that they were communicating, for the words they used were different. In the study of emotion there continues to be an illusion that workers are speaking the same language and discussing the same phenomena simply because they use the same words. As a result, instead of construction of emotion theory built on an accepted foundation, various workers each had unique sets of premises, but believed they were dealing with the same matters as everyone else.

The imprecision in thinking about emotion is exemplified in a collection of "significant papers on the psychoanalytic theory of affect" following

Freud. *The World of Emotion: Clinical Studies of Affects and Their Expressions,* edited by Charles W. Socarides,[10] are papers selected as the most illuminating group of papers on the subject over a period of eighty years. Socarides says that "Patients have difficulty in three areas relating to affect: in feeling them, in recognizing them, in expressing them." His list omits what I would consider a fourth category—the most important difficulty people have— their inability to use their emotions. The inoperative utilization of emotions, unnoticed, has blighted the human race for millennia. If we compare the varieties of subject matter in that outstanding book, we can note that the articles deal with varieties of subjects crossing the categories of emotions, emotion motivated actions, attitudes, complex emotion states, and manifestations of affect expressions. Much less is devoted to the functional utility of specific emotions. Little effort was made to adopt or even seek a commonality in parlance among them. Recognition of taxonomic systems is absent.

If the editor had made a categorization of those studies that were included by recognition of the distinctions between pure emotions and the para emotions, by pointing to distinctions among affective states, affective attitudes, pseudo affects, and affect evoking situations, the intrinsic usefulness of the studies could have been better recognized for their specific contributions to the field. The existence of taxonomy, even when imperfect, does promote understanding and inspires questions and hypotheses.

We remain with a muddle of disconnected bits of ideas and findings. Our overlooking distinctions where there are meaningful differences may be the obverse of overlooking clusters of meaningful similarities, leaving us to treat likenesses as if they are different. Both sorts of overlooking exist in the common theories. Consideration of similarities and differences can aid our understanding of cause and effect. Our unclarity in attempts to communicate with each other impairs progress. It is a reason that most of the existing professional literature on emotion is of little relevance to the ideas put forward and discussed in this book. For instance, we can use a recent book to illustrate how far apart those active in the field of study are from each other in agreement on the content of their field, in their digressions from applications of scientific logic, and in the murkiness of distinctions that keep them from having the advantages of a useful taxonomy of the elements and processes we wish to explore. *The Handbook of Emotions,* edited by Michael Lewis and Jeannette Haviland,[11] is offered as "a benchmark for research and thinking about emotions—one of the most complete and authoritative discussions of the human affects" and as "a basic research source for what is known about the emotions." A few of the instances in various chapters:

Exhilaration (which would be better understood as an attribute of any of a number of emotions) is considered as if it is itself an emotion.

Embarrassment (which would be better understood as an awkwardness in behavior that may or may not accompany shame, surprise, guilt, fear, and some other emotions) is mistakenly considered as if it is itself an emotion.

Humor (which is something more than a witty playfulness with words) is taken to be an emotion although it is actually a perspective-aided sensing of incongruities or our own ridiculousness. It is not itself an emotion even though it may arise from and usually produces emotion of amusement.

Confusion of mood with emotion, which is the special weakness of biological studies and biopsychiatry, appeared in several of the studies. The applications of neuropeptides that can produce sham emotions, lowered or heightened moods, fretful states, or sense of satiety do not produce or reduce emotions, nor do they create changes in personality organization.

Inclusion of complex emotion states as the same as pure emotion implies the mental processes as well as the instigators are equivalent. *Inclusion of attitudes as if they are cognitive elements* especially in the cognitive psychology chapter overlooks their affective component. *Inclusion of circumstances or conditions that evoke emotion as if evocative circumstance is itself emotion blocks the possibility of meaningful theory.*

Obliviousness, Introspection, and Self-observation

Individual variations in observing capacity in some people and consequent deficiencies in awareness of their inner life is worthy of much study. It has been a crucial factor in creating a barrier to understanding some vital processes. The number or percentage of people in the various categories of qualities of self-consciousness has not been studied. The reasons for that omission are important in what is presented here. Some of those reasons tell us much about the lack of progress in the science, but also tell us much that is of vital importance about psychological processes in some pathologies.

While most people appear to have some awareness of their own mental content, an undetermined percentage of people are oblivious of their own thoughts and feelings. Those people rarely consider that they think and feel. Regardless of degree of intelligence, education, or whatever useful talents they may have, they live simpler lives by being incognizant in that sense. Because that is the state of their intrapersonal experience, they have catalogable, noticeably distinct interpersonal and social qualities. Those capable of introspection—having awareness of or familiarity with their own mental content (thought and feeling)—must exist in great numbers, although no surveys of such a matter have described the proportions. Probably most psychologists are capable of introspection, for their interest in psychology is by definition direct interest in mental content and process. Biopsychiatry and behaviorism, two fields operating at the border of psychology dealing indirectly with mind, have some interest in phenomena related to psychology, but with minimal involvement in subjectivity.

It appears that some small percentage of people are capable of self-observation, a process beyond introspection that requires, in addition to awareness of mental content, an awareness of the connections among those mental contents and the various processes—the history and the cause and effect relations among those contents.

While the oblivious person cannot be bothered with the "mumbo jumbo" of inner life that he or she cannot know, the introspective person can be aware that "I am angry because you did [that] to me and you and others have done that to me before," or "I feel sad," or "I resent . . . " and "I enjoyed . . . " and "I love. . . . " The self-observing person can know, "I got angry when you did [that] to me. It is like my angry reaction in many other situations I remember with you and with many others over my lifetime, and when that happens I think I am to blame, get ashamed, get indignant about, put myself in a pattern of reactions such as . . . , resent that I always get into such situations, relationships, etc."

These two kinds of self-consciousness, of knowing self, are very different. It must be considered a truism that only if we are aware of our inner life can we be aware of such in others around us. Conversely, those unaware of their own inner life are also unaware of what others experience.[12] An introspective but not truly self-observant person, perhaps because he or she has some awareness, does not have any basis for knowing that some others have that capacity plus additional awarenesses, but instead usually believes that his or her awareness of inner life is as extensive or deep as that of any other.[13]

Because self-observation was never a requirement in selection of psychologists (nor for selection to work in any other mental health field), the distribution of nonobservers within psychology must approximate the distribution within the population at large. That may be why the terms "self-observation" and "introspection" are casually used by most workers in the field as if the words are synonyms. Consequently, for most therapists this significant distinction has not been used to help understand some mental processes, enable more accurate prediction of treatment outcomes, comprehend the quality of transference and relationship, and other valuable implications for working effectively in the field. The ability of readers to observe process within themselves will make the contents of this book easier for them to follow.

Those who are introspective but not self-observing are likely to find some of the concepts and relations puzzling. From my experience in trying to explain these ideas to others, it seems likely that those who have not previously been aware—on their own, without coaching—that they have occasionally gotten afraid about being frightened, or ashamed about being angry about being angered, will have a harder time comprehending this work. That is not a test, but a kind of rule of thumb detecting those who will not value the dynamics of emotion because they are unaware of even the gross aspects of such dynamics within themselves. For the present, self-observational capacity may be regarded as a talent that is unequally distributed among people, perhaps existing in only a small percentage of humanity.

Past misunderstandings about mental processes arose for a variety of reasons, but those misunderstandings all led to a set of myths becoming entrenched as faulty foundation of personality theory in psychology. These errors led science of mind into useless paths or blind alleys, and enabled construction of only weak theories that have led to weak therapies. The attempts made to rationalize the several nearly futile therapeutic approaches never fully justified those theories. Inadequacies of results of the applications were taken for granted as natural, inevitable consequences of the realities of human psychology. With such limited knowledge, expectations for improved quality of life were necessarily limited.

SUMMING UP

New knowledge of emotion based on three formerly unrecognized facts creates a cluster of new theories that, with their applications, brings great hope for future improvement in the quality of life for humanity. This knowledge teaches us how the underlying processes of neurosis are only somewhat like what they had been thought to be in past theories. From our more informed current vantage point, we see how those earlier misunderstandings about emotion were culpable in creating the entire class of psychological symptom disorders instead of being the expected path for solving problems. That misfortune came about because incorrect common wisdom beliefs about emotions were incorporated into theory instead of being observed, questioned, and corrected by psychologists.

Adoption and dissemination of those common wisdom ideas of emotion, as if they had been tested scientifically, brought them full circle and reinforced that archaic faulty common wisdom among the population at large. In that way, increased psychopathology among the general population has been fostered by a sincere, misguided aim to help. False knowledge was a problem repeatedly offered as if it were a solution.

More valid understanding of emotion processes woven with other available knowledge now enables us to cure, but of far more importance, our new understanding is now valid enough to eradicate some previously refractory illnesses. The whole field of psychology is changed a little with this knowledge, for it nudges, bumps, and dislodges past false beliefs, while fitting helpfully with valid portions of existing theory. It is especially in regard to personality, health, and illness that changes seem profoundly helpful, although in the long term it will be the changed view of life and relationships and the freeing of creativity and productivity—the much greater human potential of which we have had only glimpses—that will be the greater benefit to humanity.

The remainder of this book consists of support, elaboration, and implications of the fundamental concepts and theoretical formulations, and the responses to these in encounters with established schools and authorities.

NOTES

1. My suggestion is that such narrow theories have been offered and accepted by people whose own emotions are muted, for the emotions listed are powerful enough to pierce the dampening effect from muting emotions and would be familiar even to theorists with muted emotion. Their theories must be considered as comparable to theories about color devised by partially color-blind persons. It may be expected that some emotions are primitive brain stem emotions that we share with more primitive evolutes, while other emotions may be cortical. So far, the process and function of all the emotions appear to have great similarity, although distinctions may later become apparent. The affects that we can categorize as physical appetites seem similar in some ways, but also have some different processes that do not fit as neatly with emotions.

2. People do what they consider as "abreacting" repeatedly without it being curative. Abreaction to get rid of stored feeling makes the same sense as repeated thinking or speaking a thought to rid oneself of it. It does not work in obsessive thinking. There is no logical basis for believing that repeated expression of either thought or feeling "gets it out."

3. Societally transmitted attitudes are acquired in a different manner by education that fosters an adoption of familial or community reference group attitudes.

4. It is of interest that affect ejection is almost always aimed against powerful discomfiting emotions, not against pleasant or mild emotions. For emotion theory to be useful and competent, its explanations must apply to all emotion. Multiple special theories for specific affects or a small cluster of emotions have little validity and are difficult to weave into general theory.

5. This does not change the recurring problems of transference and countertransference in self-analysis. Integrating emotion and cognition may or may not help that.

6. We can compare this to an attempt to teach people to regulate or control other autonomous processes such as vision, taste, or smell.

7. This is different from manic states in which the ordinary flow of thought also is uncritiqued and freely expressed, but occurs in a pathological kind of love of self and all its products rather than being overrun by unwanted mental content.

8. In storm disorders, when the usual continuous intellectual flow of ideation that is ordinarily generated as response to the flow of sensory data is too much for the momentarily limited energy available, there is a subjective impression of a more than ordinary flow of thought. The perceived extraordinarily rapid flow of thought, when reported by patients to psychiatrists as a problem, is sometimes categorized as evidence of a hypomanic or even manic disorder. That has led biopsychiatrists to treat simple affect storms as if they are manic-depressive disorders. The typical prescription has been lithium. I have encountered people who were treated for this transient problem by such high dosages of chemicals that they were groggy. In their zombie-like states, their lives were reduced to below a human minimum and they had all the problems of adaptation to life that is a

common result of long or heavy use of neuroleptic drugs. The mild, usually disruptive, universally experienced self-subsiding affect storms had been turned into chronic illnesses and wasted their lives. Most had become tension phobic and many were unreachable.

9. This is one of the many varieties of examples of reductionist activities in the mental health field that have led many theories, therapists, and their patients astray.

10. C. W. Socarides, *The World of Emotion: Clinical Studies of Affects and their Expressions* (New York: International Universities Press, 1977).

11. M. Lewis and J. Haviland, eds., *The Handbook of Emotions* (New York: Guilford Press, 1993).

12. In response to questions about what goes on in their minds, some people say "I don't know what you are talking about," or "I don't go for that psychobabble," or "I don't believe in that psychological mumbo-jumbo." It is usually clear that their beliefs are supported by their ignorance of inner life. The use of those derisive phrases may be consistently inferred to come from people devoid of knowledge of inner life.

13. A comparable issue arises among those with good but still imperfect color vision. I have witnessed arguments among such persons as to whether a color is blue-green or green-blue, versus simply blue. Because they each have considerable color sense they believe it is perfect color sense, equal to that of everyone else.

3

The Misguided Theory of Affect Storage and Regulation

The questions we ask depend on the premises we have adopted. Good questions based on poor premises may bring good answers that are of little or no use to us. Such is the condition for common answers to some common questions about affect. If we adopt the general premise that emotions are noxious aspects of life, we become interested in a cluster of questions about how to protect ourselves from them. If we adopt the additional premise that an emotion, once evoked, remains inside us until gotten out, a system of protecting ourselves against such a danger by discharging or excreting emotion becomes urgently necessary. If we adopt the premise that affects are voluntary or can be made voluntary, rather than involuntary elements of mind, that brings questions about how we might regulate occurrence of emotion experience.

Those issues exist only for people operating with premises that emotion is an enduring event, but an event controllable at the option of each individual, rather than an autonomous process.

AFFECT DOES NOT STORE

In the first chapter I introduced a list of five myths about affect that exist in common wisdom and contrasted them with five corresponding actualities of affect. Perhaps most psychologically sophisticated readers appreciate the idea that at least *some* affects are benign, automatic, subjective responses to internal and external events and even that they bring information to us. Few have concluded that all are benign. Fewer still seem ready to concede the rapid transience of emotion events or the constructive processes involved. The myths as common knowledge are firmly imbedded in general psychology. As stated in chapter 1, because the myths are ego syntonic they are usually unrecognized, autonomous, preconscious ego content and therefore rarely verbalized. Because they are universal beliefs, they have become (without examination) implicitly premisal to all psychological theory. That is why it is worth restating and giving further consideration to those myths and actualities to build a new frame of reference for psychological thought:

myth: affects are dangerous interferences in our lives
actuality: *affects are benign*

myth: affects are useless
actuality: *affects are vital functions*

myth: affects, once evoked, remain in storage until discharged
actuality: *affects are briefly transient*

myth: affects, in storage, damage us unless we deal with them
actuality: *because affect events endure only for microseconds, we need not/cannot "deal" with them*

myth: the necessary affect discharge must be accomplished very carefully to cause the least possible damage
actuality: *any effort to get out feelings is a waste*

   Among several long-known attributes of emotion is its impelling quality. But by knowing emotion is separate from action (even though related to it) we realize we have a choice of whether or not to act. We can be joyful without smiling. We can be angry without hitting. Realization of that difference between emotion merely impelling us rather than the belief so many have held that it is absolutely compelling is an important factor in determining our attitudes about emotion and our decisions about what we do. In fact, we can be absolutely infuriated, absolutely sad, or feel any emotion intensely, while retaining the prerogative not to act in any way. For feelings to depart, we do not have to scream, pound, break something, or even speak of emotions. It is a startling idea to many that striving to "discharge" emotions is not merely unnecessary, but is impossible because discharge is a nonoccurrence.
   The belief that emotion creates a task and a danger because it compels action is part of what gives emotion a bad name. The corollary belief is that if one has an emotion reaction, the arousal remains within until one acts. If an accumulation of emotion as either matter or potential were real, such action would, in fact, be necessary and desirable. When emotions fade they may be evoked in replication, but not "brought back," for we have no place or system for storing them.[1]

The concept that emotion accumulates and stores can make people worry about having an emotion reaction. This worry can create a negative secondary emotion reaction to experiencing an emotion. For instance, annoyance or irritation may, through such chained steps, become the basis of sequential escalation finally bringing a berserk rage. When we potentiate an emotion, for example, by being afraid about being afraid, and then being afraid about being afraid about being afraid, we may construct an emotion storm. Such a storm is not an emotion. It is a more complex irrational state that is more inclusive than emotion. Those who consider an emotion storm to be an emotion can only regard emotion as disruptive and damaging.

During a storm, intelligence becomes limited. Perhaps that is because mental energies ordinarily devoted to intellectual functioning are temporarily diverted and consumed as a person becomes distracted by and engrossed in emotion. Should it be surprising, in such circumstances of reduced intellect, that irrationalities such as phobias, compulsions, or paranoid suspicion can dominate the personality? In contrast, when people understand what emotions are and what they are not, they welcome each emotion as part of a built-in system of automatic evaluation. Whether anger, joy, loneliness, surprise, gratitude, sadness, or any other feeling, each emotion, painful or pleasurable, brings useful information. Emotion provides a flow of information about the meaning of all that goes on in and around us. It is always healthy function, never an illness or danger. When we welcome our emotions as information, regardless of whether pleasant or unpleasant information, our emotion experience becomes like a symphony of emotion throughout each day—a part of our moment-by-moment experience and comprehension. In contrast, those who reject feeling experience reduce their awareness of the meaning of what goes on in and around themselves. Thus they limit their comprehension.

THE IMPOSSIBLE FEAT OF AFFECT REGULATION

One notion that has crept into the theories of emotion (from common wisdom) is that humans must regulate emotion. One has to take a stand that emotion experience is either an automatic evaluation of what is going on in and around us, or a voluntary response that we therefore can control, modulate, and regulate. If we opt for the former, the idea of regulation is illogical. If we opt for the latter, we turn emotion into a personal choice and therefore an optional experience of limited meaning, of little value for human function, and hardly worth study.

Emotion states may last from seconds to hours and vary widely in intensity. In extraordinary conditions an emotion state of high intensity may continue for an extended period of time, but chronically intense emotion states or frequent episodes of inappropriate intense emotion may indicate psychopathology.

The dangers people attribute to emotion have been, in every case I have examined, either a presumption of danger of retaliation for action related to the emotion, or the danger of painful internal reaction to emotion, rather than danger intrinsic to emotion itself. It seems clear at this point that what can store is memory of internal and external events, memory of the emotion responses to those events, and attitudinal accretions, but not emotion itself.

Many people are distressed by the impact of certain emotions. Not only do they feel bad with the impact of painful feeling content, but they are also limited in their ability to sense, use, and integrate emotions in their lives. It is in this way that they feel badly—that is to say, they do badly at feeling. Their aim becomes avoidance of unpleasant feelings instead of acceptance and use of all feelings, including those that discomfit them.

When the antipathy to emotion is examined, we find that for each person the initial antipathy is aimed against a few emotions, but later may generalize to include other feelings. Most commonly against anger, the initial antipathy is sometimes against shame, guilt, fear or sorrow, and less frequently against lust. Some people stay with the antipathy toward the few emotions, others generalize. There is no theoretical basis for excluding any emotion from possible antipathy. The origin of the antipathy has been seen in some as coming from early experience with or teaching by parents. In most people, the specific origins have remained hidden. But we seldom see anyone distressed by feelings of joy, worrying about how to get rid of joyful feeling, or about how to channel joy carefully so as not to cause trouble.

Only when special circumstances set one in contention with some particular emotion, or when emotion phobia intensifies within a person, antipathy generalizes and those emotions usually regarded by most persons as pleasant emotion experience come to be regarded with antipathy. The notions of hedonic or anhedonic emotion experience must always be related to the perceptual matrix in which they exist. As with beauty, it is in the eye of the beholder, not intrinsic to the emotion. Thus, we can relieve ourselves of the responsibility of constructing such categories, unless we do so for each individual in relation to the time and situation.

Since one of the most common emotion antipathies relates to anger, we can use that as example. The reason for danger-fear reactions to anger seems to be that the quality of impelling to action that is part of all emotion takes the form of an urge to hurt in the case of anger. Therefore, it brings the anticipation of dangers of retaliation or painful guilt if such anger related actions are carried out. The belief that feelings, in this case anger, are stored until they are expressed (gotten out) creates a powerful motive for expression. Repeated experiences of life's daily minor irritations are misperceived as increasing the compressed supply and consequently increasing the danger of an eventual uncontrollable violent expression and a possible personal disaster. Thus, one consequence of belief in the myth is a tendency to respond to any emotion signals with some antipathy and especially to respond within some predetermined cluster of anger emotions as a danger. The development of such an attitude in relation to any emotion indicates that an irrational fear of emotion has developed. The consequent damage to the individual personality is immense.

Despite the fact that ideas of storage of emotion predominate in all human cultures, they are incorrect. We more usefully view emotion as a kind of mental evaluation of external and internal mental focuses that occurs as a rapid sequence of brief emotion event units (which we could call "affectons"). Rather than an enduring emotion state being a continuance of a unitary emotion response to perceptions, the same emotion may be produced repetitively, thus forming an emotion state and continuing as long as one's perception retains the same focus.[2]

In the same sense, light is subjectively experienced as an enduring unitary sensory event although its retinal-occipital actuality is of a pulsing or cyclical series of repetitions of messages of color, image, size, form, and intensity. That is the only way our nerve fiber mediation can operate. Emotion response, when viewed, analogously allows us a further step in understanding emotion process.

The difference between premises of enduring versus transient emotion is a basic theoretical issue. Changing our view of the nature of emotion to include the attribute of transience, because it is fundamental, causes at least a small change to everything in personality theory. The internal coherence of these new explanations of the phenomena we study is sufficient to make the new theory worth taking seriously. The astonishing results of applications of this complex set of ideas by other workers, when compared with use of any other approach, are enough to establish it as significant.

Because we subjectively experience emotion as an enduring event, the common wisdom supposition has been that the actuality of emotion comprises a single lasting feeling event. Support for the contention that emotion is transient is stronger than that developed over many years for the theory of enduring emotion. Support comes from: (1) the absence of proof for the alternative theory of enduring emotion, despite age-old belief in it, (2) the superior results from applications of "transient emotion" theory, (3) the absence of proof of any place or system for storing of emotion, (4) the similarity in function of affect processes to functions of sensory processes in health as well as disorder, and (5) current knowledge of neurophysiology.

The neurophysiology of nerve fiber function suggests the hypothesis that an affect event occurs, like other neuronally transmitted events, as a multiplicity of fractional-second pulsing responses to sensory data. It cannot be a steady state, even though the rapid repetitions fading and recurring give that impression.

The significance of that briefness of affect event fading and repeating appears in the many implications for theory of affect and the nature of psychopathology. For instance, *affect that objectively exists for only a brief moment not only need not be discharged, it cannot be discharged because it has already faded. Because affect is transient, all psychological theories incorporating concepts describing storage and discharge of affect are on faulty paths and should be reexamined and restructured.*

Because people rely on their subjective experience to comprehend their objective experience, they develop a set of beliefs that fit with that subjective experience. The myth about affect that derives from uncorrected infantile experience determines that every person becomes affect phobic in some degree.[3] Indeed, we each develop as infants in a way that makes us become wary or uneasy with some particular affects. That uneasiness is not a requirement of Nature. In infancy it is a natural developmental stage. Unsurmounted in later years, it is a pathology—affect phobia. Theorists who are affect phobic have consistently included a component of "affect-as-danger" (meaning bad, disruptive, interfering) in their psychological theories and devised techniques aimed to help people deal with those dangerous affects. It is the same affect phobia in theorists that leads them to the highly illogical aim to "regulate affects." Affect phobic theoreticians have then adopted and elaborated the notion to the detriment of the field. Ideas of affect regulation have taken researchers on side paths and wasted much effort. How much chance is there of regulating an autonomous process, and to what end?

Generally people deprecate affects as nonspecific, unreliable, interfering aspects of mind. We may attribute their attitude to affect phobia. Confusion about what constitutes an affect exacerbates the problem as well. People often say, "I feel . . . ," when they wish to give an impression of personal warmth, indefiniteness, or uncertainty to a statement. It may seem to them that, in this way, they can elude tests of verity by that indefiniteness.

There is a common proclivity for saying, "I feel . . . ," not only to describe a feeling, but also when referring to judgment, opinion, or belief. This coincides with, or may be a cause or effect of, the blurring of distinctions between affect and cognition. Theorists have brought that same blurring of distinctions into their theorizing, to the detriment of both theory of cognition and theory of affect. Unless we categorize as feeling that which is felt and categorize as cognition that which is thought, we contaminate our basic data. Theory built upon contaminated data will be faulty. In turn, therapies based on those theories necessarily will be faulty. A consequence of the common blurring of the affect-cognition distinction is that only rare persons are clear in their dealing with affect and cognition within themselves.

Commonly, people (including mental health professionals) are unaware of how cautious and tentative they are with at least some of their own affects. Because they are unaware of the absolute universality of affect phobia (in themselves and others), they fail to notice the extensive consequences of that condition.

FREUD'S ANXIETY THEORY

Psychoanalysis was invented some 120 years ago by a very bright twenty-one year old named Bertha Pappenheim, better known to history as "Anna O."[4] For several years she had suffered with "hysteric" symptoms. These included panic episodes, conversions, fugue states, and phobias. She persuaded her physician, Dr. Joseph Breuer, to come to her bedside each evening so that she could describe her symptoms of the day, her memories, thoughts, and feelings. She termed the process "chimney sweeping," indicating her belief that she was "getting them out," and thus engaging in a curative process.

She described all with great detail and at considerable length. After each session she seemed better, at least for a while. Doctor and patient worked together, apparently for several months, to view the many symptoms that kept changing and modifying within the realm of what were classed as hysteric symptoms. He listened while she talked. Hence it was the model for a "talking cure."

Later Breuer told his colleague Sigmund Freud about this interesting patient. Treatment of such symptoms had not been successful in the past. Freud found the events very interesting and began a collaboration with Breuer that creatively amplified and extended the theory and therapy of psychological problems. It also got Freud started on the path of working to cure the various neuroses, and eventually led to the development of the complex psychoanalytic theory.

Bertha Pappenheim had followed the erroneous common wisdom of the day, "that one must expel accumulations of matter to achieve or maintain health." By doing that she creatively applied the concept of the then-popular "high colonic" by displacing it to the mind. Breuer and Freud readily accepted that notion, for they too lived in a society that shared the same common wisdom that accumulations cause illness and removal of accumulations rids bodies of various noxious or toxic or waste substances and thereby enhances health.

In the nineteenth century, the perfected equipment for high colonics assured that bowel irrigation, whether medical or self-prescribed, was utilized in many households. Despite the questionable advantages, and probable harm from developing dependence on that artificial process, it seemed clear to much of the population that their physical troubles were due to the extended storage of waste in their bodies.[5] The idea of being clean inside, as an approach to Godliness, was very attractive. The concept has not disappeared. Even today some Hollywood movie stars have fallen for the faddish use of that anachronistic notion for such cleansing rather than the natural functions bestowed by nature. The current general use of multifarious concoctions as laxatives regulating bowel action, with questionable health value for most people, continues to be widely advertised.

Another system of getting out "bad" contents had been popular earlier. From the first through the sixteenth centuries in Europe, bloodletting, which involved a relatively simple process, had been prescribed for a variety of human ills—also with questionable advantage and much potential for harm.

Still earlier, beginning in some dim reach of history but continuing even today, exorcism of those possessed by demons or spirits has been practiced. The belief is that illnesses, particularly neurotic and psychotic illnesses, are caused by demonic beings who have entered and taken over control of mind and body. One of the startlingly popular current "best-seller" psychiatrists has written that if patients do not respond to his ministrations it is because they are possessed and should be exorcized and that there should be a national institute for exorcisms under management of psychiatrists.[6]

THE ILLUSION OF CATHARSIS

Catharsis was an illusion; catharsis-cures were short remissions after which symptoms often either recurred or were replaced by other symptoms. With Freud's recognition of the futility of catharsis, he moved from a base of theory in affect to a base in instinctual drives instead of shifting to different issues within theory of affect. However, in this step, Freud added a series of imaginative theoretical notions that were very useful organizing contributions to the study of mind. Among his many contributions may be his most enduring idea, his conceptualization of an organized dynamic unconscious mental realm. He formulated the construct of three levels of awareness—conscious, preconscious, and unconscious. He developed theoretical constructs of forces in process as mechanisms of mental operations—like repression, reaction formation, denial, projection, etc. (see Anna Freud, *The Ego and its Mechanisms of Defense* and J. Sandler with A. Freud, *The Analysis of Defense*[7]). He asserted a description of developmental sequence, which he put in terms of psychosexual stages, oral, anal, phallic, and genital. Devising the constructs of id, ego, and superego organized an explanation of the interworking forces within mind. He discerned variables of ego mechanisms as defense of ego integration and support of adaption. From these ideas and others, he built a technical approach to the study of personality functioning and malfunctioning.

The solid entrenchment of common wisdom about affect storage made it a part of every psychological theory, sometimes explicitly and sometimes implicitly. In the beginnings of psychoanalysis, Breuer and Freud pointed to the concept of affect storage in their famous 1893 paper "On the Psychical Mechanism of Hysterical Phenomena: Preliminary Communication."[8] They used the concept of affect storage in what they called *strangulated affect*. They had translated the concept of "chimney sweeping" formulated by Anna O. to describe her idea of clearing out accumulated idea and affect that were obstructing her mental channels and "causing" her hysteria. That was only a slight recasting of long-standing common knowledge beliefs.

These various concepts of indwellings and ejections are examples of the general pattern of beliefs that form a comfortable foundation for the fallacious concept of affect storage and make it more acceptable. Unfortunately, with the disappointing recognition that abreaction[9] was ineffectual psychotherapy, instead of the logical action of dropping abreaction from affect theory, affect theory *in toto* was essentially discarded as a central issue in psychoanalytic theory and not subjected to continuing study. This leap to drive theory may have been one of Freud's few blunders. He trivialized affect in general by subsuming it under anxiety, and further by asserting both as derivative of drives. Affect never regained the place in theory it held during those first days. Psychoanalysis had moved from a failed affect psychology to a drive psychology and now made affect a subordinate part of drive theory. Psychoanalysis as a drive psychology has obviously made tremendous progress in the utilization of issues of drive and inhibition of drive as central in personality development and the analysis of normal and abnormal function, but in so doing missed the value of affect.[10]

The psychodynamic theory (oversimplified) may be described as follows: When young children confront conflicting forces within themselves, they make the best resolution of the conflict their limited experience, intelligence, and circumstance allow. Those resolutions of conflict become enduring characteristic patterns of response for use when encountering internal processes to similar-seeming situations over a lifetime. There is great advantage in having such a readily available repertoire of responses gained from experience. These, however, may become an encumbrance and later difficulty. The character patterns ingeniously worked out by infants may not be appropriate for situations of the adult who develops from that infancy. What had been facilitative in early life situations may either continue to be facilitating or become hampering in later life situations.

Drive theory focused on anxiety, thought of as the feeling experience from frustration of drives, as the master affect, and paradigm for other affects. *Psychosexual level* became the skeletal structure for ego development. *Transference* became the keystone to psychoanalytic therapy process.[11] *We always see something of similarity or differences of past relationships in our present relationships.* No one can be totally free of transferences unless free of memory. That too makes for efficiency of mental function, easing but complicating our adaptation.

Once Freud had accomplished the tethering of the theory of psychopathology to anxiety, and anxiety to drive, that enabled construction of a treatment method having the aim of questing for the roots of anxiety. Though it is not considered nice to call attention to defects of such a productive, heroic figure, his tethering of the theory of psychopathology to anxiety was due to a significant personal limitation—muted emotion. *It is important to recognize this problem because untethering from the single affect theory releases psychoanalytic theory to encompass the full range of affects and their dynamics.* That shift enables us to switch from our past ability to treat to the very advantageous ability to cure. The limitation of affect muting appears to have been shared by many people who were as affect muted as Freud (perhaps many around him were more so). Certainly many professionals today, active and even eminent in the field, give similar evidence of being restricted by limited awareness of affect as process. None has perceived the affect problems in the theory of personality, because they did not perceive within themselves a broad enough range of affect process. In contrast, becoming free of the limitation of working with anxiety as the only hypothetic construct of emotion, we have the unparalleled benefit of working with some affect processes as literal variables in symptom formation. We have moved from a morass of hypothetic constructs to a solid base of direct observations of emotion process gained from the minority of people capable of such observation. Having an observable process obviates the need to use a hypothetic construct, except for those affect blind people who are unwilling even to consider these *invisible* variables as truth.[12]

AFFECT BLINDNESS

The difficulty encountered in this shift may be illuminated by supposing an analogous hypothetical situation, color blindness and its consequences. We can assume that approximately 2 percent of the population is totally color blind, and then add some larger percentage as having color vision but with deficiencies. Because the majority of people have adequate color vision, those who are color blind are persuaded that most people have a visual capacity for distinguishing something they call "color" that gives them advantages in some situations. Because they are outvoted, the color blind do not dispute the existence of color, although they experience color only as a vague intellectual abstraction. They have no comprehension of what it is they are missing.

Let us imagine that the percentages of color-visioned and color-blind population were reversed. If 98 percent of the population were color blind and only two percent were color visioned, that majority would, in their ignorance of color, be quite haphazard about anything that involved color because it would be invisible to them. Those with the capacity to distinguish color might, among themselves, discuss the aesthetics of pleasant and unpleasant combinations of color, discuss the relative ease of selecting ripe instead of "green" fruit, the uses of color in clothing, buildings, furnishings, and decorations, and enjoy many significant advantages from the use of color, but it would be puzzling to everyone else.

The color-blind majority might be perplexed and derogate the so-called distinctions in color: "It's not important (or not even real)." The color blind would be likely to decide by consensus that the concept of color is non-sense—nonexistent pretense by a few charlatans with some kind of trickery. The remainder would not understand those few with color vision. That majority would deride them for claiming distinctions where "everyone can see there are none." The color blind would work out life in the world in terms of what they could know. Their formulations for explaining and understanding the world would be in terms of other attributes, and there-fore less complete, less comprehending. Yet they would assume, declare, and righteously defend the idea that they were including all existing factors of importance.

In psychology this is precisely the case in terms of affect, affect sensitivity, affect awareness, affect distinctions, affect theory formulations, and some other aspects of mental functioning that are within the awareness of some, but not all, people. Freud made the error of assuming that each time anxiety is present, it is the initial and only significant emotion present and active at the time, rather than what we now know to be a medial point in a complex sequence of affective mental events. Thus, the processes that may lead to anxiety are unobserved as affect process precursors, and therefore are regarded as if nonexistent. Our new knowledge suggests that in the several "anxiety disorders" the anxiety is an effect rather than a cause, as a part of a sequence of responses to preceding pathological affect dynamics. We also see that some of these disorders are not even related to anxiety. *From this view, anxiety is not an illness to treat, it is not the central issue, and the term "anxiety disorder" is a mistaken popular appellation.* Instead, the affect dynam-ics and the precursor affective events are usually the appropriate focal points of the treatment.

Those persons whose affect awareness is muted know only the intense affects that occur within themselves and know the other less powerful affects as intellectual abstractions if they know them at all. Following our analogy of color blindness, it is appropriate to term this widespread dis-ability "affect blindness," as we might for infrared or radio-wave blindness.

Thus, affect muted persons, when acting as theorists, do not have a full scale of emotions with which to work. They construct their theories out of only that portion of possible data of the processes that are available to them—but that is insufficient data about the process. Freud's own emotion storms (which can be inferred from the reported manifestations of agora-phobia and reactive depressions) and his affect muting (which were mani-fested in his inability to comprehend the significance of a full range of affects to include in his theories) may be considered a consequence of his sharing the universal affect phobia.

It is also thus in our world that affect blindness and affect awareness seem to be distributed with more people having the former than the latter. It is an unfortunate imbalance. To the extent that this is a result of affect muting rather than a genetic deficit, there is hope that dissemination of knowledge can remedy it. Affect muting reduces the span of emotion awareness in a way comparable to a reduced span of color vision in the partially color blind, who have a lesser and somewhat distorted color awareness. This is a widespread difficulty comparable to what would be if the partially color blind had the final say in theory of color. The difficulties arising from this topsy-turvy situation in psychology will be returned to in chapter 12.

Even though affect was reduced to a secondary role in psychoanalysis, the notion of strangulated affect and discharge, arising from theorists' own affect phobia, was retained tacitly as an underlying concept, although it receded from the spotlight and generally was discarded as a verbalized term. Theorists in psychosomatics had relied heavily on it as the basis for a series of illnesses that they termed psychosomatic.[13]

PSYCHOSOMATIC DISORDERS: A LAST GASP OF STRANGULATED AFFECT

The biologists' discoveries of genetic markers for each of the "psychosomatic" disorders during those same years have been shielded from the serious attention of the psychosomatists and have not yet distrained their views.[14] They continue to believe that these disorders, which actually have genetically based propensities, occur because of strangulated affect.

Biological studies continue to point to a genetic propensity activated by either infection or as physical response to some inhaled, ingested, or infectious substance that brings the disorders into action. Asthma (noxious substances usually from inhalation), the trio of rheumatic fever, rheumatic heart, and ulcerative colitis (either streptococcal or salmonella bacterial infection), and duodenal and peptic ulcers (helicobacter pylori bacterial infection) are examples.

It is not surprising to any who know the biological findings that decades of psychological treatment to cure "organ neuroses" has been a total waste. The completely ineffectual psychological treatment of "organ neuroses" since the 1930s has strangely continued without sacrifice of credibility within the mental health field. Again, the test of time has not served to persuade professionals away from nonsense fictions and toward useful truths. Early in the 1970s, the discovery of the bacterial infection that triggered peptic and duodenal ulcers led to the modest cost, antibiotic six-week cure of those disorders. But few patients received the superior new treatment. It took twenty years before such treatment gained much notice among the various health care professionals. Even now many internists continue the past interminable palliative treatments or horrifyingly sanction surgical removal of ulcerated gut that is quite capable of healing and functioning, instead of curing patients through use of the new knowledge.

Psychological treatment could neither prevent nor cure genetic disorder and should never have been offered except experimentally or in relation to somatopsychic problems. Scientific logic and careful research design would have precluded several decades of unfortunate excursion into psychological treatment of biological problems. The investigations that had been done to support fallacious theories of "organ neuroses" were poor science.

We can understand that the story of affect phobia is the story of a universal reaction to mistaken beliefs about emotions, about what they are and about what they are not. Extended past descriptions of the processes of the many psychological disorders have sometimes been complex, although explanations of the notions of being possessed by spirits, having faulty conditioned responses, being damaged by undischarged affect, having distorted cognizance, etc., are in themselves simple descriptions. But the dialectical discussions used to amplify each of these always become lengthy and complex. However, the symptom disorders become simpler to understand when we incorporate the concept of affect phobia in our basic frame of reference for understanding emotion.

Knowing the implications of affect phobia in psychopathology increases the clarity of our understanding. The new theory of emotion complicates theory of symptom and neurosis somewhat, but simplifies treatment and makes cure and even prevention possible. Discoveries about the fundamental nature of psychological disorders form the starting point for some subsequent descriptions of psychotherapeutic approaches that are in some ways contrary to long-held beliefs about the path to and importance of conflict resolution in therapy. With our new knowledge we can take a direct path to deal with psychological disorders.

NOTES

1. Many pop psychologies sincerely offer special training to gain the benefits of "getting out feelings," despite the impossibility of such processes. A hopeful public is attracted by authorities promising the impossible.

2. In contrast see C. Brenner, "Depression, Anxiety and Affect Theory," *International Journal of Psychoanalysis* 55:1 (1974): 25–36.

3. K. S. Isaacs, "Feeling Bad and Feeling Badly," *Psychoanalytic Psychology* 1 (1984): 43–60.

4. She was the person who creatively brought together the ideas of storage of mental process and catharsis by speaking to remove accumulations to free mental processes. Though she was entirely wrong, these seminal ideas were adopted and tried by Freud, although later rejected by him, but served as the starting point of a scientific field and movement.

5. H. Garrison, *An Introduction to the History of Medicine*, 4th ed. (Philadelphia and London: W. B. Saunders & Co., 1929).

6. M. Scott Peck, *The Road Less Traveled* (New York: Simon & Schuster, 1978).

7. A. Freud, *The Ego and its Mechanisms of Defense*, trans. by Cecil Baines (1936; New York: International Universities Press, 1946). J. Sandler, with A. Freud, *The Analysis of Defense: The Ego and the Mechanisms of Defense Revisited* (New York: International Universities Press, 1985).

8. S. Freud, *The Standard Edition of The Complete Psychological Works of Sigmund Freud*, vol. 2 *Studies on Hysteria by Joseph Breuer and Sigmund Freud*, trans. J. Strachey (London: The Hogarth Press Limited, 1955).

9. Freud shifted from his physical term "catharsis" to the psychological term "abreaction."

10. H. D. Lee, "On Theoretic Interest in the Affects" (unpublished).

11. Transference is simply a part of the tendency of human minds to retain memories of experiences as frames of reference for viewing new experiences. *It means that we always see something of past relationships in our present relationships.*

12. Additionally, we can develop a more useful taxonomy than Freud was able to use and notice the useful distinctions between anxiety, fear, apprehension, jitteriness, edginess, and worry, etc.

13. F. Dunbar, *Psychosomatic Diagnosis* (New York: Hoeber, 1944); Franz Alexander, *The Medical Value of Psychoanalysis* (New York: International Universities Press, 1984); Otto Fenichel, *The Psychoanalytic Theory of Neurosis* (New York: Norton, 1945).

14. Z. Harsanyi and R. Hutton, *Genetic Prophecy: Beyond the Double Helix* (New York: Rawson & Wade, Inc., 1981).

4

Affect Phobia: A Universal
Human Condition

Despite being unnoticed over the years, affect phobia is a universal human pathology that is a major factor in the genesis of psychological disorders.[1] Those disorders that we can attribute to the existence of affect phobia have been estimated to afflict and disable at least 10 percent of the world's population, but the actual figure for these disorders seems likely to be at least half again as high or even double. Surveys among some highly susceptible populations would be difficult to carry out. The cloudy criteria for the various disorders, and some additional manifestations added by this writing, make the statistical information even more uncertain.

Because affect phobia is a natural developmental stage that could and should be surmounted by everyone—but rarely is—it blights life for everyone. Probably because it has existed for so long a time as an accepted universal human characteristic, there is the added cultural support for affect phobia as ego syntonic. That syntonicity is another important reason its disruptive role in psychological functioning remained unexamined despite its probable existence over the entire span of human history. Our patterns of affect language, even in earliest written history, demonstrate the long-term burden of our foggy understanding of emotion. The fact of this unnoticed existence of affect phobia and the human failure to examine a salient feature of personality has been, in some part, a result of the influence of common wisdom.

We learn through common wisdom, for it is a major method of transmitting understanding of the world from each generation to the next. That process gives humans vastly more knowledge than they would have if they, like all other creatures, were limited to the combination of their instincts plus their personal experiences for understanding the world. Yet common wisdom, while providing advantages, can also create formidable barriers to advances in knowledge. When common wisdom enters science as premisal to a theory (a frequent occurrence), only the remainder of the theory, the part that does not have its basis in common wisdom premises, is carefully examined and tested. Common wisdom not only carries the comfort of ego syntonicity, at times it seems to be regarded as God-given. Whoever dares to question, delete, or revise such "truths" confronts a mighty host.

EMOTION AS A DANGER

Affect phobia, as an irrational unease with emotion, appears to me to be a universal condition in all societies and, as far as I can determine, throughout written human history. It should not surprise us that the concept of emotion as a danger is integrated into theories by theorists sharing that attitude in all schools of psychology that consider affect.

Nothing universal is likely to be due solely to social learning, for social learning does not cross cultural lines easily or uniformly. The more likely explanation is that affect phobia is a natural stage of development. Such an infantile stage could and should be regularly surmounted in human development, but rarely is. That omission seems to be due to a universal failure in parenting. That perdurant pattern exists only because generation after generation of parents have themselves grown up with affect phobia that was not dispelled. They in turn do not disillusion their children.[2]

The suggested revisions in affect theory strengthen general psychological understanding and make it more broadly useful as a theory of the dynamic unconscious and developmental process. It is of considerable importance for the future that these revisions of psychological theory enable preventive efforts to become feasible and highly useful.

The profound effect of the addition of "transient affect" theory to general theory of psychological processes brings changes in theories of all schools. Several disorders that have been mysteries subjected to lengthy useless treatment (useless except for the comfort patients derive from the attention of therapists) now become simpler to understand and therefore permanently curable. As therapists get increasingly serious about the place and process of affect in human life, about a careful taxonomy of affect, and rigorous standards of logical thought supplant mellow fictionalizing, therapeutic and prevention activities will become highly effective endeavors. The eventual result can be that many psychological disorders that occupy hundreds of thousands of therapy sessions each year will no longer exist in significant numbers. Psychologists will find other applications for their knowledge.

It is possible for everyone on earth to learn what will surprise some, that they not only do not have to do anything about their emotions, but that they cannot do anything about them. That is because emotions are built-in automatic responses that appear and instantly dissipate. The typical pattern is for an emotion to be evoked by an event as helpful information about that event. Affect phobia makes the affect seem both bad and more important than the event that evoked it. For instance, a danger is sensed and evokes a natural, useful response of fear. Without affect phobia, that useful fear experience would turn our attention to the danger and give us opportunity to respond to it—to confront, flee, or disregard it. With affect phobia, we divert our focus to the experience of fear as if that, not the dangerous circumstance, is what needs to be confronted, to be "dealt with." This latter response is a pathological sequence of events that is so common it usually occurs unnoticed in most people as if it is a natural, necessary, and constructive part of life. That is what is connoted by the famous but seriously pathological statement repeated over thousands of years and intended to be inspirational: "We have nothing to fear but fear itself." The healthy statement is, "There is terrible danger. But our fear will bring courage so that we will prevail."

Affect phobia distorts our view of emotion and in its pressing us to fuss with instead of use emotions serves to generate the totally unnecessary, unnatural, pathological potentiation of emotions. Potentiation often builds emotion storms. Storms are trouble. How they create the varieties of psychological problems, how they can be cured, how they can be prevented, and how life can be different for humanity are matters well worth careful study.

How the fantasy of the workings and meaning of emotion got that way takes us well back into human history. A funny thing happened to the human race along its path of development. The whole race got entangled in a misunderstanding of emotions. The more they puzzled about it, the more convoluted the explanations became. Confusion grew. Attitudes that were devised to fit with the misunderstanding about emotion created and maintained the entanglement. Affect phobia became a way of life.

Emotion was considered an enduring, disruptive, wasteful, interfering burden—a trouble. Theories failed to recognize the natural, transient, benign, constructive function of emotion. The blessing of emotion provided by nature became universally regarded as an evil opponent in our lives. Emotion became something to cure. Medicating of anger, sadness, fear, and guilt—as if they were illness—became commonplace.

Humanity would have been far better off with a clear understanding of the nature of emotion. We should have distinguished para emotions from true emotions. We should have made careful distinctions when talking about emotion. True emotion is different from pseudo-emotions (as in "*I feel* that the economy will improve"), from emotion evoking conditions (as in "I *feel* frustrated"), and from actions related to emotions (such as hitting or smiling). We should have distinguished complex emotion states from emotion (e.g., phobia from fear, depression from sadness), and all these from simple or pure emotions (such as sadness, surprise, anger, or joy).

Previous views ignored the parsimony of nature. Inexorably all organs, systems, and processes yield constructive functions either enhancing survival to the point of reproduction of the species or are at least neutral to it. Otherwise, they drop out of the gene pool. If emotion did not have constructive functions, it too would have disappeared long ago instead of remaining universally distributed.

Various special theories had been devised to deal with small portions of emotion theory, such as discharge or signal, or some particular emotion, such as anxiety, shame, or anger. The differing premises of those special theories precluded construction of coherent general theory of emotion from pieces of past theories. The internal incoherence of premises in attempts at such combinations assured that no matter how complex the aggregation of special and partial theories became, they provided no path to information about human life.

Some psychological disorders were correctly categorized as emotion disorders, but despite that were inappropriately treated as if they were disorders of intellect, biology, or behavioral habit pattern. Techniques of treatment within each school of thought were applied with religious devotion, even though those techniques were based on erroneous beliefs about mind and achieved questionable results. Certainly the application of techniques of several schools in hundreds of thousands of hours of treatment of psychosomatic illnesses epitomizes how ludicrous and wasteful erroneous theory can be.

Freud's discoveries gave us a therapy that explored the etiology of character, which enabled us to find the beginnings of patterns, developed from resolutions of conflicts. The reawakening of formative experiences, through transference neurosis effects, gives opportunity to form a new resolution of the old conflict from the vantage point of adult intelligence and experience.

The reality of the memories and of the events and reactions that served in the formation of personality patterns gave credence to other aspects of Freud's theories that were not as well grounded or testable as these. The aura from the apparent verifiability of the psychodynamic patterns produced an illusion of knowledge about matters that should have been called into question long ago. In turn, illusion of knowledge often generates overconfidence in pretenders of wisdom. This has inspired applications of the whole theory even for purposes for which it was not useful.

Despite the current primitive state of psychological science and its several related fields, there is some promise that eventually we can make the field valuable. At present we know too little to be able to agree well on matters of diagnosis, health, illness, and etiology. We have rarely cured psychological disorders that torment people; often we ameliorate them, but too often we worsen them.

The funny thing that happened during the development of socialization of the human species is that everyone became at least a little ill at ease with one or another emotion. Depending upon the person and individual experience, different emotions became the object of antipathy. That antipathy is why emotion is consistently and universally regarded as a disruptive aspect of life. Apparently that attitude has prevailed over millennia. There is evidence in the written records of over five thousand years of history that it has long been a part of human life. Psychologies that include emotion process in their theories tend to suggest that emotion is a discharge phenomenon, and once aroused, remains within—stored either as some sort of matter or as an energy potential for some kind of action. From that view, emotions have been considered a source of damage while in storage. Worse yet, they are thought to become a disposal problem the more they accumulate. That, in itself, is a source of distress for many people.

The implications of the different fundamental premise changes the theory of emotion process and through that the theories of symptom formation, neurosis, health, and therapy. These theoretical explanations alter and markedly improve the potential of therapies. They enable us to cure some disorders rather swiftly, instead of slowly ameliorating them. Further, and of far greater importance, they provide a basis for effective prevention programs for symptom disorders and some other psychological problems. Eventually they will be the basis of eradication of many psychological disorders, including all the classic neuroses that were the never-attained object of Freud's initial efforts. Instead, Freud discovered the marvels of processes related to the development of personality and important issues of character and personality formation. He made the mistake of inferring that these were the most important factors in the classic neuroses. In so doing, Freud stopped the further search that might have brought him to the factors described in this book, which would in turn have brought the sought-for cures then, instead of one hundred years later.

THE ORIGINS OF AFFECT PHOBIA

A more general understanding of what affect phobia is, how affect phobia starts, and the variety and seriousness of consequences of affect phobia increases our understanding of health and illness enough to cure, instead of treat, symptom disorders. Astonishing to some, it makes our children immune to symptom disorders, finally to eradicate these disorders from the world. To do that we need to understand the workings of our two important mental processes—affect and cognition.

If you watch newborns and young infants, you will see that they are quite unabashed about their emotions. They seem instantly aware of anger, grief, joy, and all their other emotions as direct responses to their momentary mental content, and their whole bodies portray the reaction. Emotions appear and, as the inner or outer situation evoking the emotions changes, new emotion appropriate to the new situation replaces the existing emotion in a continuing sequence. Emotion and thought processes are similar in that they have a continuing flow that is rarely interrupted. So it appears to be with most of earth's creatures. Emotions are used by all of this world's creatures in a direct manner that gives them guidance and comprehension of their circumstances. Once past infancy, only humans (because of greater capacities for discernment of others and anticipation of their reactions) significantly tangle themselves in reactions to their own emotions. Our complexity of mind and our complexity of interpersonal situations have moved humans from the natural primitive, conscious or semiconscious use of emotion, and we have made that move in some unfortunate ways.[3]

We can speculate that one of the paths by which this happens is that as children develop, and especially after they attain some autonomy, what they want may conflict with what the parent wants. Parents prohibit. Sometimes they do so necessarily to protect child, property, or others. Sometimes they do so unnecessarily—because parents have needs and limitations. Parts of such conflicts are visible, but the more consequential aspects go on inside the child as the child internalizes the parents' attitudes. He forms internal representations of parents and has a dialogue and conflict with those. Instinct pushes one way. Relationship pushes another way. There is an internal contest. The solution of the conflict of will is more often a defeat for the child's urges, a painful but often necessary part of the process of learning about realities of the interpersonal world. It is the internal accompanying process that develops an enduring structure.

We can conjecture, along with many other observers, that children until this point have understood "thought-feeling-impulse-action" as an indivisible entity. Therefore that brings the hypothesis that it is the combination—a unity of mental elements—that is unacceptable to parents. They are unaware that parents are not proficient mind readers who have a clear view of the first three elements, and therefore they do not discern that it is only the actions (not thoughts or feelings) that ordinarily concern them. Nor are children aware that their parents have separated those elements that they themselves have not separated. Children do not necessarily comprehend the degree of freedom they have. That infantile idea of undifferentiated mental content may lead to bewilderment within the child, but is the basis of much pernicious consequence when continued into adulthood. It is the basis of ruinous aims to manage, control, deny, release, fight, expel, discharge, suppress, or tolerate autonomous processes of emotion. Starting early, children set themselves that task of trying to manage, control, or deal with the whole complex entity rather than the simpler useful and feasible task of trying only to manage, regulate, or deal with action that is unacceptable to parents. How unfortunate that trying to deal with this conflict is an energy consuming and attention diverting activity. It is a monumental effort, whether for children or adults! How could the impossible be less than formidable?

After such confrontations have occurred enough times, a child develops a pattern of diffidence to emotion—becomes uneasy and discomfited with some emotions. I have termed this unease affect phobia. Parents rarely correct their children's misunderstanding about emotion, for they themselves have not, in childhood or later, had their own misunderstanding corrected. Because they do not understand the benefits of emotion experience and emotion knowledge, nor recognize the problem of confusion in their child (and themselves) about actions versus inner experience, the emotion phobia that should have been left behind as an early natural stage of development has become a lifetime pathology for each human being, generation after generation.

A simple piece of knowledge, if provided by parents to each child, would protect that child and fundamentally change his or her path of development for the better. *It is the knowledge that emotion is a mental system providing useful information without ever being dangerous, damaging, or disturbing except when contended with, a system related to but separate from action.* This is a crucial issue we will return to throughout the book.

The pattern of interaction in which this initially takes place may be that of mother and infant, with later generalization to father, other family members, and beyond. Fear of abandonment, before development of confidence in the direct interpersonal relation to mother,[4] soon internalizes as part of the first object representation of the mother. Any affects that impel to actions of a sort that an infant may perceive as a threat to the object-relation (mother representation) are a powerful basis for subduing action. Such restrictions of action, when thought of as merely delay rather than extinction, create an uneasiness. Every infant develops the hypothesis that he or she stores any unexpressed affect as delayed action, and this becomes an unexamined premise for beliefs about emotion process.

In this sense, an emotion that threatens to disturb the relationship with the internalized mother representation, and later with object relations in general, will be considered a "negative" or "bad" emotion by the infant. The impelling emotion itself (because it equals action) may then be perceived to be the same danger to the relationship as the action would be. The perception of danger may, in sequence, be the basis of a secondary emotion response such as guilt or shame. Painful emotion thus serves as motive for defense. Otto Fenichel notes correctly that ego defenses are based in affect rather than instinct,[5] but then he wavers, declaring that the organization of drives is of more importance in the psychogenesis of neurosis. Experience tells us that analysis at the basic level—affect—is more fruitful than at the level of defense against instinct.

The intensity of affect phobia ranges from mild unease with some emotions to a paralyzing terror of emotions. The most convincing hypothesis of the genesis of affect phobia is as follows: the belief that emotion stores appears to begin in the earliest stages of individual development. In the undifferentiated (id-dominated) stage of infancy, *to think is to act*, for feeling and thinking are fused with doing. It appears that the instant an infant feels something, he or she is moved to act upon that feeling. But, of course, that is the condition for most of earth's creatures, all less evolved than humans. The sequential tie between feeling and acting appears to include no decision point between mentation and action. That appears to be the healthy state for less evolved creatures and gives those simpler minds no problem. In the complexity of evolved human minds and situations, however, with action viewed as simply an aspect of impulse, the belief develops that *refraining from feeling-impelled action is merely delaying an inevitable action*. From that belief, if there is no action, a part of the feeling-action entity is still waiting. The implication is that we retain the feeling as either substance or potential until some action ejects it.

THE TROUBLED LITERATURE OF EMOTION

In all the various writings that attempt to provide understanding about emotions, the common weakness is the failure to consider emotion as a built-in, natural, useful function. Without that basis, either the ideas are isolated from other aspects of theory or are integrated into a theory of personality that describes affects as disruptive aspects of personality and thus distort the conclusions. Additionally, there has been an egregious failure to notice and comprehend taxonomy and dynamics of emotion. Sylvan Tomkins has written extensively on the subject of affect.[6] When closely examined, however, his ideas are not persuasive. What may be a fatal limitation in his work is his premisal assertion as a fundamental notion that emotion derives from facial expression. That view involves fusing feeling with expression without a choice-point between them. He follows Darwin's path about the origin of emotion in facial expressions[7] and grimacing, but in error. No convincing description of that origin is presented for the large number of emotions that have no visible physical action. It is what we can now recognize as an infantile idea carried into science as fundamental. That highly illogical conceptualization is a flaw that limits almost everything Tomkins has proposed about affect. It is again the fact of existence of a choice-point between central function process and action as process that we must regard as critical for understanding affect process— what it is and how it works. Not recognizing the distinctions between central function, experience, and expression limits Tomkins' ability to answer a number of important questions. The concern with positive and negative emotions also places him in an illogical position, for the issue he is trying to get at is the positive and negative attitudes about specific emotions—but any affect, for a specific person in specific circumstances, may be experienced as pleasant or unpleasant. The categorization of positive and negative emotion is a nonsensical digression for many attempting to work in the field. He has fused affect experience with affect expression and created a comprehensive misunderstanding of emotion. He is also stuck with the notion of affect storage that shuts him off from the advantages of use of affect dynamics and the ability to understand the usefulness of transience as a fundamental explanatory premise. Again, as with his student Caroll Izard, the undifferentiated view of affect experience is a serious limiting factor.

While facial musculature allows one of the many sorts of expressions of affect, it is only one of such, and there is no absolute requirement for such expression. Nor does it seem logical that emotion moved inward from an origin in facial expression to become a central psychic process. That would call for something central to start an action to create a facial expression in the first place. Furthermore, the entire array of dozens of emotions do not each have describable distinctive facial expressions. Tomkins' sequaces seem as trapped in the same limitations as he.

As one of his propositions, Tomkins states that "affects are not private obscure intestinal responses but facial responses that communicate and motivate at once both publicly outward to the other and backward and inward to the one who smiles or cries or frowns or sneers or otherwise expresses his affects." In this he declares that emotion originates in the facial expression and moves backward and inward rather than originating in cortex or mind and then moves to various manifestations. However, the relative similarity of facial expressions from person to person and across cultures makes the tie to central function as a built-in tendency more logical as the origin rather than to either social learning or the facial muscles and nerves as the origin.

Beyond his weak taxonomy, in which he mixes affects, affect states, affect attributes, physical actions, and conditions for affect arousal all as affects, this strained logic does not jibe well with his proposition that affect is a motivator of mental and physical activity. In some ways, Tomkins' theory is actually counter to Darwin's theory of evolution. The bicameral brain has been a part of animal life from very early stages of evolution. Those earliest ancestors of ours are not noted for facial expressions, despite that.

There is a long list of workers who have attempted to delineate affect process over the years. They all appear to share a belief in affect mythology. Even the more recent spate of affect articles fall in line with their predecessors. Various workers have made suggestions of relevance in their attempts to understand emotion, but none has noticed some elements that are particularly crucial. Izard,[8] for instance, agrees, as so many do, that affect is a primary motivator of human behavior, but views the issue of transience and stability of emotion with disregard of neurophysiological fact and therefore can state the following: "Emotion states may last from seconds to hours and vary widely in intensity. In extraordinary conditions an emotion state of high intensity may continue for an extended period of time, but chronically intense emotion or frequent episodes of intense emotion may indicate psychopathology."[9]

Izard's theorizing is limited by a number of serious flaws: (1) He does not recognize the actuality of the continuing flow of conscious and unconscious emotion as a parallel to the continuing flow of conscious and unconscious idea. (2) He views transience of emotion as a relatively brief steady state instead of its reality as a repeatable microsecond event. (3) He has not come to the important distinction between an emotion state which is made of sequences of emotion events and the individual emotion events themselves. (4) He fails to recognize the repeated brief fractional second pulsing that is the only way our neurophysiology can function. (5) His theory founders on the failure to discriminate among processes and kinds of events that are dealt with as emotion. (6) He fails to recognize high intensity of affective experience as healthy response. Izard's failure to surmount these limitations has obscured the consequences of transient affect that explain far more validly than could be known using the expansive time limits he has espoused. It is the consequential cascade of implications of the actualities of emotion—which Freud, Tomkins, and their followers have omitted or distorted—that informs and enlightens us about psychological health and illness.

The discovery in 1960 of *micro-momentary facial expressions*,[10] events that occur at a speed physiologically beneath visual limen, showed facial expression as one of many possible occasional consequences, rather than the cause (and certainly not the central source) of emotion. That is precisely the reverse of what Tomkins claimed. Those autonomous momentary facial expressions seem to register on the expresser or viewer, if at all, as facial tension because they are too rapid for the particular expression to be perceived by the viewer. It would seem likely that if affect and facial expression were as tightly bound as Tomkins and his sequaces suppose, all persons, including psychopaths, would manifest such autonomous hidden expression as continuous accompaniment of the continuous flow of emotion. That does not happen.[11]

It does not seem to matter much whether we search the most recent or early literature about affect, it all has a similar basis in common wisdom. Both the recent and long-existing literature with its muddled taxonomy creates a wandering through ideas of emotion sorts of processes based in common mistaken premises about emotion. Consistently, the theorizing also includes emotion as dangerous, disruptive, and enduring. The arguments among theoreticians are sometimes fierce battles between propo-nents of differing ways of discharging affects (that cannot be discharged), differences in how to regulate affect (that cannot be regulated), and differing views of anxiety processes in symptom formation (although anxiety has little to do with symptom formation). These are teapot tempests, for the opposing positions are issues that are of little scientific import. They are viewpoints about nonexistent or minor processes, or are struggles about entities that are not comparable elements. The "fierce, impassioned battles" within psychology are of little meaning for the subject matter of this book.

Over the years, many writers have offered ideas on affect theory. None I know of has worked with the necessary preliminaries of careful definition of the various elements of emotion. A few years back, for instance, Magda Arnold wrote on affect from the phenomenological and cognitive view-points.[12] She adopted the notion of a brief steady state of emotion, did not separate emotion-events from emotion-states, and did not understand emotion as an evaluative response to sensory data concomitant with the continuous flow of intellective evaluations of that same data. Melanie Klein described the relationship of envy and gratitude, pointing to the mutual interferences of either with the other.[13] She is one of the few who considered emotion function. There are, however, omissions in all the writings of what I regard as necessary elements for understanding emotion process.

None of these writers or any of those following them demonstrated that they had any conception of the varieties of intense emotion experience, nor of the important distinctions and functions among pure and para emotions. Theorists did not seem to discern emotion and idea collaborating as equally valuable simultaneous mental events. Instead most considered emotion a kind of second-class thinking; a subaspect of cognition. Recent publications (including those announced as forthcoming publications) echo again and again the structures that are founded on past errors and omissions.

Some psychoanalytic writers have dealt with affect in ways that super-ficially appear closer to mine, but that are still crucially different for they omit important aspects of affect process and their meaning. Henry Krystal, for instance, seemed aware that the popular belief is that there is a necessity for affect discharge.[14] He declared that tolerance of affect is a more appro-priate aim of psychoanalysis than control of affect. In this step toward—but not quite reaching—reality, his view retains the unfortunate implication that emotion is a formidable matter that must be dealt with, rather than being something benign, constructive, and functional. The espoused aim of tolerance unfortunately proposed by Krystal is an affect phobic pathology deviating from a healthy acceptance of affect as useful and nonpathological. Tolerance means putting up with something that is unacceptable. While tolerance may be a tactful or politic stance for people to take, it is an energy consuming masquerade, not health.

In his systems approach, Michael F. Basch understood affects within an information system, thus seemingly crediting them with having healthy useful function, but omits what this writing describes of that usefulness.[15] He also has not addressed the implications of transient affect for symptom formation processes and theory of illness. Howard Shevrin is aware of feeling as a kind of "knowing" and thus implies a sort of usefulness.[16] This is consistent with my view of affect as evaluative information. He does not address or seem to be aware of the issues of transience, the important distinctions between affect event and affect state, the important benign and transient attributes of affect, nor of emotions and para emotions. Charles Brenner's view fits the theoretically limiting common psychoanalytic idea, disregarding physiological fact, that affect is included by idea in an undifferentiated fusion of the two rather than what I regard as a crucial fact for understanding emotion—the independence of the two processes.[17]

Those examples of failures of theorists to make distinctions where there are important differences are examples of infantile mental contents being carried unnoticed and unexamined into adult common wisdom and then taking their place as science—accepted without examination. None of these various contributions include comprehension of the functioning of our dual mind, which explains affect as necessary, useful, concomitant, but relatively independent of ideation and equally important and necessary. Nor do any of those contributions include awareness of the issues I described as myth and actuality of emotions. The inclusion of several new premises and principles lead to theories that make the science of personality move to a more advantageous level. The old and the new descriptions and applications are far different.

A recent book is touted by the publisher as "One of the most complete and authoritative discussions of the human affects," suggesting the writings win careful critique as to their completeness, logic, and meaningfulness as authority.[18] When we use the filter of our concepts offered about benign, transient, constructive emotion, *The Handbook of Emotions* articles, in their attempts to describe aspects of emotion, are remindful of the attempts by early scientists to understand the phenomena of fire and process of burning, which resulted in a residue of ash that was heavier than the substance that had been burned away. A series of fictions were devised in failed attempts to explain the phenomena. Only after a new concept (oxygen) was described and used in new studies could it be understood that combustion created oxides and thus answered that particular question and many more. Comparably, it is the addition of a beginning conceptual taxonomy of emotion used with some rigor and the addition of use of an instrument (self-observation) to enable new questions and beginnings of answers that we can begin to bring order and more knowledge for the science.

From the philosopher's viewpoint, in the same volume (*The Handbook of Emotions*) Robert Solomon appropriately presents an overview of a history of thought about emotion, offering a broad description of contributions of the concepts, including their errors and limitations, from the writings of philosophers over the ages as they groped for understanding of emotion phenomena as a continuous part of human experience over each lifetime. His discussion enlightens us to the consistency with which all thinkers on the subject failed to pursue the distinctions between emotions and other emotion sorts of things, failed to separate emotions from various attributes of emotions, and failed to work at breaking down the "molecule" of emotion, as a compound of pure emotion combined with a wide variety of emotion related matters, into its subparts to better their understanding.

The presentation points to the belief that Aristotle and so many following him shared in considering emotion a subaspect of intellect. It was an unfortunate error that over centuries acquired a devotion hard to counter. Nowhere had emotion obtained recognition as having its own kind of rational basis to make it fully equal instead of subordinate to cognition. Nowhere does emotion gain recognition as an equal partner in the functioning of our dual mind system.

Solomon's first paragraphs put the same issues I have struggled with over decades within the terms of his discipline of philosophy. He points to the same questions and the necessity for answers within his discipline that I have considered as being vital to the progress of psychological theory.

What is an emotion? This question was asked in precisely that form by William James, as the title of an essay he wrote for *Mind* over 100 years ago. (James 1884). But philosophers have been concerned and often worried about the nature of emotion since Socrates and the "pre-Socratics" who preceded him, and although the discipline has grown up (largely because of Socrates and his student Plato) as the pursuit of reason, the emotions have always lurked in the background—as a threat to reason, as a danger to philosophy and philosophers, as just plain unreasonable. Perhaps that is why one of the enduring metaphors of reason and emotion has been the metaphor of master and slave, with the wisdom of reason firmly in control, and the dangers of our impulses of emotion safely suppressed, channeled or (ideally) in harmony with reason. But the question, "What is an emotion?" has been as difficult to resolve as the emotions have been difficult to master. Just when it seems an adequate definition is in place, some new theory rears its unwelcome head and challenges our understanding.

The master-slave metaphor displays two features that still determine much of the philosophical views of emotion today. First and foremost there is the inferior role of emotion—the idea that emotion is much more primitive, less intelligent, more bestial, less dependable, and more dangerous than reason (all arguments that Aristotle and other enlightened Athenians used to justify the political institution of slavery as well). Second, and more profoundly, there is the reason-emotion distinction itself—as if we were dealing with different natural kinds, two conflicting and antagonistic aspects of the soul. Even those philosophers who sought to integrate them and reduce one to the other (typically reducing emotion to an inferior genus of reason, a "confused perception" or "distorted judgement" maintained the distinction and continued to insist on the superiority of reason. It was thus a mark of his considerable iconoclasm that the Scottish skeptic David Hume (1799/1888) in the 18th century, famously declared that "reason is and ought to be the slave of the passions." But even Hume, despite an ingenious analysis of the structure of emotions, ultimately fell back on the old models and metaphors.[19]

Thus David Hume is a rarity among philosophers for his placement of the "passions" as being as important as "reason" and suggesting the importance of the interactions between them. But his ideas did not sell. It is different today. We now understand the bicameral brain, have neuroscience discoveries of independence of processing of emotion and cognition, use the theory of organization of dynamic unconscious mental processes, and recognize unconscious as well as repressed affective processes. From our current vantage point, we can offer psychological answers to some of the questions philosophy wrestled with for so long.

With our modern knowledge of brain and mind, we can consider the implications of emotion and cognition as equal in importance, with an interworking that sustains that equality.

NOTES

1. The reasons for its invisibility must include individual differences in distribution of talents for self-observation and even the absence of self-observing function in the majority of people. This crucial issue is very difficult to study. It may very well turn out to be a genetic issue, a constitutional issue, or a matter of faulty development.

2. K. S. Isaacs, "Feeling Bad and Feeling Badly," *Psychoanalytic Psychology* (1984): 1, 43–60.

3. There is the story of the more primitive versus later developed affects yet to be worked out. We share some of our affects with many of our fellow fauna, but also seem to have intra- and interpersonal affects they do not have. The processes of the various affects have similarities, even though many of our affects appear to be related to the new kind of world in which we live. We may discover that emergency affects are related to primitive brain areas and social affects are tied to later cortical development. There is much yet to study.

4. As described by T. Benedek, "Adaptation to Reality in Early Infancy," *Psychoanalytic Quarterly* 7 (1938): 200ff.

5. Otto Fenichel, *The Psychoanalytic Theory of Neurosis* (New York: Norton, 1945), 161.

6. S. S. Tomkins *Affect, Imagery, Consciousness*, vol. 1, *The Positive Affects*; vol. 2, *The Negative Affects*; vol. 3, *The Negative Affects: Anger and Fear* (New York: Springer, 1962, 1963, 1991).

7. C. R. Darwin, *The Expression of Emotion in Man and Animals* (1872; Chicago: The University of Chicago Press, 1965).

8. C. Izard, *Human Emotions* (New York: Plenum Press, 1977).

9. Ibid.

10. E. Haggard and K. S. Isaacs, "Micromomentary Facial Expressions as Mechanisms in Psychotherapy," in *Methods of Research in Psychotherapy*, ed. L. A. Gottschalk and A. H. Auerbach (New York: Meredith Publishing Co., 1966), 154–65.

11. A number of our subjects were free of such facial action. In the famous presidential campaign debate between Kennedy and Nixon, for instance (unpublished study), Kennedy had no micromomentary expressions while Nixon showed many. Unaware of the brief facial expressions, Nixon later attributed his visible tension to poor makeup. Other studies of psychopaths suggest that they have their central emotion system disconnected from the peripheral processes—which also allows similarly absent physiological responses. That makes measures by the so-called lie detectors quite worthless. We do better in studying central functions of mind rather than peripheral manifestations when we seek knowledge of internal process.

12. M. Arnold, *Emotion and Personality*, vol 1. (New York: Columbia University Press, 1960).

13. M. Klein, *Envy and Gratitude: A Study of Unconsious Sources* (London: Tavistock Publications Limited, 1957).

14. H. Krystal, "The Genetic Development of Affect and Affect Regression," *The Annual of Psychoanalysis* 2 (1974): 98–126, and idem, "The Activating Aspect of Emotions," *Psychoanalysis & Contemporary Thought* 5 (1982): 605–42.

15. M. Basch, "Toward a Theory that Encompasses Depression: A Revision of Existing Causal Hypotheses in Psychoanalysis," in *Depression and Human Existence*, ed. E. J. Anthony and T. Benedek (Boston: Little Brown, 1975), 485–534.

16. H. Shevrin, "Semblences of Feeling: The Imagery of Affect in Empathy, Dreams, and Unconscious Processes," in *The Human Mind Revisited*, ed. Sydney Smith (New York: International Universities Press, 1978), 263–94.

17. C. Brenner, "A Psychoanalytic Theory of Affects," in *Emotion, Theory, Research, and Experience*, vol. I, *Theories of Emotion*, ed. R. Plutchik and H. Kellerman (New York: Academic Press, 1980), 345–48.

18. M. Lewis and J. Haviland, eds., *The Handbook of Emotions* (New York: Guilford Press, 1993).

19. Ibid., 3.

PART II

PSYCHOLOGICAL DISORDER AND TREATMENT FROM A NEW PERSPECTIVE

5

Psychological Processes in Disorders

It seems to surprise many psychologists that a shift in premises about emotion changes the theory of personality as much as it does. Yet it should hardly be surprising to us when we remember that the two major aspects of mind are the fundamental endowed processes, affect and cognition. All else is function related to (or from) these. Any theory attempting to explain mind with only one or the other process will be incompetent to the task. What follows brings affect into the center of processes of human functioning. It illustrates how this change in thinking about fundamental process changes everything at least a little.

PSYCHOLOGICAL DISORDERS AND THE VICISSITUDES OF AFFECT PHOBIA

A sequence of effects follows the advent of knowledge of affect events as transient, benign, and useful. From recognition of the existence and meaning of affect phobia, we gain a very different view of emotion processes. Implications of emotion processes explain various psychopathologies more clearly. From some new truths we understand that many disorders are different from what we had thought they were. *In large part the story of psychological disorders is the story of universal uneasiness with emotions.* Actualities of all the symptom disorders are at great variance from past truths about psychological disorders. Having these new explanations of psychological illness enables us to move various psychological dysfunctions from a loosely related assemblage of disorders with minimal organization into a pattern of orderliness not previously apparent. That new knowledge of those illnesses in turn changes our ideas of what treatment should be, gives us the ability to bring true cure instead of merely treatment of illness, and even informs us how to prevent occurrence of such disorders.

CHARTING THE PATHWAYS OF AFFECT PHOBIA

It is possible to describe a great deal about psychopathology in terms of various possible manifestations of the various results of affect phobia. We can describe a number of effects in terms of increasing intensity of affect phobia and the counter-affect processes that may arise. The purpose of the chart (see Table 5.1) is to help clarify similarities of disorders within clusters, and differences between clusters of psychological impairments, so that

Table 5.1
Vicissitudes of the Pathways of Affect Phobia: A Tentative Formulation

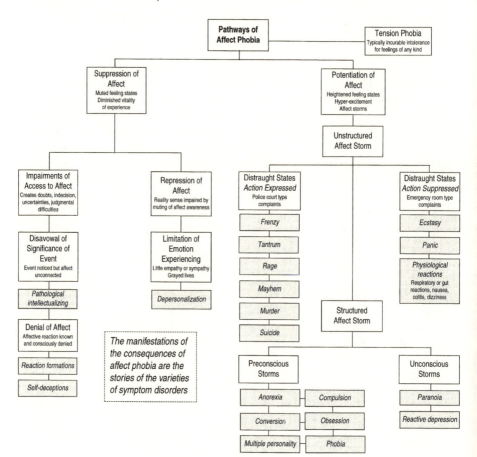

readers can group disorders according to their identical underlying aspects instead of their more variable, incidental surface manifestations. Table 5.1 can allow readers a reference when studying the descriptions of the psychological illnesses as described on the following pages.

Affect phobia varies in intensity from individual to individual and within a person from time to time. It creates distractions and disruptions in everyday life. There are some problems that are direct manifestations of that unease with emotion and many more problems and illnesses that are indirect manifestations. One terrible illness that is the direct result of intense affect phobia is tension phobia. It is a chronic disabling disorder that is rarely curable. A lengthy description of this illness is given in chapter 6.

Several interfering consequences of affect phobia, however, have not been noticed previously for what they are. They are listed here as part of a cluster although they are not as disabling as some others within the same cluster. They are usually curable.

The first general category is consequential to affect phobia leading to *suppression of awareness* of emotion. It is a cluster of minor psychological problems related to a moderate degree of muting of emotion that determines quality of life, relationships, and successes in endeavors. In varying degrees of intensity they mute awareness of and therefore the use of emotion in its necessary functions. This creates doubts, indecision, uncertainties, and judgmental deficiencies. Timorousness, aimlessness, and inability to commit to persons and principles also arise from the absence of clarity of preferences and aversions. This degree of muting creates psychological problems, but rarely creates psychological illnesses.

A further intensity of affect phobia, when it leads to greater muting, is serious enough to get people in trouble with themselves. Such a matter as a *disavowal of significance* of an event makes an event noticed but with no emotion consciously connected to it, and brings a spurious indifference to what is going on in and around the person, regardless of the significance of the events. Sometimes pathological intellectualizing occurs because emotional participation is lost.

When affect phobia leads to *denial of affect*, affective reaction, even though consciously known, may lead to self-deceptions or reaction formations.

Another pathway is affect phobia leading to *repression of affect* or *emotion muting*, creating severe impairment. At the least, emotion muting leads to *limited emotion experiencing*, with impaired capacity for empathy and sympathy. With extreme muting of affect, *depersonalization* results. This is usually a transient but always terrifying illness.

Instead of muting emotion, the unease with emotion may lead to *potentiating of emotion* by getting excited about getting excited. Chained reactions of emotion response to emotion response can occur in a variety of sequences. Thus, being afraid about being frightened, or angered about being angered, or angered about being ashamed may lead to a self-sustaining storm of emotion. These emotion storms may be unstructured or structured.

Unstructured emotion storms may create a distraught state in which *action is carried out*, leading to a frenzy that can result in mayhem, murder, suicide, berserk rages, tantrums, ecstasies, or obnoxious behavior of the type that ends in police courts.

Other unstructured emotion storms create distraught states in which *actions are suppressed* and result in panic episodes, hyper excitements, and hospital emergency room type of complaints in which there may be physiological reactions (gut reaction, nausea, colitis, dizziness, and frantic states of every sort).

After such distraught states have occurred several times, they may become a crystallized form of learned reaction giving a brain pattern structure to the episodes, leading to structured emotion storms. When the process is preconscious, these storms can develop as phobia, obsession, compulsion, conversion, multiple personality, or anorexia. When the process is unconscious, these storms can become reactive depression or paranoia.

Underlying Psychological Processes

When we categorize psychological disorders according to underlying process instead of surface manifestations, we have considerable advantage for guiding treatment applications to the central aspects of the disorders. Far too often, errors in diagnosis have occurred when similar surface manifestations arose in different disorders or when different surface manifestations arose in the same disorder.

We can start by recognizing four sources of psychological problems and the many disorders that derive from the processes in each. The first two have been long recognized as relevant to the basis of psychological disorders. They are:

1. *Maladaptive development and socially imposed restrictions*
2. *Psychic insufficiency from genetic or constitutional basis*

These two sources of psychological problems have a significant part in the production of distorted character formations, sociopathy, psychopathy, and a variety of pattern disorders that include antisocial personality, perversions, and personality insufficiencies. Recognition of the origins of insufficiencies and maldevelopment have long been parts of many theories. The derivatives are psychological troubles recognized as character neuroses and character disorders and have been most ably dealt with by the psychoanalytic and other psychodynamic approaches. However, they have not responded well to other schools of therapy. Because they are genetic, constitutional, or pattern disorders, they are not taken up as a significant part of this book.

The next two sources of psychological problems are the basis of a broad array of disorders we can now recognize as affective disorders, although they had not previously been recognized as such. They are:

3. *Muted emotion*
4. *Potentiated emotion*

We can observe and recognize the mental processes involved in muting and potentiating emotions as being consequences of affect phobia. That brings us to a redefinition of psychological disorder, includir.g crucial elements that had not been a part of psychological theory.

Because the crucial personality variable, affect phobia, by its very nature impeded recognition of its own existence, it was glossed over in previous attempts to understand psychological health and illness. Noticed or not, over the millennia the universal existence of affect phobia had a pernicious effect. It appears to have impaired psychological functioning and, by doing that, reduced creativity, productivity, and physical health in most people over thousands of generations. Often it created disabling illnesses. Finally this pathology was implicitly and explicitly incorporated into scientific psychological theories as if it is intrinsically natural to mental functioning. From that inclusion in psychological theories, misguided therapeutic approaches often aggravated rather than cured illnesses and continue to do so. In contrast, anyone understanding the processes derivative of affect phobia would be both free of symptom disorders and able to cure others.

It is of no small importance that the increased use of street drugs over the last several decades may be ascribed to the increased tendency toward affect phobia in the population. The wish is to be free of at least some emotions. Avoidance of awareness of emotion can be achieved artificially by use of drugs. In some others, it is muting of emotion that creates a sense of estrangement—with a consequent reduced sense of well-being—and that dysphoria brings a wish to feel again. For them the use of drugs brings them, so to speak, back up to zero. It is a kind of liberation, but without health. In both these instances, the underlying problem is the preventable and curable affect phobia. Without affect phobia, drug use would be less.

Blame for some portion of the increase in affect phobia may belong at the doorstep of the psychotherapy community to the degree that it has fostered affect phobia. Misguided belief in common knowledge has intensified that universal problem instead of relieving it. Affect phobic mental health professionals heighten affect phobia when they advise: "Get out your feelings." "Release your emotions." "Don't hold in your feelings." "If you feel it do it." "Your old feelings from childhood are burdening you." "Feelings you have held inside yourself are causing your neurosis." "Anger is a formidably dangerous emotion." "Feelings must be managed and controlled." "Take this medication so you will feel less." "You need treatment for your loneliness (grief, anger, sadness, guilt, etc.)"

One part of the definition of healthy personality functioning now can be stated as the free functioning of affect and full acceptance of emotion experience as constructive, benign, transient, natural function—all denoting freedom from affect phobia. Psychopathologies commence with even small amounts of contention with emotion and have an increasing degree of seriousness in correlation to the intensity of that affect phobia.

Recognizable problem states ranging from minor interferences with personality functioning of the sort that are tolerable to most persons to the extreme of severely disabling psychological symptom disorders that can lead to the vicissitudes of affect phobia allow us to view the broad scope of evolving processes that result from degrees and kinds of unease with emotion and the consequent interferences with natural functioning.

In preparation for the description of a variety of illnesses, we can restate the two kinds of interferences derivative of affect phobia, which are of particular interest in symptom disorders, and then elaborate upon the processes involved.

1. *Suppression of awareness of emotion and consequences of such muting of experience*
2. *Potentiation of emotions and consequences of varieties of intensification of experience*

Minor degrees of muting of consciousness of emotions result in minor but unequivocal interferences in personality function, such as doubt, indecision, or an inability to declare preferences in minor matters. These may appear in moments of emotion suppression or as a person's consistent tendency over time. Severe muting of consciousness of emotions changes a person's overall experiencing of the world. One's vitality of experience and clarity of perception of self and others is hampered by such muting or damping down of emotion experience. The degree of such muting determines the degree of interference that occurs.

With extreme degrees of muting, the very intense internal forces can ban from awareness all but the most vigorous exigent emotions. Doing that creates havoc in personality functioning. The resulting state is called depersonalization. It occurs as a transient condition far more commonly than has been generally noticed. It is so common that I have yet to meet anyone who has never experienced depersonalization. In muting there are several possible consequences. An event may be noticed by the person, but the ideation about the event is not integrated with emotion about the event. Pathological intellectualizing occurs. Muting, by omitting emotion participation in decisions, also plays a part in the uncritical acceptance of ideas that do not fit with consensually validated positive or negative perceptions.

Minor degrees of potentiation of emotion result in mild degrees of distress that disturb functioning and may briefly unsettle clarity of thinking, equanimity, and poise. People are temporarily "thrown off." With greater potentiation, the person may endure hyperexcitement, anger, tantrums, or berserk rages that move people to murder or suicide.[1] For those whose propensity is to withhold action, there is a tendency for the person to develop physical symptoms of hyperadrenal states, a focus on ideation, and various transient distraught states such as panic episodes. These all foreshadow the conditions that appear with structuring of storms. Structuring of storm processes seems to occur after potentiation has occurred many times, so that a pattern of response develops to move a person into an idiosyncratic standard repertoire of excitement and activity or physical reactions.

Partial Theories of Mind

To understand the new explanations, it is worthwhile exploring an overview of some past ways of viewing psychological disorder. Each previous view of pathology has attempted to understand pathologies by centering attention on whatever factor was believed by its adherents to be key to the processes of function and dysfunction of mind. Each specific treatment approach was designed to accord with a particular view of pathology. Those views of pathology and their derivative treatment techniques now can be reconsidered in relation to limitations arising from past errors or omissions in personality theory. We can better understand a broad variety of disorders as essentially affect disorders.

Fundamental Faults in Partial Theory. Emotion excretion theories, with a basis in belief that emotion, once it is aroused, remains inside us (in some kind of storage for whatever length of time) until it is expressed or discharged, carry the implication that emotions are unfortunate, interfering disturbances that become especially dangerous when we store, strangulate, hold in, or hold back. The theories form a cohesive description of mental process without convincing basis for connection of theory to mental process or consequences of application.[2] The idea of emotion discharge may, however, because of its fit with common wisdom, be the most widely believed psychological process. Even so, these theories do not bring together enough explanations of psychological processes to make them a school of psychology. While these excretion theories have the merit of working with a significant mental factor, emotion, they consistently misunderstand the fundamental nature of emotion, and diminish the value or even exclude the equally important factor of cognition. As with any partial theory, they are limited in their explanations and, from an erroneous premisal view of emotion, fail in the intention of utility of applications. The several excretion therapies, using techniques to "get out feelings," have a discouraging treatment outcome record.[3] We know now that the excretion of emotion is a charade of discharge of something that existed for only a fraction of a second—something that appeared and then immediately disappeared by itself.

Each of the many theories constructed in attempts to explain the diverse psychological disorders that plague the human race has protagonists proclaiming its validity. Unfortunately, all of those theories have severe limitations. Most of them have a "clay foot" problem stemming from common wisdom beliefs offered in the guise of scientific fact. Many theories are poorly tested fictions that have been so persuasively presented that they gained undeserved credence. Descriptions of pathological process have been illogical in some theories and chaotic in others. We now see discontinuity in their descriptions where meaningful continuities should have existed. Many of the descriptions are not amenable to scientific tests. The explanations do not explain well enough to cure. None has succeeded in providing a basis for cure of the troubles they attempt to explain, although to their credit a few have provided some comfort and amelioration.[4] Indeed, the incapacity to cure gives such a dismal record, proponents of some schools attempt an apologia by making a virtue out of deficiencies, declaring that the nature of the disorders is such that they could not be curable. Within that view, ambition to fully cure any of such disorders is a pathology of the therapist. That view gives no consideration to the possibility that it is the tentative state of the theory—not understanding the disorders—rather than the nature of the disorders that makes them incurable.

The viewpoint that the disorders are not truly curable myopically (and unimaginatively) assumes that existing descriptions of the disorders are the ultimate understanding. With such a belief, it makes no sense to aim treatment toward "impossible" cures; amelioration makes more sense. Partly because of that belief and partly from the pharmacological approach to psychological problems, an unfortunate trend has occurred in which amelioration, palliation, and symptom suppression during episodes of psychological illness have become thought of and spoken of as cure, thus obliterating distinctions between such limited outcomes and literal cure.

In truth, all therapies have produced amazingly little curative effects for patients despite intense, sincere efforts by both patient and therapist. Palliation should never have been considered a curative result. The protagonists for those theories are wrong. Most psychological symptom disorders are curable. The errors in the past are from poor science, faulty premises, faulty observation of facts, faulty hypotheses, faulty logic, and based on these as foundations, creation of faulty explanations leading to sincerely intended error-filled technical approaches to psychological disorders.

Biological Psychology. Because the faulty psychological theories infrequently brought cures, biologically oriented professionals have staunchly asserted that by reducing psychological processes to a biological level they can find physiological basis for the illnesses and therefore can appropriately classify psychological illness as psychiatric illness. For those believing that, the obvious approach is to treat brain function with the assumption that mental dysfunction (as a simple direct derivative of brain process) will be cured. If mental function is narrowly a function of the electrochemical processes of the brain, the chemical (or indeed electrical) applications will change the mental contents. The difference between psychiatric and psychological treatment approaches is the difference between manipulating by suppressing some electrochemical brain processes with the use of drugs (or electricity) versus educationally using words about feelings and ideas within the frame of a relationship to improve people's awareness and understanding of their own mental (mind) processes. The logic of the biochemical approach to psychological disorders is wanting because, to whatever extent neurotic troubles include patterns developed from learning experiences, no chemical will, by suppression of brain activity, provide a synthetic, healthier substitute learned content to supplant memory of the actual history. [5]

A spate of research studies have offered corroboration that the processes of emotion involve the electrochemical processes of our neural system. That there are connections should not surprise anyone, for concomitant processes occur at various levels. One problem in many studies is the research design inclusion of the tendentious presumption that reducing to biology can answer psychological questions. The causal connections between psychology and biology remain elusive, with few clear answers despite highly touted error-filled answers from chemical applications.

To whatever extent personality patterns are determined by the interaction of our genetic endowment with our personal experiences, the involvement of chemical processes is as participating vehicles—not as causes—of the personality patterns. Perhaps when biologists can produce pills that create not moods but specific emotions, such as surprise, admiration, or loneliness, or pills that make us consistently joyful (not indifferent) despite unfortunate events and consistently sad (not indifferent) despite fortunate events, then they will have established that chemicals can replace inner responses to our learned personality patterns. By doing so, however, they would create a disablement of people through "happy" pills that would keep them from the true meanings of inner and outer events. Yet they would still have the task of demonstrating that chemicals drive, rather than register, our learning. The further problem in this would be discovery of an ordinal relation between specific events or event types and specific emotions. To understand psychological matters, we have to work at the psychological, not biological, level.

A major and little noticed problem in many studies of emotions and mental disorders carried out by biologists is that although they have demonstrated an admirable rigor about chemicals, controls, statistics, and quantitative measures, sadly, when they attempt to deal with psychological issues, that rigor often dissolves. Their typically undifferentiated use of psychological concepts, diagnoses, and their omission of the distinctions among various emotions, as well as the lack of distinctions between emotions and other mental events (seemingly but not appropriately includable) moves many of those studies out of the realm of good science.

Despite meta analyses of such studies almost invariably suggesting that the theory is on the right track, the research design, faults in taxonomy, and confusion of cause and effect reduce the meaning of the results to relative insignificance. This is true despite the fact that, if a study is of large enough size as typical in meta analyses, the confidence ratio becomes encouraging even with weak correlative findings.

The extent of the misunderstanding of the differences between the two types of disorder (psychiatric and psychological), the difference between treatment and cure, and the uses and results of the biological and psychological approaches are exemplified beautifully in the introduction of a currently popular guidebook called *Psychotropic Drugs: Fast Facts*.[6] The author offers the erroneous common biopsychiatric description, which misconstrues the fundamental nature of various disorders, glosses over the distinction between palliation and cure, and ignores the important differences between psychotherapy and counseling. He displays well the biopsychiatry confusion about the important differences between augmenting levels of substances natural to the body (e.g., insulin), which have been seriously diminished by physiological dysfunction, versus imposing drugs (such as psychotropics) that normally either have no presence or have only minor presence in the human system. Flooding the body with such drugs, which are unnatural in kind or amount, have serious additional effects. The aimed-for effects in using unnatural drugs or unnatural amounts of natural drugs are alleviation of symptoms through suppression of brain function. But such a suppression of natural, necessary brain function is hard to defend as health building. The implied notion that the psychological disorders are the result of chemical imbalances is an unverbalized undertone throughout this reference guide. The better analogy for what the chemicals do, if, as in *Psychotropic Drugs: Fast Facts*, insulin is to be used as an example, would be that of injecting unnatural amounts (overdoses) of insulin to treat insufficiency of natural insulin (diabetes). One does not have to be a physiologist to comprehend the danger in that path.

Psychoanalytic Psychology. The psychoanalytic school, as a broad theory, is a rarity in a sea of partial theories of personality. It contains a broad cluster of truths about psychological functioning, including its faulty attempt at a single-emotion theory of affect. The breadth of the theory might be an advantage in the necessary transformation. It could achieve this, as a few of us have done, by substituting new affect theory for false truths of old affect theory and integrating the myriad consequent changes in theory of neurosis. Yet that might also be an insurmountable difficulty for many professionals, for that is not a simple change; it requires a double process of change first to abjure many past false truths and then espouse a multitude of new truths. The move from ignorance to knowledge is a less difficult path than the move from firmly held false knowledge to better knowledge. That may be a reason why cognitive theory (as a limited, partial theory) could have an easier path to transformation of itself to a whole theory—only having to add vast complex theories of the organized dynamic unconscious mind and of affect to become a whole theory without the task of first having to displace existing sets of ideas in those niches. It would have to make a considerable change in its view of psychopathology by constructing a far more complex theory of personality, health, and illness than it has previously recognized. That, of course, may be insurmountable for those professionals who have been content to build and utilize a theory ignoring the dual mind.

Cognitive Psychology. The cognitive approach, currently attracting a great deal of interest, has a laudable advantage, that of dealing with the surface of a fundamental aspect of mind—cognition—but has the fatal deficiency of omitting an integration of valuable knowledge about the equally important aspect of mind—emotion—into the theory. That restriction and the relative indifference to unconscious cognitive and affective processes keep that school of thought a partial theory. The fact that affect and cognition are independent, concomitant activities means that we should consider both equally in building an effective theory. If the cognitive school began to utilize knowledge of affect and commenced to deal seriously with those parts of cognition and affect that are out of awareness, it would move toward the breadth and depth of psychoanalytic truths and become a whole theory. It remains a partial theory of mind because it omits affect in general and omits the vast content of unconscious processes of both affect and cognition. It too ignores the dual mind.

Behavioral Psychology. The behavioral approach to mind focuses on visible products of mind because they are consensually much more verifiable, and eschews attempts to directly consider the contents and experience of mind (affect and cognition), because they are much less easily observed or consensually validated. But it is the central function of mind, to whatever extent that is recognizable, that is more informative than behavioral manifestations for understanding mind. As a partial theory of psychology, behaviorism has the laudable use of actual variables, including some that are relevant to the problems studied. That is why behaviorism is useful in some aspects of psychology. For psychotherapy, those variables are consistently immaterial to the mental processes of the illnesses. The effectiveness of behavioral treatment applications through conditioning or deconditioning processes has been of minimal consequence. Relief from episodes can come from interrupting and distracting, or from the natural fading of symptoms that comes with the self-subsiding of storms. Relieving episodes of psychological disorder is not the same as curing the disorder. Proponents have extolled those treatment approaches, although they have been ineffective for most of the various symptom disorders and of inconsequential effect in character pattern disorders. It remains a partial theory by exclusion of all subjectivity.

The Fundamental Nature of Psychological Disorders

Counseling aims to calm and ease people, but more important, it aims to guide them about living with or changing specific situations or their participation in those situations. Psychotherapy aims to enhance mental function and eliminate pathologies or other interferences in ways that enable the individual to guide themselves.[7] Dosages of chemicals that have profound effects on the body in the name of curative efforts need to be considered carefully. The *Psychotropic Drugs: Fast Facts* manual professes to inform readers about applications of psychopharmacology without touching upon theory. But it cannot be read by any whose orientation includes the question "why" of the scientific attitude, who want to understand processes, causes, and effects, without them noticing the book's undertone of pessimism about an actual cure. The author offers a sophisticated set of psychopharmacological facts and an amazingly naive set of psychological ideas, as in the following passage:

> Although *Psychotropic Drugs: Fast Facts* focuses on drugs, this does not mean that only drugs are effective. Medications function best to alleviate specific symptoms (e.g., delusions, panic attacks). Psychotherapy, in contrast, functions best to resolve specific issues (e.g., marital fights); issues may accompany, cause, or result from symptoms. Psychotherapy addresses the content of symptoms (e.g., "the homeless spy on me"). Psychotherapy clarifies how medications reduce symptoms (e.g., "I understand why I'm taking this drug"). Psychotherapy puts life into perspective (e.g., "My elevator phobia is fearsome, but my wife is fantastic!"). Psychotherapy explores how to behave with a mental disorder (e.g., to tell one's husband, not one's boss, about hallucinating). If one has diabetes, a medication, insulin, would reduce blood sugar; a self-help group, a psychotherapy, would discuss the stresses of living with diabetes. Insulin and a self-help group do not conflict, but serve different, albeit complementary, purposes. The same applies for psychotropic drugs and psychotherapy. To compare the two is akin to asking whether the length or the width of a football field determines its size. [8]

Thus the author trivializes aims of psychotherapy, and glosses over the vast complexities of mental function and the nature of psychological disorders. He does not consider the differences between psychological problems and psychological disorders nor meaning of psychotherapy. He can then blithely offer the use of pharmacology as if the comparatively simple biochemical ambiance that controls mood and suppresses function even deals with the complexity of psychological issues. He, like much of the public, does not yet recognize that for physiologically based endogenous depressions or schizophrenias a psychiatrist's knowledge may suffice, but for psychological disorders one needs help from someone with knowledge of complex mental processes in psychological health and illness.

Others writing about psychological disorders describe a psychological basis. Mathews, Gelder, and Johnston[9] discuss neuroses with the premise that anxiety is the etiological basis. Marks[10] describes a set of definitions of emotions that are somewhat at variance with those in this book, but that enable him to construct a coherent theory not otherwise possible. Some of the definitions he uses restrict his theorizing. For instance, he considers phobia to be "fear out of proportion." That definition creates problems in understanding both phobia and fear—and thus limits his theory.

Depression May Be One of the Most Overused Diagnoses of the Present Time. One of the reasons for overuse of depression as diagnosis is use of the check-list system of diagnosing disorders from surface manifestation signs listed in the standard diagnostic manuals. These are typically used instead of direct consideration of patient information about the mental processes that are the disorder. (The signs are what the professionals, as outside observers, detect and use as indicators of an illness, in contrast to symptoms that patients can objectively or subjectively detect.) The signs in the manuals and screening surveys mistakenly include various manifestations that may also be from inhibition caused by conflicting inner forces consuming energy (as in various distraught states) or could be consequences of unconscious affect storm in which energy is consumed by heightened emotion (as in reactive depression) or that could be from anergy due to reduced production of mental energy (as in endogenous depression). Use of such false signs from ignorance of inner processes have turned healthy sad, lonely, or grieving people into chronic patients diagnosed as depressed.

The diagnostic manuals even include healthy feeling reactions to some untoward experience. Indeed the manuals mistakenly include "sad and empty" and "appears tearful." If we recognize "sad" as an emotion and "empty" as an attempt to describe painful loneliness (meaning lonesomeness) from separation or loss of a relationship, we do not, should not, consider diagnosis of depression. Also we know that tears are rare in true depression. Instead, weeping portrays presence of a considerable intensity of felt emotion experience (probably occurring more often with hope and joy than with sadness) or relief that comes with resolution of conflict, as well as occurring with sadness.

A patient was sent to me for consultation because over the past year she had not been able to continue with her college work, was having trouble thinking clearly, could not concentrate well, and had stopped being as socially active as she had previously been. She was unable to work and did not get along well with family or friends. The trouble was triggered by conflict with her stepfather. Overwhelmed, she retreated to her room for much of the time, stayed in bed, frightened, bewildered, weepy, and saw herself as helpless. She consulted a psychologist and a psychiatrist at her college. She was diagnosed as depressed, given imipramine, and urged to leave the home. After moving, she improved in general functioning. However, her intellectual capacities diminished and her social life became nonexistent. She dropped from three courses to two courses and finally to one, and could not even manage that work well enough to pass. At the point she came to me she was planning to drop that course, abandon her plans for a college degree, and take a simple job.

Putting her story together, I viewed her original episode as a transient distraught state—a psychological problem rather than an illness—not depression. My suggestion was that this diagnosis indicated she could function better by understanding some of the processes within her mind. To do that she would have to taper off the mind-suppressive medicine with some medical guidance for doing so. I offered her the alternatives of continuing with the psychiatrist and medication, or working with me. I told her that I would be glad to work with her, and that if she wished she could make a further appointment. Because she rushed out without a word, I assumed she preferred to take medication and not study her inner world and that I would not hear from her again.

She returned a month later, smiling and more energetic, told me that when she had gone home she wept and was angry, frightened, and resentful. She stopped the drugs on her own, and within a week was able to think more clearly and was much like her old self. Her friends had commented favorably on her improvement. She had taken on two jobs to pay off the debts she had accumulated over the past year and was planning to go back to college. Her improvement, as she thought of it, was solely from being cured of drug effect, from dropping the unfortunate use of medication for the distraught state— indicated from misdiagnosis as a psychiatric disorder. She also was affected by hope from my statement that her troubles appeared quite curable. The psychiatric treatment appropriate for the supposed disorder had worsened rather than bettered this young lady's actual condition and wasted a year of her life. There are no grounds for assuming this is a singular instance of misdiagnosis or mistreatment.

Depression is an erroneous, much overused diagnosis currently applied for sadness, unhappiness, insomnia, hypersomnia, low energy or fatigue, low self-esteem, concentration difficulty, indecisiveness, dispirited states, sense of hopelessness, mourning or grieving, and inhibited states as well as correctly for reactive and endogenous depressions. In contrast to settling for palliation or alleviation of symptoms, knowledge about the fundamental nature of psychological disorder enables us to comprehend aims and processes of treatment, what works or fails, and why.

What this writing presents about psychological disorders is new knowledge of the dynamic processes of emotion woven with some portions of existing theory. Valid understanding of those processes can free a person from any of a very large cluster of disorders,[11] prevent the development of those disorders, and finally eradicate those psychological disorders from the face of the earth.[12] Such a valuable consequence is worth whatever effort is needed by individuals to replace their old ideas about emotion, health, and illness with new and more valid knowledge. Proponents of partial theories have much to learn about people. These new ideas are, like most fundamental truths, essentially simple; but because the implications touch on everything in personality function, the overall theory is extremely complex. Understanding the first part of this writing requires understanding some of what is described later. It is because of that complexity of interdependence of ideas that few can absorb and integrate these ideas in their first encounter with them, no matter how bright they are. It is a large task, but one well worth the labor.

NOTES

1. Many adolescent suicides are the consequence of such minor emotion storms. These are likely to occur when, during an emotion storm, the adolescent loses his perspective and for the moment believes there are no alternatives to suicide. Without the loss of critical judgment from depletion of intellectual energy, the probability of maintaining perspective would be much greater. Such occurrences among adolescents are far more likely to be the explanation than the commonly asserted basis of adolescent depression, and is far more curable and preventable. By treating affect storm with medications, the probability is exacerbation of the illness and an increase in the likelihood of suicide. Many instances of spouse abuse are also manifestation of rage storms. The exceptions are the coldly calculated cruelties of controlling unresolved (Delta) characters.

2. B. C. Finney, "Say It Again: An Active Therapy Technique," in *The Handbook of Gestalt Therapy*, ed. Chris Hatcher and Philip Himelstein (New York: Jason Aronson, Inc., 1976). Finney describes his view:

First and foremost, I emphasize feeling and emotion; faced with a choice I will always follow a feeling over a thought, I believe in the concept of emotional re-education, and for it to be re-education, it must be emotional. To be emotional, it must show the physical signs of mid-brain activity—tears, trembling, flushing, muscular activity, heart and breathing activity—all the familiar indices of autonomic response, including the facial expressions of the type described by Darwin and the primate ethnologists. Furthermore, I think that emotions are the particular domain of the "inner child," and the re-education of the "child" is the goal. All these notions lead to the idea that the goal of therapy is to free up the expressions of feelings—to get the block of natural emotional reactions removed; the more intense and prolonged and repeated the discharge of feeling, the better. This is of course catharsis of feeling—where Freud began; I think he left this procedure too soon. My experience has convinced me that when a person is able to experience and discharge in a controlled but intense way all the hurts and pains and the new ones occurring daily, he will lose the symptoms and anxieties that limit him. I agree with Janov (1970) that insights follow the discharge of feeling; when the conflicts and pains are experienced directly they cease to be unconscious. In general I find that it is not necessary to go through the symbolic and fantasy expressions; if one can get in touch what the "inner child" he will experience them without distortion. And I find I can talk directly with the "child." (446–47).

3. Is "feeling better" or "less anxious or bothered" equivalent to cure? Few patients, even if pleased about having some relief, would think so. The adherents of the excretion theories seem more beguiled by dramatic therapy process that they consider as meaningful improvement.

4. Among these are the beautifully written fictions contrived by Franz Alexander (*The Medical Value of Psychoanalysis* [1936; New York: International Universities Press, Inc., 1964]) and those by Flanders Dunbar (*Mind and Body: Psychosomatic Medicine* [New York: Random House, 1947]) describing "psychosomatic illnesses." These are marvelously persuasive with their breadth of coverage of psychological formulations of the basis of a variety of physical illnesses. The persuasiveness collapses, however, when one thinks of tests of the formulations, considers the logic of the arguments, notices the reversing of cause and effect, and the absence of any tie of those fictions to outer reality. Additionally the factors of genetic predisposition and the bacterial infection as triggers now make those past formulations untenable.

5. Medications that change moods have been used in psychiatric disorders, as in endogenous depressions, and other drugs have reduced hallucinations in schizophrenics, allowing them to function with less interference from "voices." In both instances, despite distressing side effects for some percentage of users, drugs have greatly benefited many. The unfortunate extrapolation to use of drugs for psychological illness makes a jump in logic and a distortion of facts about the nature of psychological disorders and may be an attempt by reductionists to arrogate the mental health field. To the extent that a psychological disorder is related to learned patterns intrinsic to personality, or related to learned patterns of fallacious beliefs, or related to failure of comprehension of knowledge that has effects on their personalities, chemical applications offer an unlikely curative prospect and always bring risk. A flood of poorly designed studies using inadequately defined control and experimental groups has been used to promote the use of drugs to deal with varieties of psychological disorders. In close examination, they appear to be insufficient basis for justifying the use of billions of dollars per year of psychotropic drugs. Those studies with their conclusions and recommendations deceive the majority of physicians into the belief that they have a superior understanding of psychological disorders and therefore sufficient knowledge for capacity to cure them. The public trustingly believes the same medical experts to have sufficient knowledge to deal with the issues.

For the character neuroses and character disorders that are properly routed to psychoanalysis to examine etiology to restructure patterns, the problems do not have to do with mood or biochemistry. Applications of drugs to change learned patterns in psychological disorders is analogous to use of some medication to take before traveling to a foreign country, so we could speak like a native when there, and then taking another medication upon return to restore ability in our own language. There is a world of difference between manipulating mood and reformulating personality or other psychological content.

6. J. S. Maxmen, *Psychotropic Drugs: Fast Facts* (New York: W. W. Norton & Co., 1991).

7. This is a difference in aim and process, not in people or profession. Many counselors do psychotherapy and many psychotherapists do counseling.

8. Maxmen, *Psychotropic Drugs*, vii.

9. A. W. Mathews, M. G. Gelder, and D. W. Johnston, *Agoraphobia: Nature and Treatment (New York: Guilford Press, 1981).*

10. I. M. Marks, *Fears, Phobias, Rituals: Pain, Anxiety, and their Disorders* (New York: Oxford University Press, 1987).

11. This has already taken place with several dozens of patients who remain free of all storm and affect muting disorders.

12. The theoretic basis for prevention programs is clear in this theory of psychological disorder.

6

Symptom Disorders

It is in affect phobia that we find the basis for creation of a significant portion of psychological disorders. These disturbances include all the symptom disorders that for a century have been considered "classic neuroses," plus discovery of other disorders suggested on the following pages. The knowledge presented provides the foundation to be used for adding to knowledge of psychological health, illness, treatment, and prevention.

Two extremely disturbing psychological illnesses that have been mysterious and puzzling have sometimes resulted in lengthy hospitalizations sometimes of several years in duration. With our new knowledge, the mystery disappears. The illnesses are, simply put, disorders consequent to suppression of emotion awareness. Neither hospitalization nor medication has been helpful for either. To the contrary, unless there are complications, hospitalization is unnecessary and medication usually worsens these disorders.

TENSION PHOBIA

When affect phobia results in sufficient discomfort so that a person seeks treatment for a healthy emotion (sadness, fear, loneliness, anger) or for a distraught state, physicians kindly offer medication to make a patient "feel less." Several medications shield people from feeling experience, making them less complete persons. Doing that is consistently destructive psychologically and brings the risk of destructive consequences biologically. Despite the kindly intent of the prescription, considerable risk arises from the

heightened iatrogenic possibilities of palliative drugs creating the psychological disorder I have named tension phobia. Tension phobia is an extremely painful state that sometimes results from affect phobia being
treated with medication (or from use of street drugs) over a period of six
months or more. The length of time this requires must be a result of several
factors that finally brings suppression of feeling awareness caused by most
of these drugs.

When drugs shield a person from emotion over some length of time,
reducing their sense of reality, it results in that person becoming both
unaccustomed to the normal, continuous, sequential flow of feelings and
the vitality of sense of self and the world around him. Although to most of
us such nonfeeling (muted experience of emotion) is a strange, uncomfortable state, it can become the usual and expected experience, no longer
strange, for a person drugged for an extended period. With adaptation to
muted experience, that emotion-anesthetized state makes sensation of any
sort come to be perceived as a dangerous intrusion into the refuge of
peaceful quietude of nonfeeling. Thus, anyone preferring a nonfeeling state
becomes extremely uncomfortable with any sensation of any sort, whether
physical or emotional. He comes to regard such sensations as noxious
encroachments. For those persons, what is often considered an addiction to
medication (or street drugs) may be an "addiction" to the quiescence of a
nonfeeling state.[1]

The enormity of this disorder and its horrible effects came with recognition of the troubles of a patient approximately thirty years ago. His horrifying experience is a dramatic example of the extreme degree tension
phobia can reach.

He was a 30 year old man who had been in treatment for several years
because he had not "found himself" after finishing college and had
worked out no vocation or career. His wealthy family, wanting the
best for him, inquired among physicians and followed a recommendation to send him to a prominent psychiatrist. That psychiatrist,
indoctrinated in biological psychiatry, upon meeting this patient decided that the patient was ill. He apparently did not discriminate
between psychological problems and psychological disorders, or
make distinctions between those disorders and psychiatric disorders.
Therefore, the physician turned this healthy but unambitious young
man, who enjoyed the somewhat indolent leisure of a wealthy life-
style, into a patient. Having a personality pattern devised to fit with
being raised to be taken care of in "the lap of luxury" without instilled
motivation to work to support himself other than to watch over his
investments, he was viewed as being ill. To the contrary, what he had
done was adapt by learning his pattern well: to be amiably unaggres-
sive, to expect to be taken care of, to be always congenial and affable,

to learn many facts for vignettes to use in small talk, but without pressure to apply knowledge in productive ways. To me it seemed not a neurosis or psychosis but an appropriate style of life for a genial member of a fortunate nobility. In no way was this a psychiatric disorder.

The physician, from his belief that the problem was brain, not mind, tried several medications over the years in the hope these would activate the patient's ambition. It was to help the patient "find himself," to "balance" those chemicals that had left him aiming only to use his considerable inherited funds to enjoy life. There was, I thought, some moral view that it was more proper for this contented young man to energize his brain to make socially productive use of his intellect and make more money than he could use. Over the eighteen months preceding my seeing him, the medication used was Prolixin, at that time a popular antischizophrenia drug, prescribed for the young man despite absence of any indication of that disease. The drug, like several others that had been tried, brought no remedial effect. The logic of any chemical creating changes that would turn a pleasant, passive, bright but unambitious young man into an empire builder like his grandfather is still not apparent to me. With hope that increased dosage would create the desired effect, the physician had finally raised the amounts to ten times the recommended usual dose (thus giving him three times what the manufacturer recommended as maximum dosage). The patient, with this medication, developed serious side effects of somnolence, muscular ataxia, retinal deterioration, and other problems that effectively disabled him. At that time, he could sit quietly with friends, converse a little, sleep long hours, and do little else. Perhaps the psychiatrist thought the patient was deteriorating despite the medication instead of because of it.

A friend of the patient told him of my work, and since the ideas made sense to the patient, he came to see me. I suggested that the amount of medication he was taking interfered with a very useful function, his being able to notice his emotions. To be able to work effectively with me to gain understanding of his emotions would require noticing them. He would have to reduce the medication. He was fully aware that the dosage prescribed for him was well beyond safe limits, was aware that the excess medication had damaged him, and was skeptical of what he had been told—that it was "an extreme measure to overcome his neurosis." He favored the idea of being free of drugs. I sent him to an internist to supervise that process. The internist was concerned with both the dangers from the excess drug use and the dangers of stopping suddenly. He decided that of the two dangers, the dangers of the high dosage made the considerable danger of rapid reduction the lesser of the two. Because of the great excess, he brought down the amounts of medication rapidly to moderate levels while staying very alert for detrimental physiological effects of rapid reduction.

The patient started to work with me in observation of his emotion. With reduction of medication, as is usual with most people coming off drugs, he began to recover his awareness of emotion. What happened from this point on is illustrative of the enormity of misusing drugs. After the years of affect anesthesia from the several medications that had been prescribed, he found each sensation to be strange, an intrusive "pain." What most of us consider ordinary sensation he considered agony. Each mild emotion experience and each bodily sensation of any sort—to be hungry or thirsty, hopeful, angry, or sad—was experienced as an assault. It was an agony for him. He had become accustomed to a nonfeeling state as his natural state. Affect anesthesia now was normal for him. The iatrogenic disorder was chronic.

We conversed much about feelings and sensations, their usefulness in enabling us to know when we are thirsty, hungry, sated, hot, cold, in danger or safe, to know the congeniality of companions, that we have lost someone, or that we find someone desirable. He could consider these as logical abstractions, could occasionally briefly experience the vitality of an affect experience, but could not consistently accept affect experience as a functional part of himself.

Despite the circumstance of long-term extreme drug use, he began making progress in awareness of feeling. I had been content to tutor him on the uses of emotion while he decreased use of the medications. The courage with which he faced the agony evoked by any tension was superb. After a few months of this, however, he wrote me a letter saying that he understood how my approach was right, but that it was too late for him. He could never stand to feel anything again. Instead of continuing with me to discuss this, he had returned to the psychiatrist and the anesthetic refuge of three times the maximum allowable medication. Some months later I learned that soon after returning to his overdose of medication he had gone to his family's summer home. One morning his boat had been found on the lake—empty.

Over the years I have seen many persons with similar but less extreme tension phobia. They had settled into a life of semiawareness of self and the world around them, and most often they had developed an arrangement with a kindly intentioned internist to take one or another psychotropic drug (addictively) for the rest of their lives to limit their experiencing.[2] In many instances, patients taking various of the neuroleptic, psychotropic drugs over some period, but who, for whatever reasons, had not developed tension phobia, could reduce medication and learn from me to use their emotions free of affect phobia. In no instance, so far, have I been able to bring severe tension phobic patients back to an affectively vital life experience. That task is theoretically possible. It may be that by contriving a special situation that offers a great deal (twenty-four hours per day) of augmentive support without drugs of any kind, there could be a reversal of the pattern of flight from emotion that had originated in childhood, later became intensified as affect phobia, and then by drug usage had crystallized into permanent "necessity." Undoing that may be possible in a contained environment, to do what is antithetical to "usual and customary" medicine and is rare in hospitals: to free people from the iatrogenic destruction of inappropriate medications while providing affect educational tutoring. That will be an arduous task. The far more feasible task is that of prevention of affect phobia and thus keeping people away from naive, sincerely intended destructive drug treatment.[3]

MUTED EMOTION: UNNOTICED DISORDERS AND "NORMAL" IMPAIRMENTS OF ACCESS TO AFFECT

There are several psychological problems that are related to suppression of emotion awareness, but are not as severe as tension phobia and depersonalization. Because these are quite common, they are often dismissed as unimportant, accepted as idiosyncrasy, or disregarded. The common attitude is that they are misfortunes to be lived with. These troubles are important in that they blight, rather than disable, lives. When they have been mistaken for pattern disorders, the intensive psychodynamic treatment has been exploration of etiology (as if they were personality disorders). The biopsychiatric treatment has been medication (as if they were mood disturbances). Muted emotion troubles appear to me to be most frequently misdiagnosed as depressive conditions and treated with chemicals that worsen it. If instead the muting tendencies are dealt with, the more serious emotion muting disorders might never arise in the person. Emotion access is imperative for ordinary as well as momentous decision making. Among the thousands of little decisions that each of us makes each day, we use that sense of meaningfulness and significance to press for decisions one way or the other. Without emotion participating we have doubt, indecision, and judgmental error. We may be uncertain what to select from a dinner menu, which city to bomb, what career to follow, or whom to marry.

Most of us have on occasion sat at a restaurant table while one of our companions scans the menu up and down, tentatively considering one and then another entree, sometimes cycling back to previous items. They indicate they cannot decide, ask others what they will get, and finally when forced to do so, select among the alternatives. For them it is like throwing a dart at the menu and taking whatever is nearest to their hit. When the dinner is served, they observe what others have selected and might indicate, "That looks better than mine. I probably should have gotten that." It is easy to see that they would be easily persuadable by any others who might set out to convince them of the merits of a specific choice. That suggestibility is one difficulty consequent to emotion muting.

Those persons appeared to be making up their minds and then changing their minds again and again, but that was not what they were really doing. They had not made up their minds at all. They had made a selection without making a choice. They did so because they were operating with diminished emotion awareness. It takes specific emotion experience as a feeling system indicator to inform us of our preferences and aversions along with our cognitive evaluations to make a selection also be a choice. That cannot happen when the voice of emotion is even slightly muted.

If this were a problem that occurred only with matters as minor as restaurant menus, the subject could be closed. It is because the muting of emotion occurs in all life situations that the necessary vitality of experiencing is reduced at times in some degree and in varieties of ways for most of the people on earth. That is often to their serious detriment. In matters of decision, the dithering by a president, for instance, may be followed by a seeming decision that is really an impulsive selection of some policy statement or action that requires later reneging. Such basis of actions by government officials has been costly to many countries. When presidents or other leaders have this defect, their personal limitations are of great cost to the public. Frequently legislators whose emotions are muted are persuaded to vote for legislation that later proves disastrous because they have temporarily succumbed to suggestion rather than adhering to principle.

It is that inability to know their feelings (be aware of and use the information of emotions) integrated with ideas as guidance that puts people in trouble with themselves. It is just as much a source of trouble as inability to think and be aware of and use the information of thought as guidance. I have known people to marry the wrong person, or turn away from the right person, because their feeling experience was insufficient for them to have enough of a sense of assurance about loving or not loving. They later realize they committed their lives to a less favorable path. Some people repeat that error in a series of marriages. Because it is emotion that determines our sense of certitude or doubt, use of emotion makes us confident of judgment and sure of our aims and activities. We need inner guidance from knowledge of preferences and aversions many times each day.[4]

A woman who came to see me wore a cashmere sweater with a price tag hanging from it. I asked her if she was not concerned that the pin attaching it might scratch her. She said, "I always wear clothes a few times before I can decide whether I want to keep them." It turned out that this was a common practice for her. She returned far more merchandise to the stores than she kept. While I am sure the assumed right of free use of stylish clothing was consciously chosen, it was in large part a result of her suppression of awareness of her emotions that made her unable to decide. Without such awareness she had to take a week or so until preference or aversion became apparent and allowed her to come to a decision, or until an array of opinions from family and friends assured her that her decision was "right." Much of her life in other aspects was just as uncertain.

Without emotion participation, we may even notice the event but not connect the evoked emotion with it and thus disavow the significance of that event. We may, under the same circumstance, engage in pathological intellectualizing. Symmetrically, without intellect participating, we may be impulsive. We do not operate well when we try either using intellect for what only emotion can inform us, or using emotion for what only our intellect can tell us. Sometimes a person denies the emotion he or she experiences—as in a vehement, "I never get angry!" These may be conscious deceptions, or they may be unconscious self-deceptions of the sort that sometimes lead to reaction-formations.

Emotion phobia leads us to all the various difficulties that are described in the preceding paragraphs. Those difficulties may be easily understood as varieties arising according to the proportion of suppression of awareness of emotion. When muting is of minor degree, most people live with impairments as simply their way of being. When they interfere with one's daily activities, or create great discomfort, it becomes a different matter. As episodes that run their course, these usually are self-cured in a short time. On the other hand, when brought to practitioners, most have received the current "usual and customary" antitherapeutic sorts of treatment. Tragically, practitioners who do not understand their nature have turned minor variations in the sense of reality into major lifelong disturbances. Such destructive "treatment" activity has been the disastrous standard in some circles.

Depersonalization: Varieties and Degrees of Emotion Muting

The second rather simple, troubling psychological disorder we have long regarded as a mysterious and incurable human trouble is depersonalization. There is in this disorder a sudden advent of a sense of strangeness about self, other, or surroundings.[5] Within a moment, a person shifts from being comfortably aware of who and what he is, where he is, and whom he is with, to being oppressed with a weird impression of uncertainty about the who, what, where, when, and how of his situation. It is as if he had been suddenly transported to another place (such as another planet) in which there is an exact replication of his previous situation, including substituted people in his life. The experience is that it is a precise replication, except that something is suspiciously different, somehow alien about the situation, person, or place. The weird, strange, and unreal impression of self and world often makes the person frightened that he is going crazy.

The sudden sense of strangeness disturbs the sufferers. Their descriptions often point to a sense of weirdness about themselves (or the world) that comes over them. They describe the world about them as frighteningly distant rather than immediate. Experiencing of life is grayed-off and less vital. The experience of loss of what has been known of self and surroundings is often terrifyingly ominous to them as their anxiety is aroused. The horrifying danger of losing their personality appears imminent to them. To them it is as though they are no longer directly participating in the world they have known. Sometimes they have a dizzied sensation or a sense of faintness. So many have declared that the world seems "weird" to them that I always consider the possibility of depersonalization when I hear that word from a distraught person. They commonly believe they have lost their sanity. Shame and fear about going crazy often makes people reluctant to reveal their mental state to others.

With our new understanding of emotion, we can perceive that depersonalization is a disturbance that is simple to understand and simple to cure. We can also understand why practically everyone has had such experiences—most often in adolescence. It is important to note that it can occasionally be a reaction to any of several other disorders, although usually it is self-curing. Commonly, it is a little noticed, complicating part of episodes of what is often called panic attack.

To understand this illness we need to consider the processes by which humans comprehend reality. Again it involves our concomitant dual mental processes. The crucial process of reality testing is a cognitive function, for our cognitive functions carry the main load in discerning what is real and what is illusion. Cognition evaluates the up, down, right, left orientation—the who, what, when, where of life.

Deficiencies in reality testing may seriously hamper our ability to function by blurring or even eclipsing distinctions between our fantasies and what others might consensually agree upon as the reality. Interferences or failures in reality testing may at some point reach a degree serious enough to move us from eccentricity to psychosis. It is the process of delusions.

The cognitive evaluation of what and where, even if working perfectly, does not help us much in comprehending the significance or meaningfulness of whatever is discerned. *That comprehension of meaningfulness is brought to us only by our emotion system. It informs us of meaning by the particular emotion quality, and informs us of how significant an event is for us by the intensity of that particular emotion.*

In schizophrenia, with reduced reality testing, we have diminished ability to perceive what is real and what is illusion. A schizophrenic (or drug intoxicated person) who believes he can fly might therefore leap from a window to his death, not comprehending why he is plummeting to earth. That would occur not because he seeks death but because he misunderstands the reality of who and what he is and what his circumstances are.

It has not previously been well recognized that emotion evaluation is what gives us the sense of reality, nor how crucial the "familiarity" provided by that sense of reality is for our healthy functioning. Although Paul Federn[6] described "sense of reality" and his student Edoardo Weiss[7] amplified it somewhat, neither described enough of the implications for these ideas to penetrate the mainstream thinking as having the importance they do have in understanding human health and illness.

We can hypothesize that the normal processing of sensory data involves channeling sensory data to two branching pathways for concomitant ideational and affective evaluation.[8] In depersonalization, use of data from the affect branch is blocked. This may be because totally suppressing awareness of the affect branch is simpler than repeatedly selecting and suppressing single emotions before or after passage through the branch.

Reducing the affective component diminishes the sense of reality. The world and self appear "real," but are experienced as "different." Though our reality testing operates primarily on the basis of an intellectual appraisal, our sense of reality operates on emotion evaluation of the same data. The estrangement that occurs in depersonalization is because, in this state, the perceptual image has a cognitive, but not an emotion component, and is therefore left incomplete. Although cognition is sufficient for reality testing, it is incapable of the task of reality sensing.[9]

It could have been further recognized that to guide our adaptation to whatever we encounter we need the continuous cognitive process of testing the real and distinguishing it from the unreal. We normally relax this testing process only in dreaming, fantasy, in reading or writing fiction, or when immersing ourselves in a play, movie, etc. We abnormally relinquish it with fever, use of alcohol or other drugs, and in illness. A serious disruption of reality testing is a mark of psychosis. Where that disruption occurs along the series of steps we use to keep track of reality determines what kind of disturbance will appear.

Our awareness of emotion is diminished in depersonalization, but is not ordinarily stopped. There is instead a degree of modulation of feeling awareness. It is a degree of muting. When the muting of emotion awareness is sufficient, it creates a condition in which only an intense experience can produce an emotion strong enough to emerge through that suppression and reach awareness. With such muting we may experience terror, fury, etc., but are less likely to be aware of apprehension or annoyance or any other of those mild emotion experiences that more subtly guide us throughout the day.[10] Thus, in depersonalization there is not a total absence but varying degrees of diminution of emotion. The degree of that reduction determines the experience of a person within the broad area ranging from minor impairments to disabling depersonalization.

Because we need both affect and cognition, absence of affect and the resulting diminished sense of reality makes our experience weird. It therefore brings anxiety into play with consequent "crazy fears." That "crazy fear" is often one component in painful panic episodes.[11] Biopsychiatrists consider panic episodes to be "attacks" and therefore treat panic episodes with medication to "stabilize" patients in relation to the physiological manifestations that are consequences of the psychological disorder. The medications so often used to "stabilize" the patients unfortunately worsen and usually seem to prolong both depersonalization and panic. Damage from their use can be considerable. In the light of our new understanding, it is clearly wrong treatment even though it is the usual and customary. Eventually it must be considered malpractice. If the physician response to medication-intensified depersonalization is then to increase the dosage of a substance that suppresses affect awareness, that in turn increases the depersonalization and further frightens the person, and thus further increases the panic. It is a path by which the usually brief problem of depersonalization has often been iatrogenically turned into lifelong trouble. Our new psychological understanding is simpler and offers cures more rapidly and without danger.

Probably the reason depersonalization has been misunderstood is that the concept of reality testing—keeping track of the reality around us—has not usually been distinguished by theorists from the concept of reality sense, the feeling of reality. When we understand these as two different concepts and how the processes of each work, we are well on the way to understanding and curing the disorder. Reversal of the process of emotion suppression has brought instant permanent cure of depersonalization in many patients. This has usually occurred in one or two treatment sessions when the patient's observation of affect expunging and recovery processes within him became a part of his knowledge of emotion processes. Patients who have been medicated have consistently taken much longer. Some of those have become unreachable because medication for depersonalization led to tension phobia that doomed them to lifelong illness. When reality-sensing functions well, it provides us with the crucial emotion experiencing of what is perceived. This operates in relation to both inner and outer reality.

For decades depersonalization had been regarded by some as an element of schizophrenia, as a prepsychotic condition, or as a mental disturbance requiring hospitalization.[12] Some people suffering with that disorder have been hospitalized for years without improvement.[13] Medications used have not cured and more often appear to have been the singular factor that worsened the condition. Because depersonalization episodes are universally experienced as transient ordeals at one or another time in life, and since only a tiny percentage of people have been treated for it, it should have been clear to professionals that most untreated episodes have been self-curative. Knowledge of that last fact should have aided recognition of depersonalization as a psychological disorder that is not psychosis and not prepsychotic. As such, it should have been treated without medication and without hospitalization—as a psychologic rather than psychiatric disorder.

Sadly, diagnosticians who do not understand its psychological processes frequently overlook depersonalization. They then treat the patient for another disorder—whatever has been mistakenly diagnosed. This brings the likelihood of the treatment being worthless for cure of the depersonalization, but worse, it can be seriously damaging to the patient by leading to other psychological disorders. Those who fail to understand the process of the illness unfortunately tend to think of depersonalization as a bothersome but insignificant aspect of some current illness believed by them to be the significant matter to treat. Those commonly misunderstood "more important" illnesses are often the more dramatic schizophrenia and panic.

POTENTIATION INTO STORM: UNSTRUCTURED STORM AS BRIEF EGO STATES

A further large class of disordered emotion processes—distraught states—also starts with emotion phobia. These are disorders that afflict many millions of people and on which billions of dollars are spent each year in treatment. The treatments used have been only palliative, because the distress usually moves people to consult internists and other general practitioners who prescribe sleeping potions, tranquilizers, or at least some neuroleptics. Those practitioners are the most likely to believe drug companies' tendentious descriptions that psychological disorders are psychiatric (brain function) disorders, and deceive themselves by assuming, therefore, that their knowledge of brain makes them sufficiently knowledgeable about psychology. They do what is best for their patients according to drug company recommendations and thereby risk making the patients' conditions worse or even chronic. We can now understand all these disorders as varieties of consequences of people contending with their own emotion experience. That is not a physical disorder. The unfortunate universal unease with emotion creates a propensity for reacting against and fighting against our useful built-in adaptive responses.

The disorders in this category may best be considered as a variety of distraught states resulting from such emotion response to emotion response. These are simple disorders that do not occur in anyone who understands his or her own emotion processes. These disorders are usually curable with our new knowledge about emotion, unless an unfortunate antitherapeutic treatment is first applied.

Potentiation of Emotion

Although an initial emotion response to events in and around us is healthy mental functioning and always constructive, our secondary emotion responses, if they are against those initial responses, are invariably pathological, even though this is a common human event familiar to most self-observing people. These reactions follow in the pattern of being irritated about being annoyed, angered about being irritated, furious about being angered, and enraged about being infuriated. That excitement moves a person from the healthy initial emotion response that offers information about the person's situation into a fight against that initial emotion. That potentiation can create an emotion storm.

Potentiation of emotion occurs as a consequence of the belief that emotion is a big event. That belief distracts the person from focusing on his situation to focusing on his emotion evaluation of the situation. Getting excited about emotion potentiates the emotion state. Potentiation of emotion draws mental energy away from intellective activities to sustain a storm of emotion for a time, until it subsides and mental energy is again appropriately apportioned between feeling and thought. During the intellective deprivation in a storm we can only resort to habit, rote memory, or ideas that call for little mental energy. Critical judgment is reduced for the time of the storm. The content of the flow of thought that is always a part of us may, as a result, be uncritically accepted or uncritically rejected. Those storms, brief as they are, are severe pathology. That is why for those moments, we function at the level of idiocy and appear as if psychotic.

Unstructured Storm Disturbances

These unstructured storm disturbances fall into two general types of distraught states in accordance with the temperament of the individual: (1) those people whose genetic attributes push them to internal (mental) action when they are distraught, and (2) those people whose genetic attributes push them to move into external (physical) action when distraught.

Unstructured storms in persons who tend toward internal action yield a frenzied hyperexcitement. Such persons become frantic and have physiological responses. Some have respiratory difficulty, including dyspnea, become dizzy, develop an attack of colitis, generate excess hormonal activity as in a hyperadrenal state, shake, tremble, become weak, and some manifest helplessness, sleep disturbances, or panic episodes. They include most of the sorts of difficulty that lead people to hospital emergency rooms for what turn out to be psychological difficulties.

Unstructured storms in persons pushed into overt action lead to destructive effects: threatening frenzy, mayhem, murder, suicide, berserk rage, tantrum, or other obnoxious behavior of police type complaints. The typical hostage situation, in which a man with a gun is holding his own family or others hostage, is a too frequent example of such a storm. Most police departments have learned to wait out the hostage situations. The storms soon subside, except when they occur in a psychopath or psychotic. None of the storms would occur in a person who observes and understands his or her own emotion processes. The typical spouse abuser is either in the category of susceptibility to rage storm episodes or is manifesting the cruel controlling behavior of primitive (Delta level) personalities acting coldly toward a spouse they "own."

While a theoretical time limit is uncertain, in either type of storm, whether action is suppressed or executed, the usual storm ranges from only a few minutes to (rarely) more than a few hours. The distress is such that the sufferers experience a dreadful agony during the episode. The storm usually subsides by itself, and the persons resume the experience and behavior of their ordinary state. People who become apprehensive about a return of the storm state are often persuaded to turn to drugs to protect themselves. None of these distraught states would occur in anyone who understood his or her own emotion processes and could observe these processes within himself or herself—a fact that suggests the preferred remedy.

The woman was distraught. She frantically rushed to the hospital emergency room complaining of difficulty breathing, a frightening sense of estrangement, and fear that some catastrophe would occur. She was trembling, sweating, and weeping. She portrayed her agitation by pacing back and forth, and by garbled talk in which she was trying to discuss several things at once. These all suggested mental derangement.

Such scenes are not rare in hospital emergency rooms. People in pain of every sort look for comfort in the wisdom they expect there. This woman's disconnected phrases and agitation would make most casual observers believe she was crazy. They might then have medicated her as a psychotic. A few minutes of questioning her, however, was enough to decide that the woman was not psychotic, was not physically ill, and did not need medication. She was in the midst of an emotion storm termed "panic" in the hospital records. The escalation of emotion had brought physiology into action. Hormonal actions had produced the rapid pulse, and made her gasp for breath as if she had run a hundred yards. Of most importance, the storm diverted mental energies toward emotion—and away from intellect. Then she could not think well, and her judgment was insufficient to allow her to assess her condition.

Her fear of fear had brought the sequence: being afraid of being afraid about being afraid. The whole episode was like several others she previously had; it all started with her misunderstanding about emotion. She did not comprehend the usefulness of feelings.

Sometimes, in less enlightened facilities, people in this condition are hospitalized, medicated, and treated for months. Their lives are disrupted. Worries about their sick spouse, child, or parent torment their families. In this particular hospital, where the attending resident physician knew of my theories, the emotion storm was disassembled in a few minutes by staff helping her understand her emotion system, without applying drugs.

What have just been described are some self-dissolving distraught states that occur in almost everyone from time to time and that are, for most people, usually transient unless mishandled. But these same distraught states can be transitory to structured affect storms. The shifts from unstructured to structured storms occur with repetitions, although people vary in number of repetitions required for that to happen. Some people have seemingly unending repetitions without fixing patterns of response. This is an aspect that needs study.

POTENTIATION INTO STORM: STRUCTURED STORMS AS RECURRENT EGO STATES

Beyond the emotion suppression disorders, we now can recast our formulation of other pathologies in the light of implications of affect phobia. The new view of psychological disorder separates the overarching category that had been termed a single general category, neurosis, into two general categories.[14] One category consists of the long recognized varied manifestations, classically termed character neurosis, which we can rename more descriptively and plainly as pattern disorders. These are described in a multitude of psychoanalytic writings. The second category is a group of disorders, including what had been categorized as the various dissociative disorders (phobias, conversions, multiple personalities, fugue states, obsessions, and compulsions) plus several other disorders, such as reactive depression, heterophobia, and paranoid episode, which can now be grouped descriptively and plainly as *symptom disorders*.

Symptom Disorders

Pattern disorders can be thought of as characterologic problems. They are personality distortions developed from inadequate or maladaptive drive-conflict resolution. They are characterological in the sense of being ready-made patterns for response to inner or outer circumstances. Those refractory disorders are, in effect, intrinsic to the personality of the individual. They cause people to get in their own way repetitively, defeat their own aims, be consistently in conflict with others, or have unsatisfying lives. In a real sense, these disorders are the personality. Such troubles include character neuroses, character disorders, adjustment disorders, developmental disorders, and some others. These disorders have manifestations that vary broadly from person to person so that they are hard to define specifically in categoric descriptions. Often they are seriously disabling. Treatment of these by the psychoanalytic approach has been the most successful. Other approaches have not helped and more often have wasted time, effort, and money.

Symptom disorders, however, now can be seen as very different troubles created by previously unrecognized emotion dynamic systems converging with psychodynamic patterns. Considering these disorders to be based in personality is no longer justified. These disorders are a result of failure to integrate affect and cognition. Emotion potentiation can lead to affect storm and result in formation of symptoms—producing symptom disorders by exaggerating the individual's normal psychodynamics.

Our new view of affect places the symptom disorders, such as phobias, compulsions, obsessions, conversions, multiple personalities, and several other troubles, as merely varieties of manifestations of occurrences of the same simple curable disorder—affect storm. With this understanding these disorders usually become simple treatment problems, despite the extreme pain and serious disablement they had involved. The new understanding may eventually remove these disorders from the category of illness. Without proper treatment, however, patients can retain such disorders for decades as chronic incapacity. With inappropriate treatment, many people with minor psychological problems, such as distraught states, have been turned into permanent patients with entire lives wasted.

Each repetition of a storm, in response to inner or outer circumstance, increases the likelihood that it will form an enduring structure. This appears to be similar to structuring of the rituals we all develop to make our lives more efficient. They become engram organizations that endure unless deliberately changed. Those patterns create inactive structures ready to be evoked by occurrences of a similar situation. It is those enduring patterns that, when activated, become what have been considered the classic neuroses. There has been enough experience so far to include the disorders listed above as curable storm disorders. Work with several other disorders appears to show the same process and as likely to become as convincingly demonstrated with further experience.

When storms form into any of the classic neuroses, the choice of a particular kind of neurosis may be determined by genetically based patterns of the individual. Some people seem temperamentally inclined to overt action and others to internal activity. This is not a matter of intelligence versus muscle, for there have been no demonstrations of superior intelligence in those who tend toward internal activity or of better coordination or dexterity among those with a tendency to respond physically. These are merely styles of response in which people rely more on intellective (inner activity) or on physical (outer activity) tendencies.

When in a storm, individuals who have an action-oriented character structure will produce one or another of the "hysteric" disorders. These are typically what have been called dissociative states, such as phobia, conversion, fugue state, compulsive disorder, multiple personality, anorexias, etc. Those disorders are more readily visible to people around them.

Persons with an intellective oriented structure, when in a storm, are more likely to produce an internal process disorder, such as reactive depression, paranoia, or obsessive disorder. Those disorders are less observable to others.

For some persons, the unstructured storms continue, rather than being limited to brief episodes. They develop a standard pattern of emotion reaction to events that evoke certain anathematized emotions in them. That tendency toward potentiation of some specific emotions, which are triggered in specific situations, makes casual observers infer that the situation rather than the readiness for potentiation is the important element. It seemingly becomes a situation-induced psychological disorder rather than an affective disorder in which the situation is an incidental trigger. A sensitized circumstance produces emotions that fail to be accepted as information about what is going on in and around the person. When an emotion is not acceptable to us, we may have an emotion reaction to that emotion and create a storm episode.

Instead of past theory that considers neurotic disorders the result of childhood trauma, we now can substitute a more valid explanation that psychological disorders take a general form from genetically based temperament, a triggering pattern from personal experiences, and an excitement from affect phobic contention with particular emotions creating emotion response to emotion response. In our terms, an emotion storm exaggerates a personality pattern and thus creates a psychological disorder. Chemical imbalances are not the disorder nor the cause of the disorder, but are one possible consequence of the psychological disorder. The personality pattern is not the disorder. The character tendencies active in the personality are not the disorder. Instead, it is the convergence of three psychological factors that create the specifications of the illness—emotion dynamics, personal history that creates trigger sensitivity, and emotion phobia.

The use of this knowledge has enabled us to cure such disorders in more than nine out of ten instances. We could not do that if the problem were some weakness in the makeup of the person or a deficiency of any kind other than lack of knowledge about and acceptance of emotions. That is why tutoring the suffering person about the knowledge they need is most effective for these disorders. (My tutoring approach to psychotherapy will be described in subsequent chapters.) It is far more curative than putting patients through a process of desensitizing in relation to the superficial, manifest situation as triggers (which does nothing for conversions, multiple personalities, and anorexias), attempting to bring them intellectually to a more sensible, realistic view of the trigger situation (open space, social groups, bugs, heights) as benign, shifting moods with chemical dosages to subdue physiological consequences of psychological disorders, or questing through free associations about childhood experience.

Storms always start with impairments placed in the path of access to one's emotions. Most people make the mistake of trying to "deal with" their emotions. They mistakenly try to manage them, control them, suppress them, tolerate them, or get them out. But we operate more healthily when we understand that acting on them is optional. Instead, we are better off noticing our emotions and using the information they bring before deciding whether action or nonaction is appropriate. All attempts to "deal with" feelings are unfortunate.

In some instances, storms can lead to mayhem or murder. From structuring patterns of response to storms we develop neurotic phobias, compulsions, physiological disturbances, depressions, paranoia, and other intensification disorders.

When mental health professionals learn more about emotions, they cease the futile and sometimes destructive medication of these conditions and turn to the simple and rapid cure of the disorders. That is better for patients than costly, long-term ineffectual treatment.

Phobia

Phobias in all their many variations are the most frequently presented structured affect storm disorders at the present time. Bringing the knowledge of vicissitudes of affect phobia into the explanations of these disorders allows us very useful explanations. The disorders are far less mysterious, treatment can be very direct, and prevention becomes possible. Several types of phobias (agoraphobia, claustrophobia, heterophobia, acrophobia, bug phobia, and others) have been responsive to this understanding. The successes in varieties of phobia are sufficient to suggest that emotion storm is at the basis of all phobias and offers us both the understanding and potential for cure.

The technical literature on phobia provides a long list of types of this category of disorder. The varieties of creatures as object of disorders span the known species. The varieties of situations span multifarious varieties of situations and circumstances. The objects of phobia for some persons include entities that most other people view as benign or even desirable. With the impressively large variety of objects of phobia, it is logical to infer that the object of phobia can be only incidental—a minor aspect of the illness.[15] With the recognition of the processes and effects of emotion storms, we can move to the crucial issues in this psychological disorder. We find the most critical issue to be potentiation into storm. Without potentiation, we have no phobia.

What happens in a bug phobia may be useful for describing some aspects of process in phobias and informing us about cause and cure of storm disorders in general. Those who suffer with a bug phobia, when confronted with or even anticipating such an encounter, may undergo extreme distress, with psychic pain and physiological agitation in several systems. Anxietous expectation that their self (personality) may be dissolved or demolished, heightened heart beat, dizziness, weakness, nausea, visual difficulty, and any of several other reactions may occur.

It is difficult for those among us who have not themselves experienced a phobia how terrible the experience is and how brave those afflicted have to be to carry on with their lives while undergoing such an experience. The many descriptions of the disorder that therapists hear conveys the psychic pain that is produced in any person with any of the various intensified or suppressed emotion reactions. Such disorders as depersonalization, and any of the phobias, are agonizing experiences to the sufferers. It is easy to understand why those compassionate professionals who do not understand the disorder are led to offer immediate reduction of the pain by brain (and mind) suppression, even though that "help" is destructive over the long run.

The bug-phobic person is reduced to a nonfunctional state when confronted with the idea of bugs, photos of bugs, the expectation of seeing bugs, or the actual presence of bugs. At its extreme, the terror reaches the maximum possible for any person. Confrontation with a bug is experienced as so threatening that it compares with the threat any of us would experience if given credible information that we are in the target area of a nuclear attack due to occur in three minutes. The emotion is real. It does not matter that the danger from a bug is infinitesimal. The feeling reaction is appropriate to the perception, not to the reality of the danger.

For whatever reasons any particular emotion has become anathematized, the arousal of that emotion to some critical level may be automatically subject to potentiation. The potentiation may occur in a chained straight line sequence, *as in fear of fear of fear*, or the potentiation may occur as a variegated emotion sequence, as from fear to shame to anger to guilt. At some point in that sequence, the potentiation is to such a degree that for a time it is self-sustaining and continues as a storm of emotion for minutes, hours, or even days.

It is during such storms that the energy necessary to drive our mental functions of affect and intellect is insufficient to power the increased affective energy needs. In all storms energy appears to be diverted from intellect to affect to sustain the storm, thereby depriving intellectual processes of sufficient energy to function well. The capacity to critique or evaluate the thoughts that arrive from our ever-flowing memory, ever-flowing sensory processes, and ever-flowing associational processes is reduced. The data are received without evaluation. It is as if we are inundated by a flood of ideation, for with our decreased energizing of intellect there is far too much to be processed or set aside as it ordinarily would be. During a storm the ideation is uncritically accepted or uncritically rejected and the consequence is a disordered state. That is why in bug phobia, the tiny bug is accepted as being as dangerous as a nuclear attack. In paranoia, whatever occurs is readily, uncritically accepted by suspicious persons as part of an overall plot against them. In agoraphobia, the unenclosed is accepted as immensely dangerous. For these disorders the temporary loss of intellect makes us not gullible, but absolutely suggestible to our own misunderstandings.

While there is a great deal more that goes into the selection of phobia versus obsessive disorder, and, within the category of phobia, the selection of spider as object, instead of air travel, the major element in phobia is the potentiation of emotion due to the person's affect phobia. That is the major element in the several storm disorders. The various anorexias (in the assorted subcategories of eating disorders) have the same potentiation and storm processes at work. It is consistently the loss of judgment and reduction of intellect from the impoverishment of energy that is at the root of the problem. In some disorders, such as paranoias, the manifest distortions appear as if psychotic and not merely temporary idiocy. As we think about it, however, we can recognize that the distortions in paranoid episodes are no greater than the distortions in anorexia or phobia. They are all matters that can be considered stupid beliefs (delusions) rather than beliefs due to disordered thinking. The difference between psychosis and temporal stupidity is the difference between thought process breaking down and thought process momentarily not being sufficiently energized to operate. Psychosis is a proper diagnostic category for energized thought that is chaotic. That is different from unenergized and underpowered thought that is therefore currently inadequate. When diagnosticians become confused about this distinction, they make errors.

Most of the times when people say "I feel depressed" they have confused both endogenous and reactive depression with emotion and really mean they are sad, lonely, dispirited, down-hearted, or disappointed. Reactive and endogenous depression are, nevertheless, a frequent disorder of the normal population. In reactive depression, an untoward event in the person's life serves as a trigger. (Self-observing persons usually recover memory of a cluster of untoward events rather than merely a single triggering event. It can be argued that such multiple causation is the rule rather than the exception.) The process of repression is an additional step that plays a more important part, especially in reactive depression and paranoia and somewhat in obsession than in phobia and compulsion.

A middle-aged man whom we will call Mr. Jones told the following story of his personal experience.

Upon arriving home from work one evening, Mr. Jones was greeted by his two small sons. The younger one had a bruise on his forehead and the fluid gathered around it between the skin and skull distorted the shape of the little boy's whole head so much that it looked grotesque. Jones immediately called their pediatrician to discuss whether the child needed further attention, but they decided that was not necessary in the absence of any signs of concussion or interferences of other sorts. The man thought, "How am I going to protect and take care of these tiny boys by myself?" He actually had two housekeepers living in the home to attend the children's needs and share their care so that the children would never be alone. He ate dinner with the boys and enjoyed their company, although all were sad because two months earlier they had lost wife and mother to a long, painful, slowly debilitating illness. They were not only lonesome for her and saddened by their loss, but the boys were also frightened about being without their mother, frightened that they might themselves contract the same illness and die, and frightened that something might happen to their father so that they would be absolutely alone. A phone call from a distraught friend interrupted their dinner. She weepingly told of her dog, currently the only real companion in her life, having been struck and killed by an automobile a few minutes before. Because she was inconsolable, he agreed to meet her the next day to talk. After the saddening phone call, he sat with the day's newspaper and was shocked by the headline with his name in unusually large type as the top half of the front page:

"JONES INDICTED"

The story was about a high government official having been caught embezzling great sums of money and performing some other misdeeds being considered a criminal. Seeing his own surname in that newspaper headline (although it was about someone completely unrelated to him) seemed to taint him and was distressing. It resonated with his guilt about the limitations on his ability to take care of his children, his guilt and sadness about the painful illness of his much loved wife, and added a weariness to his experience of life. He decided to make a cup of tea. He heated water, poured it into a cup, and found he could hardly move his hands, fumbling although he was usually adept. He had extreme difficulty manipulating the tea bag so it would go into the cup. He noticed that he was thinking very slowly, with no particular content, and without his usual speed. It was only then that he asked himself the question, "What is wrong with me?" "What am

I doing?" "Why is this happening to me?" "What is making me so incompetent?"

He began to recover the memories of the untoward events of the evening, which he had repressed as he moved from one painful situation to the next. There was a moment's hesitation as he struggled to recall. With the rapidity of thought process, by pulling one memory out of repression, it was as though the series of memories were on a string (perhaps because of their grievesome quality or their temporal contiguity), and he quickly knew what had happened. Then he could again allow himself to feel sadness and lonesomeness for his wife, fear for his sons' care and safety and make plans to help them better, sympathy for the woman who, like he, had lost her most loved companion, and relaxed about the headlines that, after all, had nothing to do with him other than the coincidence of names. The process took only seconds. His whole mood lifted. The reactive depression was gone. His functioning recovered and he was able to enjoy the rest of the evening with the boys, together going through the mourning process that would eventually allow them to live life and have the satisfactions of their relationships. He has never again over the decades experienced a reactive depression.

From this account we can put together the process of the sometimes very serious illness of reactive depression. The self-observations of this man give us the opportunity to notice the buildup of painful emotions on top of the underlay of painful emotions that are a part of healthy mourning process. To carry on our daily activities, we need to pick and choose, and suppress some mental contents or our minds would bog down. When we are already busy with our sadness and begin feeling guilty about fear for someone else, and then both afraid and guilty about our limited capacities, and finally angry about the situation evoking the guilt (in this world everyone's situation is unfair in some ways), we are already well into a storm process. Especially when we are weary we may want to push the whole thing away, and we do so. Suddenly the storm is unconscious. That not only does not reduce the storm or its effects, but instead gives it a free rein. The reduced intellectual capacity during the unconscious storm made it plausible that the coincidence of the name in the headlines turned similarity into identity. He combined his guilt about protecting the tiny tots, the guilt about failing to protect his wife, the grief over her loss, anger at the world, fate, the careless driver who killed the dog, and guilt about not being able to protect his friend from her loss. He suffered both emotion storm and a dystonic emotion chord. All went into the whirl of his unconscious emotion storm. Reaching into the unconscious by reviewing the events of the evening and the reactions to those events allowed him to bring the storm back into consciousness and instantly disassemble that storm.

Anyone with self-observing capacity equivalent to this man can begin to disassemble the depressions, phobias, compulsions, anorexias, etc., on their own. Anyone with introspective capacities can be helped by a therapist to disassemble such disorders. On the other hand, for those who may have been born with no potential for capacity to view within themselves, adoption of a framework of comprehension or acceptance of emotion is likely to exist only if they have grown up with that view within a family that teaches the uses of emotions. The childhood training can provide an unconscious frame of reference that they use automatically, without insight. In that way they too can be immune to affective disorders.

The conclusion may be drawn that symptom disorders are disorders of preconscious awareness. This brings a possibility that those who are quite oblivious of thought about feeling and feeling about thought, thought about thought and feeling about feeling are, in their simplicity, free of the likelihood of storm disorders, although often fragile in other ways. They suffer problems related to insensivity through lack of awareness and are more often perplexed by those around them. Those who are highly self-observant are typically able to notice the feeling sequence in process and free themselves of potentiation, or can usually do so with minimal guidance. Those in the middle of this sequence—people who are not self-observing but who are introspective—suffer symptom disorders most often. Whether they are constitutionally incapable of observation or have somehow been forced to restrict their observation, the impossibility of disassembling their storms or capping their potentiation of emotion makes them vulnerable. Thus, symptom disorders seem to be preconscious disorders of introspective people.

Many people are being treated for illnesses that have become popular to have or are popular diagnostic choices among professionals. Therapists find such disorders as "multiple personality" exotic and such disorders as "panic disorder" (which is dramatic and painful) to be interesting and treatable, but unfortunately incurable. Both are overused diagnoses. Anorexia's former popularity has given way to bulimia. Currently the most common diagnosis appears to be depression. Anyone who has a down-spirited moment, or a time of sadness or grief is liable to be categorized wrongly as depressed. Additionally, high-incidence unrecognized, muted emotion is very often mistaken for depression. A few decades ago a common diagnostic choice was psychosomatic organ neurosis, which we now know is not a psychological disorder. A hundred years ago, hysteric ritualistic dramatizations were quite common. Patients rarely produce that form of storm disorder currently. It is not acceptable to most persons.

NOTES

1. One of the serious defects in the typical drug abuse counseling has been the failure of drug counselors to notice this important distinction. Treatment outcomes can be improved by use of this knowledge.

2. This medication will make you feel less.

3. One of the common errors made by those with insufficient training in psychological functioning is the acceptance of a lumping of psychological problems together with psychological disorders, and then erroneously considering those to be brain disorders that require chemical treatment. That is a common path to turning healthy people into chronic patients or worse. This has occurred with people who healthily grieve, are healthily lonely, healthily angry, healthily guilty, etc.

4. One difficulty in the work aiming to create artificial intelligence has been the use of a faulty model of mind. Thus decision-making computer programs have been designed as though it is increased power of intellective activity that enables human-like decisions. Even though computers have been devised to function in ever more complex ways, the systems have not yet been developed to coordinate processes and functions of dual human minds. It is a failure to find proper premises upon which to base questions that has stood in the way of finding useful answers. Solutions not previously possible become possible by moving study of artificial intelligence to include use of the dual mind (the use of both cognition and affect), with coordination of the evaluations of these two major functions as equally important interworking parts of mind. Until the artificial intelligence experts adopt that, their achievements will continue to fall short of the mark.

5. Although current usage includes the splitting of sense of reality of self and sense of reality of surroundings as separate diagnoses, at the base of each the issue is the muting of emotion, which makes the appropriate treatment for both to be the same. They are the same disorder—emotion muting.

6. P. Federn, *Ego Psychology and the Psychoses* (New York: Basic Books, 1952).

7. E. Weiss, *The Structure and Dynamics of the Human Mind* (New York: Grune and Stratton, 1960).

8. There are complexities to this that are outside the scope of this book and not dealt with in this writing. Some affective evaluations appear to be cortical, but some clearly are subcortical.

9. But dysfunction in reality testing often impinges secondarily on sense of reality and dysfunction in reality sensing impinges on reality testing as well. A double problem often occurs in schizophrenia. That may be why schizophrenics, especially during the early stages, appear to be so bewildered. It also may be why some schizophrenics I have worked with and have helped with their sense of reality have suffered less deterioration over years than is typical in that disorder.

10. These latter emotions may not exist in the consciousness of emotion muted persons. It is to them as if these are insignificant abstractions that they have heard about but do not know. The appropriate comparison is that of the existence of color to the color blind person. The term "affect blind" is just as appropriate as the term "color blind" and brings us understanding of those persons who are content with an affect theory centered on intense affects such as anxiety, shame, guilt, fear, surprise, or anger.

11. The dynamic path is to a condition of muted emotion, which when occurring in sufficient degree evokes anathematized fear that escalates to a storm. Following the several microsecond psychological steps the hormonal system is activated. For instance, adrenaline and other emergency substances prepare the person for encounter with a formidable situation bringing rapid pulse, raising blood pressure, and the other common signs of the episode such as dizziness, perspiration, etc. That is the panic episode. It is not an "attack from outside."

12. Grateful acknowledgment is made of support by the Scottish Rite for a 1957 study of depersonalization as a prepsychotic condition. That study gave no support to the hypothesis that depersonalization is a necessary or consistent prepsychotic condition in the patient group studied.

13. L. Wurmser, "Neurotic Depersonalization," in *Clinical Psychopathology*, ed. G. Balis (Boston: Butterworth, 1978), 309–25.

14. The term "neurosis" connotes a functional disorder of the central nervous system. We have known for some time that these disorders are not an aspect of nerve function and are not related to nerve dysfunction but are a mental dysfunction. It may take a long time to supplant this misnomer, but eventually it will fall out of use as error. In this writing, other terms deemed more accurate and more descriptive are used as much as possible wherever it is thought not to confuse.

15. A paraphrase of the poetic statement by Gertrude Stein is appropriate here: "A phobia is a phobia is a phobia." Treatment of any phobia needs to be very much like treatment of any other phobia. That treatment should be directed toward fundamental issues of the disorder in order to be effective.

7

The Meanings of Psychotherapy

How we arrived at a situation in which healthy human responses are considered illnesses, subjected to psychotherapy, blunted with medications, and considered worthy topics for research on means to regulate or eliminate them all begins to be understandable when we consider basic premises of the mental health field. A crucial, little-regarded problem arises from the use of mental health theory organized around psychopathology. Because the field has always been in the hands of those who treat illnesses, the field of study we have is really the field of mental illness, but it has acquired the more acceptable optimistically euphemistic title of its very opposite—mental health. The detrimental consequences of this distortion are vastly greater than the public and most professionals have realized. How human health and illness are viewed, what is acceptable, what is treated, what is deemed an appropriate basis for confinement in treatment centers, and what is seen as normal development are very different when we take our orientation from a core of understanding of processes and conditions of health rather than illness.

THEORIES OF MENTAL HEALTH AND MENTAL ILLNESS

How strange that the mental health field is mainly in the hands of professionals who are trained in and think of themselves as experts in mental illness—the opposite of the field in which they are positioned as authorities. Certainly that developed in response to the horrifying disturbances of deranged people. For millennia the deranged "mad" were disparaged, feared, abused, left to die, and in the last centuries placed in madhouses. Their miserable conditions resonated within puzzled sympathic persons as insistently demanding some kind of solution. Many people were moved to attempt to understand and help those hapless folk. From that beginning we now have a field in which mental health workers declare what mental illness is, but have never produced convincing, organized descriptions of what mental health is.

Shifting the Focus to Natural Processes

A major shift in thinking about theory would occur with a move from pathology-centered pathognomonic approaches to a functional health-centered approach. Prevention approaches, having definitions of health and how to maintain it, would give us great advantage in helping people to productive and creative lives, would improve interpersonal and intrapersonal relations, and would change our understanding of diagnosis and psychotherapy. *Not only is it just as possible to consider usable diagnoses in terms of deviations from healthy processes as it is from diagnosing pathologies from presence of signs or symptoms, it would offer significant advantages over the common current system.*

At first blush this may seem to be a distinction where there is no difference, as if this is only a matter of starting at different ends of the same continuum, but when you begin exploring the possibilities, the differences become recognizable. Once understood, we see it as two different journeys, starting from different locations and heading for different destinations. In the current system, health is considered as a residual condition in the absence of illness or what exists after signs and symptoms of illnesses are cured or removed. In the other, health is a definitive state with built-in natural processes performing adaptive tasks within an optimal range. This allows for variation of function within and between individuals. In the health definition, the manifestations are considered first as natural variations in useful functioning. Using the illness definition, we seek any aspect of mental function that shows tainted attributes (signs and symptoms) of illness. If no pathognomonic taint is found, the person is considered healthy.[1] The more signs and symptoms that are found and cured or removed, the healthier the person is considered to have become. In contrast, using the health centered orientation, we work to strengthen the natural, built-in mental functions to enhance healthy processes and so prevent illness or free people from illness. The same processes guide our lives and either cure or decrease the vulnerability of each person to psychological illnesses. Because most people occasionally manifest some declared signs or symptoms, some pessimistic professionals are led by strained logic to the view that everyone adapts by using considerable effort to hold psychotic chaos at bay. To them, health is a successful fight against illness.

Those without knowledge of the dynamics of mental processes resort to manifestations of signs and symptoms to identify a disorder process. That is the current approach in both behaviorism and biopsychiatry. Pathognomonic reading can lead to a quick diagnosis, but too often it is a quick erroneous diagnosis.

A patient was sent to me to provide her with psychotherapy concomitant with medication for her depression. She had been diagnosed the day before by a psychiatrist in a brief interview. She had complained of fatigue and insomnia, and said she was worried in general about her future security. Her job was not assured. She and her husband both worked long hours for little money. They were struggling financially. She said she was happily married to her hard working husband. She had used the phrase "depressed about our financial situation." The psychiatrist took that phrase to mean depressive illness. I took the "about" to mean "saddened," "disappointed," or "worried." He gave her some imipramine.

Her manner and demeanor, ease of flow of thought, bright and alert responsiveness instead of the dull, drooping attitude of a depressed person also suggested this was not a depression. She worked a full week managing a housekeeping staff at a hotel, took care of housework at home, guided her teen age daughter, and also helped her husband on their farm. Her husband also had a second job three nights a week to bring in more money. To me that sounded like a full work week for both. She also used the medication Slobid, which can cause insomnia, for her asthmatic condition. Insomnia often causes fatigue.

Instead of adding imipramine for her fatigue, insomnia, and improbable depression, as planned by the mental illness expert, exploration of the possibility of reducing or eliminating the Slobid, if that is not required for her asthma, is an appropriate first step by a mental health expert to try to help the insomnia. Telephone contact with a pulmonary specialist suggested that with her minimal degree of asthma, she might be able get along without Slobid as a regular medication. The decision awaited her visit with the pulmonary specialist. His decision was to reduce the medicine that created the insomnia and drop antidepressant medication. Her life is now easier and has continued so for a year.

The pathognomonic diagnosis is speedy. If we can check the list and there is the sign "fatigue" and the sign "insomnia" plus symptoms of apprehension and sadness, that unquestionably is the illness "depression." But following that diagnostic approach glosses over an underlying process that may have any of several surface manifestations, and the same surface manifestations may stem from any of several underlying processes. Is the problem a drug reaction or depression? Does adding a drug to modify a drug reaction lead to health or merely obscure what is going on?

By emphasizing pathology, we had tacitly accepted health as the absence of signs of pathology. If instead we emphasize normal development and healthy functioning, we adopt the view that pathology is deviation from health as nonfunction, dysfunction, or malfunction of natural processes. The pathology-centered approach brought an increasing tendency to consider all human mental function as essentially pathology, in greater or lesser degree, which often led us to spend a great deal of effort in working to cure aspects of healthy function. That is a terrible error.[2] Instead, we can view mental health as a complicated but definitive functioning condition, discernible as having many elements of normal processes functioning well, with mental elements and factors that serve purposes we can understand. We then view health as those processes aiding us to adapt and function in personal and interpersonal life. This vantage promises to be increasingly fruitful and more useful than pathology-oriented study. The work presented in this book has already brought knowledge for cure and prevention. Extension of the theory of health beyond the scope of emotion health may bring far more knowledge.

Perversions of Therapy

The "everyone is ill" belief leads to an industrial approach to mental health issues and all too frequently to a smug, condescending attitude toward patients. As one psychiatrist observed, "Every child should have a course of psychotherapy during adolescence." His belief that everyone is ill in some degree meant that he should treat everyone who came to him, to prevent catastrophic developments, or at least to make their lives healthier in some degree by removing pathology. From his illness-oriented approach, any least characteristic or element of any illness that he could note he declared to be sufficient basis for necessity of treatment.

From several of his former patients who eventually came to me, those elements of illness he detected would often have been better understood if they had been considered along a range of variation within healthy mental functioning. His approach had made healthy children into patients. Then they needed psychotherapy—to free them from being patients! His practice involved thousands of adolescents over at least three decades. His belief in the universal necessity for treatment gave him what could look like an uncanny diagnostic talent. He needed only to hear the name of an adolescent to know sincerely that the youngster should be under his care, usually in a hospital for thirty to sixty days, isolated from communication with parents (to break the parent-child bond and foster a healthy relationship with the therapist), all the while medicated with one or another psychotropic drug. Supposedly the child then could start anew to form good relationships with parents and family. The problems in that are obvious.

His view was that he "salvaged the lives" of many children. To me and some others he appears to have captured and temporarily imprisoned many children who had been oppositional, thrown temper tantrums, spoken of running away, or who were saddened or resentful and innocently used the fateful phrase, "I feel depressed." He had alienated many children from their parents. He acted as a pretender of wisdom. He and his platoon of a few dozen associates seemed to be working to implement his creed in relation to all who crossed his path. Similar to many others, he belongs in the category of those who do well, but not good. There are several like him in each metropolitan area of this country.

MENTAL ILLNESS AS DEVIATION FROM NATURAL PROCESSES

The more clearly we can specify aspects of health, the more clearly we can describe illnesses in their deviations from our view of healthy processes. Where do we place the boundaries between health and illness? How do we decide what makes a boundary between health and illness? In a health-centered approach, we tend to concentrate more on elements of process—both healthy and pathological—than on signs and symptoms of health and sickness. From a pathology-centered approach, we consider any suspiciousness a possible sign of paranoia and then evaluate how severe that piece of paranoia is. From a health-centered focus, we consider suspiciousness a healthy, functional, self-protective watchfulness, possibly appropriate for the circumstances of that person and not necessarily a sign of paranoia, even if intense. We recognize sadness as a useful emotion, not as a piece of depression. We consider a rush of ideas to be a manifestation of excitement, enthusiasm, or interest, rather than a sign of hypomania. Thus the currently commonplace attempts to cure rapid or slow thinking, excitement, grief, anger, loneliness, fear, sadness, guilt, shame, and other discomfiting but useful healthy responses become recognizably improper.

This is not so much a difference among schools of thought as it is a difference in ways of using the knowledge within each school. Health, no longer considered the reduced presence of noticeable elements of pathology, comes to be seen as the existence of functional utility of the endowed mental processes. In the past, most professionals aimed to rid patients of what those professionals regarded as pathologies, rather than aiming to enhance their processes of health. Their view has been that the absence of noticeable pathognomonic symptom aspects of pathologies is what confirms health.

We could define psychological health in a more complex but more useful way as the functional utility of many natural useful processes of mind that serve to guide lives and enable people to be and do what they want to be and do, in ways that are not harmful to themselves and others. *Actuating this view will take many years, but will finally define an ideal of mental health based on use of function rather than absence of dysfunction.* That may finally eliminate the preposterous attempts to cure people of elements of their health.

The failure to work from a basis of health is part of the reason we have therapies aiming to cure natural healthy reactions, as if they were illnesses. They mistakenly treat as pathology such natural and useful (although unpleasant) feelings or states as grief, loneliness, anger, sadness, shame and guilt. They seek to cure such natural and useful (even if unpleasant) conditions as perceived low self-esteem, inferiority, superiority, inadequacy, passivity, and shyness. None of these conditions ordinarily calls for interferences with the natural processes that are occurring in them. Attempts to cure health frequently risk transforming health into long-term illness. It can waste lives, as exemplified in the account in the previous chapter of a patient suffering from tension phobia. I know of many such instances.

> A boy discomfited with shame leading to school avoidance was treated by hospitalization, medication, and long-term treatment instead of the few counseling sessions that would likely have sufficed.
>
> A troubled young woman whose admission that occasionally she had a rush of thoughts resulted in her hospitalization and medication. That turned her into an impaired, drug-dependent, chronically disabled person. Instead, the relatively simple easing of her psychological problems (not psychological illness) with psychotherapy would have saved instead of wasted, her life.
>
> In contrast, a boy discomfited with alternating emotion muting and emotion storming, and who said he was depressed although he meant sad and lonely, required only three psychotherapy tutoring sessions to change his experiencing of life so that he could go on to a constructive and pleasing life. The others, in the right hands, would have fared as well.

The mental health field has continued to work with impaired theories of health and illness. Instead of continuing to consider mind processes as brain dysfunction, as if they were physiological troubles, we need to consider these in psychological terms to obtain useful answers. Our mental processes comprise subsets of emotion and cognition processes. Probably the theories about emotion have been the more seriously handicapped of the two basic psychological theory areas.

Two emotion theories were quite influential in the history of mental health studies. From our current view we see them as scientific blunders. Freud's theory of anxiety set the stage for a long continuing emphasis on

anxiety as the fundamental emotion. Although other emotions were studied and considered in psychoanalysis, anxiety remained the major focus as
the significant emotion. Later, efforts by Tomkins used ideas derivative of
Darwin and James to put the basic function of emotion in the arena of
communication, thus not considering its significance as a central mental
process. Emotion, along with cognition, should have been considered a
central issue. Instead, healthy growth of emotion theory was stunted by the
powerful influence of the affect theory viewpoints of Freud and Tomkins
and, astonishingly, the effective omission of affect from behavioral and
cognitive theories. It is because the twin processes of emotion and cognition
are so important to a theory of health and illness that the consequences of
the use of impaired theories are so unfortunate.

Thus, failure to comprehend the healthy processes and functional utility
of emotion, or the pathological processes of muting, emotion potentiation,
and storm—all unnoticed decade after decade—meant that they unfortunately were unavailable for understanding and helping people. These
psychological processes, discernible to some people and invisible to others,
are not generally noticed even decades after their discovery and are not yet
generally absorbed into the thinking of theorists or practitioners. A theoretical contribution encompassing the dual mind, which now enables the
field to answer old questions more ably and to raise and answer new
questions, must first catch the attention of sufficient workers to be studied
and recognized for what it is.

Various special theories had been devised to deal with small portions of
emotion process, such as discharge or signal, or some particular emotion
such as anxiety or anger. Special theories were constructed relating to
diagnostic entities as if they were specific emotions, as with depression and
phobia. The differing premises of these several special theories precluded
assembling and integrating them to construct a general theory of affect or
illness. The incompatibility of the various premises in efforts at such combinations assured that no matter how complex the aggregation of special
and partial theories became, they provided little helpful information about
human life. No extended dialectic could be persuasive.

Embarking on the study of mental function from a basis in healthy
psychological activity would focus attention on variations in and digressions from these natural processes. The aim of improving and maintaining
health and preventing illness, instead of the past central aim of restoring
health by curing illness, creates a new set of activities and attitudes
about what the mental health field is. The shift to this approach will
promote encroachment of study areas to bring many pseudo ailments
back into the territory of healthy functioning, reversing a trend of many
decades.[3]

ON DIFFERENCES WITH CURRENT MAINSTREAM SCHOOLS OF MENTAL HEALTH

Should We Treat the Peripheral or Central Aspects of Psychological Illness?

Once one notices the mental processes of emotion and observes the occurrences of emotion storms, one recognizes those as the major participant processes of psychological symptom disorders. With access to that information, we view a sequence within the disorder processes—(first) the conditions or situations that trigger an illness, (next) the dynamic mental processes that are the central aspect of the illness, and (then) the various manifestations that are the consequences of the illness.

Those of us who discern symptom disorders as a coherent group of psychological disorders based in emotion storms, and are able to observe the steps in the sequence just described, find the most effective treatment comes by dealing directly with the illness processes. In contrast, none of the four mainstream schools that currently dominate the treatment market for these illnesses view the illnesses in terms of central psychological process. Instead they each focus on other elements they regard as vital aspects of illness. Three of these schools focus on conditions that trigger illness—one (Behavioral) on external and two (Cognitive and Psychoanalytic) on internal conditions that trigger the illness. The fourth view (Biological psychiatry) focuses instead on some consequences of the illness.

We can see that the four mainstream approaches resolutely work with elements in proximity to the illness, but not with the emotion storm itself. The Behavioral, Cognitive, and Psychoanalytic approaches, each in its own way, focuses on the trigger condition as the important factor. Behaviorism works with external conditions in an attempt to dull response to the trigger by wearing it out—while it ignores the psychological process of inner experience. This attempt to wear down the triggering response is comparable to the current approach in treatment of allergies, in which we have insufficient knowledge to enable us to modify the underlying process. It is comparably weak in success. Cognitive approaches work with the internal response to external conditions in an attempt to rationally persuade or teach patients that the response to the trigger is illogical, not a sensible reaction, and not something worth the excitement. However, most symptom disorder patients react as they do to trigger conditions even though they are typically conscious of the illogicality of doing so. It is rare that they are unaware that they are making mountains out of molehills. Psychoanalysis also focuses on the inner response to conditions that trigger the illness in an attempt to change the basis of reaction so that the trigger loses its effect. In contrast to those three, the biological-psychiatry approach, needing to categorize symptom disorders as brain disorders, brings an aim to chemically suppress signs or symptoms because such consequences of the psychological illness are taken for the illness. That focus on the consequences of the illness is comparable to a pediatrician ignoring chickenpox while concentrating on a child's pimples as if that is the whole of the illness.

Traditional Approaches to Psychotherapy

All psychotherapies move as directly, swiftly, and effectively to the heart of a problem as the validity of their explanations enables them to do.[4] The manner of treating patients has always been derived from what made sense according to some understanding of the ailment. Most therapies, however, had blindly groped for solutions to problems that were partially or dimly illuminated, if at all, in their theoretical framework. A few therapies have developed from serendipitous discovery of something that seems to help people—without persuasive explanation of why or how it helped (as in eye movement desensitization). For these a rationale attempting to explain the process was usually developed later.

Each school of psychology has devised treatment strategies relying largely on whatever they have posited as the key factors in the illness. The current major groups are listed below in a simplified outline:

1. *Biological psychiatry* supposes that psychological troubles have their source in brain chemistry
2. *Psychoanalysis* considers all psychological illness as based in origins of personality development (with exceptions such as inborn deficits)
3. *Cognitive theory* postulates the key element to be faulty thinking (although in that school, workers appear to concentrate more on attitudes than on idea)
4. *Behaviorism* postulates the key element in pathology to be faulty or unfortunate conditioning
5. *Popular psychologies* consider key issues to be such matters as stored emotion, faulty self-attitudes such as inferiority complex, or temperamental difficulties such as "over" or "under" assertiveness

In fact, all those suppositions are imperfect. The treatment results for the classic neuroses, by the approaches of each school, corroborate the impression of weaknesses and deficiencies entailed in those theories. This suggests we are at an early stage in the development of the science. It needs more work.

Although some treatment approaches for psychological disorders had been presented with little theoretic basis, even in those atheoretic psychologies the techniques fit with some defined principle (such as the hopeful, religiously based, somewhat mystical but persuasive "built-in drive for health" posited earlier in the nondirective therapies and visible again more recently in Kohutian "self" theory). Occasionally specific techniques have been offered without substantial supporting theory, but by the influence of an authority declaring them to be of value, have acquired undeserved credence. Overall, however, therapy techniques are usually carefully delineated applications of elaborate theoretical formulations of mental process, psychological development, symptom formation, illness, or health. Let us make comparisons as we consider treatment processes. In the course of our examination, we will find that a new approach offers not only more efficient and effective treatment, but also the possibility of actual cure of the illness rather than of the episode.

Psychodynamic Therapies

Because they deal with process more fully than any of the other therapies, we will spend most time on psychodynamic therapies. Current dynamic psychology theories instruct us to deal with therapy process based on the belief that all psychopathology is tightly bound to personality, because early life conflict-resolutions and the residuals of those resolutions operate in compromise formation structures that become fixed patterns in a person's mental operations. From that theory of psychopathology, the techniques use the forces of transference and enable wide roaming free association to provide slow, meandering, but promising paths to insight and improved health. You can understand from our new knowledge that the quest for various bases of maladaptive conflict resolution implies a plan of restructuring psychodynamic patterns so that one by one they stop acting as triggering elements to neurotic pattern episodes. This reduces the frequency of activation of a patient's neurotic episodes. If by assembling and examining a narrative of an individual life one can find and remove enough such triggers, the patient's health improves because neurotic episodes diminish in frequency of occurrence triggered by fewer conditions.

It cannot be well argued that this is *ineffective* therapy. What can be argued is that this is *inefficient* therapy, certainly in comparison with the new approach that works more thoroughly and effectively because it eliminates episodes instead of diminishing frequency of occurrence, and routinely does so more rapidly.

Psychoanalysis is the self-declared pinnacle of understanding of unconscious mind, but it is based on a highly contrived set of partial explanations that includes brilliant truths and brilliant errors about human mind. That, as treatment, involves a very complex and difficult to manage, loosely guided searching among associations "from the couch." Because the field has part of the story, psychoanalysis provides genuine help for character neuroses. Because it does not have the rest of the story, that help has been essentially useless for symptom disorders.

The various mainstream psychological theories about symptom formation, psychological disorder, and psychotherapy have serious limitations, unclarities, and errors. These make them insufficient foundations for useful explanations of illness. The knowledge in some of these schools of psychology is valid enough to ameliorate personality problems. However, that knowledge has been incapable of facilitating an effective cure of psychological disorders. Incapability of curing by application of any of the mainstream theories is a deficiency to be remedied rather than a virtue to be extolled.

What the public has gotten follows one or another suasive formula connoting that although psychological disorders are incurable, medication or psychotherapy can help them. It is a tragicomedy that most therapists faithfully apply techniques and concepts of archaic, hallowed systems of treatment that, despite claims made for them, are scientifically unproved. They seem unabashed by the limited usefulness of the product they purvey. Many therapists have piously followed strategies out of their faith in a dogma offered by authorities in the profession who assertively made claims, but offered little demonstration of value. That is why most people with these illnesses have undergone lengthy, expensive, but ineffective and even harmful treatment that too often became interminable. From our new vantage point, most of those therapies involve a thoughtful, assiduous, relentless search for psychic material that we now know to be relevant but of minor importance for cure, or perhaps a blind application of chemicals that obscure the disorders and far too often disable people enough to waste their lives, or skillful application of irrelevant knowledge in a sincere aim to help people.

Biopsychiatric Therapies

Biopsychiatry operates from a reductionist point of view. A spate of research studies has offered corroboration that the processes of emotion involve our electrochemical system. That should hardly surprise anyone. But the electrochemical processes do not give us answers to psychological questions. The expectation that it can answer such questions comes from the tendentious pattern among those studies that reducing psychology to biology can subsume and by that comprise answers to psychological questions. That is as illogical as moving a further step more elemental—from biology to physics—and expecting that will bring answers to operative questions about biology and thus, in turn, about psychology. The answers offered in biology for psychological questions about emotion are unimpressive to any in contact with their own and others' subjectivity. Causality is not touched. The connections between mood and emotion remain elusive in those studies. We have to be careful when we attempt to find answers to questions in one field by traveling to another field in pursuit of scientific evidence. *Psychology is a genuine scientific field struggling at an earlier stage of development than most of its participants recognize.* Theorists may translate that statement to, "There are many fundamental questions that are not yet well answered." It should not be translated as meaning "the answers are else-where."

It is quite correct that chemicals can produce moods. Moods do endure. Emotions, in contrast, are microsecond events that may arise within moods, and may even be contrary to the general tenor of a mood. To whatever extent personality patterns are determined by the interaction of our genetic endowment with our personal experiences, the involvement of chemical processes is as incidental vehicles—not as causes—of the patterns contrived. When biologists can produce a (brain) drug that produces substitute knowledge for existing knowledge that we have developed as derivatives of our learned experiences, and change the patterns of attitudes and other tendencies to change a person's character, they will have established that the chemicals are the cause of our learned patterns. Without that, to understand mind, we still must work within the field of psychology.

What has happened also in various psychopharmacological studies by biologists about psychological effects of chemicals is that they display an admirable rigor about chemicals, controls, statistics, and quantitative measures. Sadly, when they attempt to deal with psychological issues, as previously mentioned, that rigor dissolves and their concepts and distinctions about psychological processes and states are quite undifferentiated. It is as if the psychological aspects of their studies are not important to them. That makes their study results rather questionable.

Unsubstantiated generalizations that do not take into account the many important psychological differences involved have made most of the bio-chemical-psychological studies less than convincing as good science. Any researcher limited to the belief that a mood is an emotion will have a hard time comprehending the important psychological distinctions such as those outlined in some preceding pages. That failure is what makes many biological studies of psychological matters a mix of science and pseudo science.

Other Therapies

Cognitive theory is another partial theory. The sincere aim is to center study on "idea" and its processes. It settles on idea as the fundamental unit of mental function because it does not recognize the equal importance of independent affect and its processes. Its literature, however, appears to concentrate on attitude erroneously categorized as cognition. The published claims for results of treatment are exaggerated by a fuzzing of the distinction between cure and improvement. The insufficiency of any partial theory approach to yield cures is obvious.

Behaviorism has great merit in its testing of actual variables in the studies of a variety of relations, but presents the logic of a claim to study mind by studiously concerning itself with effects of mind, distancing itself from content and processes of mind because those are more difficult to observe and validate. But viewing the periphery of mind does not reveal subjectivity, where each of us lives. Behaviorism is a partial theory limited by being tangential to study of mental process. Despite the merit in its use of actual variables, it loses from insufficiency of materiality and relevance of those actual variables to the basic issues purportedly being studied. Its approach is comparable to geographers diligently and carefully mapping and exploring a coastal terrain and using that to infer what exists many miles from that vantage point. Does entering the territory seem too chancy to the explorers, or do they believe it would have no advantages? Why should we expect to gain an understanding of mind worth relying upon from peripheral data?

Psychoanalysis, on the other hand, has been limited by its error-filled affect theory and many unproved hypothetic constructs, and the limitations of indirectly observed mental content.

Popular psychologies have found a place in the mental health field in large part because the mainstream theories did not produce satisfying results. Primal Scream and Gestalt treatment programs tend to concentrate on emotions by the pseudo expulsion of both emotions and pseudo emotions, plus some work with psychodynamics, forming a crude view of psychological organization. The very popular Peckian writings present concepts of psychology that could fit only with the distorted dynamics of primitive (Delta) level view of what goes on in human minds and the meanings of interpersonal interactions. Descriptions of its principles are exemplary of the combination of what can come from theorists with muted emotion working at the Delta level. Est falls into the same primitive popular personality approach, and is also believable only to those who do not observe distinctions and meaning of differentiation in developmental levels and their implications in our various cultures.[5] L. Ron Hubbard's *Dianetics* celebrates forty-five years of popular sales. That popularity raises the question of whether the public's interest stems from the simplicity of its structure. Based on an illusion of knowledge, coming from uncorroborated hypothetic constructs, it is a set of ideas that is especially believable to those with personalities organized at a Delta level of Relatability. To some people, mystical matters are attractive. They want the mystery to continue because the idea of matters not understood pleases them. To others of us, mystery is something not yet understood—a problem to be solved.

The actual basis for symptom disorders and the mental processes in those neuroses can be recognized as different from descriptions in past theories. In psychoanalysis and dynamic therapies those highly educated, sincere workers who are skillful masters of sophisticated technical approaches to matters of minor importance, or even irrelevant to curative process of these disorders, waste their own and their patients' time (sometimes they even waste their patients' lives by needlessly keeping them enduring disablement for many years) and billions of dollars per year.

Of the prominent schools of psychology, psychoanalysis has a narrow affect theory that uses anxiety as paradigm and gives comparatively little importance to other affects and especially those emotions that have lesser intensity. The behavioral school seems to regard emotions only as interferences. The cognitive school shows only a minor interest in emotion. Various popular psychologies have a much greater interest in emotion, but consistently they regard emotion, loosely defined, as a disturbing factor disrupting personality functioning. None of these schools has come to the realization that built-in processes, such as affect, continue to exist in humans only because they are useful aspects of personality.

It is of relevance that many religious philosophies also include writings about emotion as disturbances, as something to conquer, diminish, transcend, or eject. Religious philosophies typically offer a representation of common beliefs of the time and place of their origin. Consider the "Seven Deadly Sins" in Roman Catholic doctrine: pride, avarice, lust, anger, gluttony, envy, and sloth. Other than sloth (which refers to inaction) they are affects or affective attitudes. In addition to the Catholic and Jewish writings about the virtue of rising above emotions (or passions), we note the consistency of Buddhist and Zen writings about aims and approaches to transcend emotion, often with the implication and sometimes the explicit declaration that the ideal state is to be free of anger if not of all passion. Modern biopsychiatric studies carry forward that same common wisdom aim in efforts to free people of intense feeling by subduing or regulating emotion. All these are engaged in the explicit or implicit contention with emotion.

Reasons for the absence of comprehension of the usefulness of emotion have to be recognized as important, whether in religious philosophies or in attempts at scientific studies of psychology. Multiple causes for those omissions are outlined elsewhere in this book. Human variability in awareness of affect, the restriction of ability to discern distinctions among affects, and the limitation of ability to distinguish emotions from para emotions have not seemed important to those in any school of psychology. Even the most gross distinction between emotion and mood has not been a part of either biological psychiatry or behavioral science. Without acute sensitivity to this whole set of distinctions, we can have only the chaos in the twin fields of mental illness and mental health that exists today.

All human characteristics and attributes vary from individual to individual, ranging from complete absence to astonishing degrees of capacity or facility. Some characteristics vary so that, although we may properly use categories to describe degree of capacity or incapacity, there are not clear margins to demarcate the classification in such categories. For other attributes we may have a clear demarcation of boundaries and the classification is therefore solidly in one or another category. While oblivious persons are solidly classifiable as separate from introspective, it may be that we can teach some of them to become aware of their mental content in process and thus move them to a new category. Similarly, we may be able to help introspective persons expand use of minimal self-observing capacity. Because symptom disorders are disorders that occur mainly among introspective persons, rarely in self-observing people, and glossed over in oblivious people, we have the task of helping people, use whatever degree of self-observation they might have.

NOTES

1. As one example of the signs and symptoms approach, the MMPI personality test uses a vast number of signs, symptoms, and manifestations of conditions as evidence to diagnostically categorize people.

2. This is remindful of the perhaps apocryphal story of a group trying to raise money to help care for local residents who were psychotic. They put on a gala dinner with speakers for their fund drive. Over the stage was a banner reading "FIGHT MENTAL HEALTH."

3. An advertisement for a mental health clinic offered treatment for such "disorders" as loneliness, anger, grief, sadness, guilt, and several other such troubling experiences. The view of the clinic staff is obviously that emotions are psychological disorders rather than healthy responses to internal or external events. They are offering to cure us of our health. If they should succeed in that, they will make us ill. It is sensible to shy away from professionals who offer such "help."

4. The term psychotherapy has gained a status as a particular form in the generality of the various mainstream schools of psychology. This book presents a somewhat different approach that is effective in achieving the aim shared by all therapies.

5. The construct Relatability (Appendix A) describes the meaning of object relations differentiation in terms of perception of self and others. Comprehension of these distinctions enables us to understand more about why popular psychologies fail.

8

Affect as a Major Factor in Psychotherapy

Each school of psychology has organized its theory around some element or process considered to be the major factor in personality or as cause of illness. The logical inference consistently has been that this will spotlight a crucial aspect of personality, the path of development, or means to cure illness. It is a reasonable inference. The effectiveness of any application, however, depends on the validity of the theory as a description of major factors.

AFFECT OR PERSONALITY?

Most psychotherapies appear to have been devised with an aim to cure what have been termed the "classic neuroses." Many have brought comfort, but none has produced cure. In the process of exploring personality while aiming to cure illness, mental structures and processes of personality derived from early childhood experiences were discovered and described. Because these are clearly important determinative aspects of personality, the erroneous inferential extension was made that they are also causative factors in psychological disorders. Instead of the quick adoption of that idea as a working explanation, it should have been considered from a scientific view and stated as a general hypothesis—psychological disorders derive from personality—then put into specific testable form, tested, and, of course, when unsubstantiated, discarded or modified. Whatever studies were done with it were done on the premise that "it is fundamental truth, therefore it must be right."

Working with personality as the central issue, diligent therapeutic activities brought some changes, but did not bring cures. From our knowledge of the ramifications of transient affect, we now know why delving into etiology of patterns of personality to construct a narrative of life is extremely helpful for understanding personality and, in particular, for making extensive modification in character neuroses and bring promising leads in character disorder. But it is quite worthless as curative activity for the classic neuroses. For decades several fundamental premises have awaited the unthinkable—rethinking! *With adherence to careful logic, by following through from the new premises about emotion to their implications for psychological health and illness, disorders turn out to be very different from what they previously have been thought to be.*

MAJOR AND MINOR FACTORS IN PSYCHOTHERAPY

In psychological disorders, as in any complex process, there is unlikely to be a single origin; several factors participate as causative forces. Each has a part in moving the person toward illness. Those factors differ in the ways and extent to which each influences health and illness. Distinguishing among forces of variable strength, and understanding the part each plays, enables us to understand better how to reverse a process. If we wish to interfere with pathological processes, we can choose between the alternatives of using a great deal of time and effort working with a weak factor or a lesser amount of time and effort working with a strong factor. It is an obvious rule that the greater the importance of the factor with which we can work, the greater our likelihood of producing wanted results.

We know now that emotion processes are stronger forces in creating symptom disorders than those residuals of early childhood experiences that set the triggers for the disorders. Our new understanding of how the various processes participate in the creation of psychological disorder finally enables us to do what was previously impossible—free the world from most such disorders. Complex storm-based troubles such as phobia, panic, compulsion, obsession, conversion, depersonalization, reactive depression, fugue, multiple personality, storm-based heterophobia, anorexia, etc., are usually readily cured, but the same knowledge, when widely disseminated, can be used to eradicate affective disorders from the face of the earth. Experimental prevention programs[1] with children are starting to test the feasibility of creating invulnerability to those disorders.

Faulty resolution of early childhood conflict creating residual maladaptive psychodynamic patterns was asserted by Freud (and apparently continues to be believed by a substantial proportion of psychologists) as the crucial element in all neuroses. Therefore, these have been considered the appropriate treatment focus as the singular basis for lasting improvement. That is error.

Our new theory includes the reality of such patterns being important in the development of individual personality—but we have shown by full and lasting cures of patients with these disorders that those patterns are of trifling importance in creating symptom disorders compared with emotion dynamics.

Also, from various schools, the suggestions of alternative bases for psychological difficulties (faulty habit patterns, distorted thought processes, stored old feelings, chemical imbalances, etc.) all turn out to be either weak factors of minor importance in disorders or pure errors. In either case, they do not constitute material with significant functional utility for curative activity. New knowledge allows us to choose to work with the strong causative forces and thereby transform the mental health field from its history of lengthy, painstaking, but minimally effective therapies into a science that can eradicate the various psychological symptom disorders and ultimately bring more pleasing and vital lives to all humans.

Working with strong forces gives therapeutic advantage analogous to the advantage of making a swift and sure voyage in a square rigger with full sails instead of a lengthy and uncertain voyage in the same ship, but using only one small sail that catches less wind than the ship's hull. If you did reach your destination in such a disadvantaged vessel, it would be the result of amazing good luck and great feats of seamanship over a long span of time.

The work done by the typical psychotherapist fits that analogy. Heroic effort using a great amount of highly sophisticated knowledge about a factor that is of minor importance to the disorder may yield changes in personality, but miss cure of illness. Results are chancy and limited.

From the perspective of advanced knowledge, the pattern of heroic effort that has been the ideal is a tragicomic charade of caregiving in which technologically skilled therapists typically have given comfort and modified some personality patterns, but too often have prolonged the disablement and worsened illnesses by sincere, assiduous, virtuous applications of false wisdom.[2] Various schools of psychology each have selected, studied, used, and taught that some relevant minor factor is the most significant factor to work with to cure psychological disorder. Those incorrect, weak hypotheses and their premises should have been transient tests—tried and discarded—that automatically made them obsolete. Instead, they were foolishly embraced as if God-given, indisputably valid ideas that would be effective if only we could learn how to use them skillfully enough. Clinging to such distortions, despite the absence of scientific support, moved the mental health field from blind faith in an offered fiction to a mass delusional reliance upon fantasy truths.

Because psychoanalysts and other dynamic therapies so overvalue their chosen minor factor, they have lost sight of the original aim—to cure illness. Instead they work valiantly to reach a different, unwanted destination, a journey they have persuaded their patients is the best thing that could be done for them. They sell symptom disorder patients on the idea that reformation of personality is the highest aim and of greater importance than the "mere cure" of illness sought by them.

MAKING AFFECT A FOCUS OF THERAPY

One reason my work has been something like a forty-year secret project, despite every effort to offer it to all willing to listen, resides in that indoctrination (the widespread proclamation of minor factors being major factors). It has created a formidable barrier to scientific advance. Instead of failures leading professionals to search for more meaningful explanations that could enable cures, their own inability to cure seems to have made many psychologists conclude that the disorders are incurable. A one hundred–year error has misled them. Their indoctrination also makes them regard the possibility of any significant advance in knowledge as "too good to be true." The idea that they could become highly effective therapists if they shifted their work to more important factors, and to work with them in a new paradigm of therapy, usually arouses their incredulity and irritation. Their belief is, *"It is not possible that we could have overlooked important fundamental aspects of human mental functioning all this time."* A religious fervor brings vigorous defense of important illusions.

Fortunately, it is possible to think new thoughts. Fortunately, the improved theory makes a rather expeditious cure available. Of far more importance than individual cures, in the long run, that same new understanding makes it possible to prevent these disorders. We can eradicate these disorders from the face of the earth, so that in a few generations we may no longer need cures for these disorders. That is what the public wants. It is now available from experts, but not yet known to authorities.

Curing the various symptom disorders calls for moving patients to the same healthy frame of reference about affect they would have had by growing up without affect phobia. It is, in that sense, a restorative process. It becomes the basis of a treatment approach. Eventually it becomes the basis of prevention of the disorders.

We will find that when each person confronts and comprehends the nature of his own affect phobia and comprehends the functions of emotions, he excludes the possibility of potentiation and storm within himself. That is why effective treatment follows these truths: *Without affect phobia, there is no potentiation; without potentiation, there is no storm; without storm, there is no symptom disorder.* Thus, affect phobia is the key to these troubles, and the key to the understanding of health. It is the proper subject of study in each therapy of symptom disorders. *A person who becomes free of storms by becoming free of affect phobia will have removed the possibility of emotion escalation, no matter how many or what kinds of maladaptive triggering patterns still reside within the personality from maladaptive conflict resolutions.* The triggers no longer start storms. That usually leaves the personality patterns or complexes, which had been triggers, to continue their existence, but from that point on they exist as merely innocuous idiosyncrasies. They no longer fit the category of neurotic complexes.

This approach has been far more effective therapeutic work than trying to dissolve the basis for any of the millions of individual styles of awkwardness in adaptation, the deconditioning of specific triggers of a phobia or compulsion, working to eject emotions that actually have long since departed, or imposing a chemical straitjacket to reduce physiological consequences of neurosis by reducing mental functioning. It is in this aspect that prevention programs in schools will change our culture by turning our children into neurosis-invulnerable persons who are more comfortable with themselves and others. Consequently they will perform better in many aspects of their lives—an outcome that cannot be predicted in detail, for the consequences will develop in sequential steps that can become apparent only as they unfold.

Treating Disturbances Caused by Muted or Potentiated Emotions

Our alternative theory, having several points of greater validity, gives more useful explanations, which is why it can suggest surer, often swifter, and consistently more effective approaches. Understanding these alternative ideas requires recognition of the scientific grounding in redefinitions of terms, reformulations of concepts, and answers to new questions of what is illness, health, symptom, and development. We are aided also in understanding personality by making the important step of adopting the construct of Relatability, a particular description of object-relations differentiation based in clear, distinct steps in evolving perceptual capacity rather than Freud's three biological organ system stages. It is a substantial augmentation of Freud's theoretical construct of psychosexual development.[3] The set of new definitions and concepts also brings new paradigms of what a therapist should be as a person and do as a professional. The same knowledge also leads to useful concepts of prevention that can free the human race of phobia, compulsion, conversion, obsession, and other symptom disorders within a few generations. That would be a hubristic aim if we were limited to the knowledge in past theories. These are expectations that are not possible from previous theoretical premises and formulations.

Where Psychoanalysis Fails

In practices related to psychoanalysis, the work involved in pursuing the quest for the origins of personality is considerable. Few outside the profession comprehend the skill, sensitivity, and the vast knowledge required in expert administration of psychoanalyses in such a quest, for it is usually invisible to patients in treatment. The careful persistence in leading a patient to focus on important areas of subjectivity may not even be noticeable. The care, quiet activity, and the restraint to abstain from distorting the flow of patient associations takes much background knowledge, training, talent, and high skill.

To the psychoanalyst, the hidden source of psychological problems can be found in the subtle nuances of "free association material." That source cannot be forced to reveal itself. Forcing in such a circumstance would be analogous to attempts to catch a feather floating in the air. Moving aggressively toward a floating feather creates swirls of air movement and reduces the likelihood of capturing it. One can only try to remain in its vicinity, within the likely path, with only a small capacity to pursue or entice it. In psychoanalysis we can provide an ambiance that allows the emergence of hidden mental content, and watchfully wait for the information to emerge. More important, we must have the knowledge and sensitivity to recognize it and respond with appropriate skill when it emerges. For the psychoanalyst, all else is secondary to such unimpeded flow of mental content as the source of vital information about personality. The therapist knows not to interfere. Theories of transference and a vast literature on process and technique of therapy guide therapists' activities in pursuing the quest for what we understand is the major factor in neurosis.[4]

Psychoanalysts "know" that such long, painstaking, etiological personality search is the only possible way to cure psychological disorders. That is why typically we tell patients who go to psychoanalysts a version of the following: "Your problems are due to maladaptive solutions to early childhood experiences. The only way to free you from that pathology is through a free association process, three to five hours a week for three or more years. In that process the relationship with the analyst reawakens your experiences, and makes it possible for you to form new patterns and make new and better adaptations."

The psychoanalytic theory of illness makes the proper aim of therapy to change mental patterns constructed by each in childhood as the best their infantile knowledge, experience, and intellect could construct for their circumstances in their aim to adapt. With the belief that all psychopathology is based in personality, delving into those original situations is therefore what makes sense for analytic explorations of personality.

The new theory agrees with classic psychoanalytic theory that characteristic personality patterns develop out of adaptations via resolutions of early childhood conflicts. However, in sharp contrast, the new theory explains that although those patterns are crucial parts of the basis of characterological structures, those psychic structures are rarely pathological and for most people usually do not even create difficulty within the person unless magnified by emotion storms. Without storms, these patterns are usually mere idiosyncratic ways of being and therefore benign, rarely calling for treatment or modification. Despite widespread reverence for the psychodynamics that are of immense importance in character issues, they are of minor importance for symptom disorders.

The astonishing results of applications of the discoveries bring confidence that these ideas will be a significant part of the psychology of the future. Those results of therapeutic applications of this new understanding of emotion are corroboration of the validity of the theory. Applications described in this writing are only suggestions for particulars of treatment method, however. They demonstrate that the old paradigms are not more effective and that their abandonment would be a gain. The implications of the theory need to be further explored before we can arrive at the best means of using the knowledge. Because the discoveries are of basic psychological theory, they are knowledge useful as underlying theory for every school of psychology. Diverse schools can incorporate new fundamental theory and express it in varieties of technical applications. The areas of psychology to which these can be applied also range widely. For instance, applications are being studied in child development and prevention programs, in work with abusive men, in studies of fatherless families, in studies of varieties of group interactions in corporations and military organizations, of process in relational situations, and other approaches to a broad scope of psychological functions.

Curing Affect Storm Tendencies

From our new viewpoint, we see that cure of symptom disorders was previously understood in dynamic psychotherapies to come specifically from enabling new and more adaptive adult character patterns to replace maladaptive character patterns that had created character neuroses. The premise had been that symptom disorders were manifestations of the personality.[5] *We now know that cures are achieved far more thoroughly and easily by freeing people from the storm syndrome tendencies that turn ordinary idiosyncratic character patterns into classic neurotic episodes.* Of the two approaches to symptom disorder, curing the storm tendency is consistently simpler, quicker, more thorough and lasting, and therefore more effective than changing the character patterns.

Those who have adopted this complex new theory have become consistently able to help their patients more completely and more rapidly than they previously had. They do not worry about disrupting the flow of patient concentration, because they are balancing the issue of expressions of unconscious psychodynamic patterns with the issue of delineating dynamic processes of emotion. They understand the important interactions between these two factors.

Whatever their school of thought, those professionals are improving the lives of their patients; they modify the atmosphere of schools, families, and ultimately will do that also for society. They understand how the fundamental nature of emotion and consequently the fundamental nature of psychological disorder and health are essentially different from past beliefs about them. Because the validity of the theory brings so much advantage to their applications in comparison to past theories, it is only a matter of time before most others will reach similar conclusions. Some hallowed traditions in psychology seem valid, valuable, and reliable, but a surprising number now seem foolish fictions leading professionals and their patients astray—at a cost of pain, time, and, money.

The problem in teaching new concepts to older therapists has been that those trained in past theories are usually less open to considering that *what they previously understood to be the sole cause is a minor factor among various causative factors, or worse, that what they have relied upon as fundamental premise is false*. The idea that symptom disorder psychopathologies are only incidentally based in personality formation issues (as believed in psychoanalysis), that they are not simply faulty conditioning (as thought in behaviorism), are not simply faulty perception (as believed in cognitivism), are not from feelings held in (as asserted in most popular psychologies), are not simply subaspects of moods due to variations in neuropeptides (as asserted in biopsychiatry), and not a problem of self-esteem (as in some wild offshoots of mainstream theories) is something so contrary to their past "knowledge" that most cannot take it seriously. Often such therapists are as much offended as astonished by the suggestion that their fundamental beliefs include error. The proponents of the schools of psychology such as those listed above that rely on a partial theory as the basis for their understanding of their field are not easily convinced to increase the complexity of their view of mind.

- *For instance, what has in the past been devotion to the sanctity of the free associational flow from patients in dynamic psychotherapy is superseded by increased freedom of therapist activity because we can use our improved knowledge of what causes and cures illness more directly to bring the cures patients seek*

- *The belief that painful, time-consuming symptomatic deconditioning creates cure can be superseded by understanding how to deal more directly with cause of the disorder*

- *The belief that changing the mood or suppressing emotion awareness and other mental activity with drugs will cure can be superseded by knowing how to offer people knowledge of their minds*

- *The ideal therapist stance now becomes very different from past beliefs*

- *The ideal treatment technique is now quite different from past beliefs*

Describing activity different from what has been standard in the training of all therapists about what a therapist should be, how he or she should comport self, surprises, sometimes frightens, and occasionally angers patients. It disturbs especially those who have gained psychological sophistication from informal or formal training about past views of what the ideal therapist and therapy approach should be. One psychology student who had chosen to become a psychologist because fifteen years of treatment with various therapists of a variety of schools had done nothing for his severe phobia said to me at the end of a brief consultation, "I have been taught what a good therapist is and does, and I don't find any of that here." He was trembling with anger at me as he left. There was no way he could, for even a moment, consider that the various therapists whom he had seen over the years had failed to help him precisely because they fit the mistaken pattern he had been indoctrinated by his teachers to seek.

We now have an alternative theory of neurosis that stems from our alternative theory of symptom formation. This theory of neurosis gives us a reclassification of some disorders. From these there is a natural development of an alternative theory of therapeutic approach that fits with the new knowledge and is both more efficient as a therapy and far less likely to be damaging than approaches used in the past.

From Cure to Prevention

I suggest we move away from traditional treating of symptom disorders in the manner of loosely focused applications derivative of past theory and instead focus much more directly on the process we know creates these disorders. We can move away from the tangential approaches of deconditioning and conditioning. We can move away from the charade of emotion discharge. We can move away from centering our attention on intellect as the singular important mental factor that subsumes emotion. We can move away from the belief that personality patterns, problems, and conflicts are the equivalent to moods and, as such, are brain conditions we can manipulate with chemicals.

Knowledge about unstructured emotion storms has not been disseminated widely enough to help the thousands—perhaps millions—of people who suffer each year. The patterns of emotion responses to emotion responses are so simple to understand that almost everyone who can observe inside can notice the process and promptly change it to their benefit. That is the hope and the difficulty.

The ever-present problem is that of individual differences among patients and therapists. For the reasons described earlier in this book, not everyone is capable of observing the emotion processes that exist within all humans. The recurring difficulty I encounter in trying to inform people about emotion dynamics occurs especially with those people who listen to my description of process, but in their minds, consider it a description of an abstract explanatory device rather than the literal process. Many people notice only that they have an intense emotion experience. They may not even know which emotion they are experiencing. They are thus handicapped by protecting themselves from themselves. Many professionals who do not notice emotions are thus handicapped in helping patients because they omit the existence and importance of these emotion dynamics in their work. Emotion blindness in patient and therapist is of far more consequence than has been recognized.

By shifting to direct our approaches to the newly outlined fundamental aspects of health and illness, we have cured many patients. By doing that we satisfy the original aim of all patients who come to us—we provide the cure they sought from us. Our newly found capacity to cure symptom disorders means that therapeutic ambition, which in psychoanalysis had been thought of as a vice, can now gain respect as a virtue. With the changes, psychological theory of personality becomes increasingly useful over a much broader span of issues than in the past.

Practitioners applying this theory are accomplishing, in short order, what even the most eminent psychotherapists over the last century have tried but failed to accomplish despite extensive sophisticated application of their knowledge. With this theory we ordinarily cure more than nine out of ten patients and in doing so change them sufficiently to make it unlikely that they will suffer recurrences or have any likelihood of developing any of the other symptom disorders. We usually accomplish this without the encumbrance of rituals from mainstream theories.

Although emotion has a history of being much maligned and feared, it is a natural, useful human mental function. When understood in terms of our new explanations, it is seen as one of nature's gifts—not a burden. Bringing discovery of that to the public so that we can raise our children free of emotion phobia will become the most appropriate and invaluable task of psychology. The consequence will be a changed world in which human functioning will not be impaired by "neurosis." This startling promise will be realized not by use of psychotherapies or "early interventions" for everyone, but without need of therapies. It will occur from *preventive education.*

If people did not want freedom from psychological troubles, they would not turn to therapists of whatever school of thought and pay billions of dollars a year in hope of relief. Those various schools of psychology claim merit for their viewpoints for whatever they value: biopsychiatry for its belief that psychological function is best understood as brain chemistry, psychoanalysis for "depth" because it deals with origins of formations of personality patterns and their unconscious influences, cognitivism for its recognition of personality in terms of a belief in "primacy of idea" in mental process, behaviorism for its "scientific approach" to observable and consensually validated matters, and various popular psychologies for their dealing with "vital" aspects of personality.

Whatever merits are claimed for an approach, the only worthy test that would please the public is production of cures. To satisfy requirements of science it would need a clear explanation of cause in addition to producing cures. Without a cure—or even better, prevention—any claimed virtues are pretentious comedy. This book describes some aspects of the set of psychological theories that offer psychology a science of cure instead of a science of treatment, and in doing so enables eradication of symptom disorders. The total theory described, with its ramifications, is complex, although its base is simple.

TUTORING IN PSYCHOTHERAPY

With our new understanding of disorders, we are freed from past constraints requiring us to be a relatively silent presence waiting for patients to arrive at helpful associations from unconscious elements pressing for expression, confronting them with troubling situations, or pressing them to release and eject their stored emotion. We can actively approach our patients with curative information that would be most improbable for them to come upon by themselves. We become therapist-tutors to help them understand emotion and its processes within themselves, the meaning and significance of affect phobia, the reality of potentiation within themselves, the self-sustaining tendencies of affect storm, the recognition that emotions are always benign, and other teaching that will change their frame of reference about emotion. When we do that successfully we witness symptom disorders *disassembling* before our eyes. The process and results are so clear that therapists need not point out the changes, and neither patient nor therapist doubts the process involved. It changes our view of health and illness. Health, from this view, is a describable state instead of merely the absence of illness.

The use of tutoring in therapy is similar to tutoring in any educational situation: We assay the student's relevant knowledge, work at filling the gaps in that knowledge when we know what they need to know, and correct misunderstandings. That *conversational* activity is in sharp contrast to helping a patient explore his mental content in an associational method to learn the developmental process for what he is and how he got there. The latter approach is invaluable in discovering *patterns* and helping people reformulate their personalities, but again is essentially useless for symptom disorders.

The new knowledge shows us that many long venerated icons of superior therapy unfortunately honor false gods. Those errors have implications that affect the entire mental health field. Even portions of psychology's ethical practice are based on the false truths of past theory. The ethical admonition to take a full history before treating, regardless of the presenting complaint, for instance, stems from the false knowledge that all neurotic problems are based in past experience. In fact, many of our patients have been cured of symptom disorders in a shorter time than ordinarily would be devoted to taking such a history. The personal history is of little relevance or importance in these illnesses. Insistence on that as a preliminary activity delays cure.

For treatment of symptom disorders, several other hallowed practices and beliefs need to be laid to rest—they are error. In psychoanalysis and the derivative dynamic psychotherapies, the standard therapeutic ambiance, the valued paradigm of a therapist intellectually alert but passively waiting for crucial associations to arrive from a fragile thread of a patient's sequential thoughts, the assumption that the psychological basis of pathologies resides in maladaptive early conflict resolutions and therefore transference resonance is needed to reawaken conflicts to help patients create new adaptations as the sole path to cure; the acceptance of anxiety as the paradigm emotion and therefore of special importance in creating symptoms; and belief that long-term treatment is always superior in its effects and thus always has greater merit—these and many other practices and beliefs have been mistakenly venerated to the detriment of the field and with devastating damage to the millions of credulous, hopeful, trusting, needful patients by consigning them to lengthy suffering of illness while enduring a stigmatized status as debile patients with diminished regard for them as persons.

Conversations with Patients

Our process of conversations with patients presents a very different picture. In the new approach, it is possible to watch people first develop awareness and then comprehension of their emotion processes. Then step by step, over a relatively short time, we observe the disappearance of the basis of the symptom disorder, and once free of that substructure, the disappearance of the disorder itself. Because the substructure that has gone away and the new substructure that replaces it as a frame of reference are understood, patients can become permanently invulnerable to the entire category of storm disorders.

Each patient has come to me with a unique life experience, unique personality, and an individual array of talents skills, and disturbances, but all have come with affect phobia. It is that affect phobia interacting with other elements of the personality that has constructed the specific type, form, and manifestations of the disorder that disables people with agonizing illness. To cure themselves, they have to recognize and understand their own affect phobia. They can then free themselves from that universal disorder and thereby free themselves of the symptom disorder and change their lives. The future generations that grow up without affect phobia will be different in many ways, besides being free of symptom disorder.

By presenting conversations with patients in the next two chapters, I hope to allow readers to see the interaction that occurs with patients, as a process of tutoring to give them knowledge about subjectivity they should have gotten from infancy on, not as a coaching of behavior. They can learn to understand themselves to see that while transference occurs, etiological issues exist, conditioned responses and deconditioning occur, and faulty thinking occurs, the most effective therapeutic process for symptom disorders is narrowly that of tutoring on use of emotion. The closer to good tutoring about affect realities and process the treatment is, the faster and more efficient that treatment process is. Patients without sophistication about treatment comfortably slip comfortably into this mode of interaction. In contrast, patients with sophistication about treatment "know" that either I do not mean this to be therapeutic, that I am awkwardly failing to perform properly, or I am contemptibly ignorant of what a therapist is supposed to be and do. I offend those people and lose them as patients.

A programmatic therapeutic technique to fit with the new view of symptom disorders has not yet evolved. A checklist of items to know is inappropriate. Attempts at formulation of techniques have not proved particularly successful so far. Undoubtedly interested professionals will put their minds to it. From the questions asked by people beginning to study the theory, it is apparent that most therapists prefer to operate as technicians who know how to apply a method rather than as professionals skillfully applying theoretic knowledge by devising a technical approach appropriate to whatever immediate problem they encounter. Therapists who absorb the knowledge sufficiently to free themselves of the problems of affect phobia change their approach.

The main operative assumption I use in my treatment approach is straightforward: *Affect phobia is at the root of symptom disorders; conversely, any person who grows up free of affect phobia will be free of both emotion potentiation and suppression disorders.* The next logical step is to attempt to help the person build a frame of reference consonant with freedom from affect phobia. The person then will possess a frame of reference similar to what he would have had if he had grown up in a psychologically healthier atmosphere. The goal is clear and well established as facilitative of health. How best to create such a frame of reference is not finally determined. *Meanwhile, a systematic tutoring of patients to fill gaps in their knowledge and to correct misunderstandings has been more successful with the variety of psychological disorders that come under the rubric of symptom or muting disorders than anything described in the literature about other treatment approaches. This has been fully effective in a few hundred patients at the time of this writing.*

In this form of treatment, we witness our patients freeing themselves of their disorder. We witness their changing their relationships, becoming better acquainted with themselves, and recasting their opinions about the meaningfulness and significance of activities and people in their lives. It is important to recognize that these changes are psychological, not behavioral, that they are mental, not biological.

NOTES

1. For the past few decades the idea of prevention programs has centered upon the injection of early intervention to work with especially vulnerable people. Early intervention is helpful for those who have the beginnings of disorders, but as synonymous for prevention it is a misnomer. True prevention would be the removal of the vulnerability.

2. Another pernicious approach parallel to this is the current move toward what is termed "brief psychotherapy." The emphasis on "brief" is at the expense of psychotherapy, for the insurance companies that foster this approach are saying, in effect, "psychotherapy does little good, but people want it, so let's give them the least we can get away with." It is a good example of a charade of care giving in which therapists offer token help to people who come to them in pain for some small part of their problems.

3. See Freud's *Three Essays on Sexuality* in *The Standard Edition of The Complete Psychological Works of Sigmund Freud*, vol. 7, trans. J. Strachey (London: The Hogarth Press Limited, 1955). The descriptions of personality in psychosexual levels are clusters of traits that are coherent and are of value in understanding personality. However, instead of those traits being derivative of the personal developmental history of life experience of each individual, they now seem to fit better with some particular genetic tendencies that are now partially defined in neuroscience findings. For instance, anal traits of character such as orderliness and neatness, resistance or obstinacy are unlikely to be derived from toilet training experiences and more likely are genetically imposed. The psychologically based sequence of object relations differentiation I term Relatability is described in Appendix A.

4. Freud had aimed to understand and cure the various neuroses. In his efforts to do so he succeeded in discovering a wealth of knowledge about unconscious processes and personality development and contrived a delineated technique for studying these and for changing personality patterns to benefit patients. That accomplishment is monumental. Because he appears to have missed gaining awareness of a significant portion of emotion process (omitted because of his own emotion muting), he failed to accomplish what had been his original aim: comprehension of the classic neuroses.

The vast knowledge of character and personality that he discovered has been assiduously but futilely applied to symptom disorders, for those are not based in the personality. He had sought and failed to discover his aimed-for understanding and cure of the classic neuroses (symptom disorders), and discovered an enormous amount of information about personality and character. He and his followers had for years adopted the fiction that all psychopathology is based in personality. They adopted further fictions about "organ neuroses" and thus considered several genetically based physiological disorders to be psychological. In full sincerity they led thousands of patients on wild goose chases while incidentally persuading them by implication that they were somehow psychologically inferior (because the professionals were unable to acknowledge an inherited propensity) for having incurred these illnesses. Regardless of those errors, the psychoanalytic understanding and treatment of disorders of personality and character remain unchallenged as the most useful approach to date.

5. The relation of personality to symptom disorder is discussed as an element in the choice of disorder, but not as cause.

9

Conversations with Patients

The treatment of a variety of affect disorders has illustrated the usefulness of valid affect theory for a range of disorders. These include the varieties of symptom disorders that are often dramatic in their manifestations, such as phobia, panic, conversion, anorexia, heterophobia, reactive depression, paranoia, compulsion, and multiple personality. But also included are disorders in which inner pain brings fewer observable manifestations visible to others. These include many disorders that have been considered problems of character, behavioral disorders, or mood disorders. Such disorders have often gotten people into long-term treatment that turned them into chronic patients.

THE LESSON OF EPIPHANIC CURE

When each week's best-seller list is assaulted by yet another book promising to reveal a sure cure for one psychological problem or another with three, ten, or a hundred things to do, wary readers are justified in becoming skeptical about any claim in psychology. In this chapter and the next, an effort will be made to show precisely how a therapy that changes the focus to problems of affect phobia, affect muting, and affect storming can help therapists become more effective and patients achieve cure of the problems that brought them into therapy. The actual process will be explored, warts and all, including a section on circumstances that make therapy impossible. Readers will be able to judge for themselves—the whether, how, and why of it all.

But what of the occasional situations when improvement is obtained even though the therapist has no direct access to the sufferer? These startling instances of cure by epiphany, or at best therapy at a distance, must force attention to the power of the central concept being employed rather than a result of persuasion.

When Knowledge Alone Can Cure

One open-minded therapist who had bothered to learn and use the theory, after telling me of a patient he had cured, described an issue succinctly, "If I can cure a phobic patient in one session, is phobia really an illness?" My reply was based on the fact that she had been disabled by her phobia for three year, and treated by two other therapists without beneficial effect. "Something was wrong with her, but it was not a challenging treatment problem for you. Compare it to a disorder like bacterial pneumonia, an exceedingly disabling and life-threatening illness that had been incurable in the past, but now is usually cured quickly with antibiotics. Once it was a formidable physical illness, but with new knowledge it no longer is."

A handful of instant cures of severely disabled patients provides an important set of facts to use as a part of the base of our theoretical framework. These are epiphanies observed occurring in moments of adding and reshuffling knowledge. The improvement through comprehension and integration of knowledge, which we more commonly see over a dozen sessions, took place in minutes. The one-session cure of a phobic woman, referred to above, was ministered by a therapist who knew and understood the theory I have described. A few such cures occurred with my own patients.

Two other instant cures are of special interest because in each, treatment was administered by people who had learned the words and ideas by rote, but did not understand the theory. It is significant that information was transmitted by people who did not understand it, but the patients were cured. This supports the view of strength of the theory rather than persuasiveness of the therapist.

A young psychologist came to me for supervision as part of his qualification for his professional license. He was bright, willing, and eager. We worked together for several months, he consulting me about diagnostic and therapeutic issues. Early on in that supervision he told me he had a new patient with "panic attacks" who for a year frequently had to stop her car by the side of the road, and typically would pace up and down for about fifteen minutes until she was calm enough to drive to her destination. The student asked, "What should I do with her?"

I outlined the issues in the diagnostic process to be sure that this was actually a panic episode, which other matters did not complicate, and then described, in considerable detail, affect phobia, potentiation, and storm. I suggested that over several sessions he could inform her bit by bit of the storm process and its sources, but that it would be too much for her to absorb in even a few sessions for that might overload her.

The following supervisory session was about as follows: The young doctor said, "I told my panic patient what you said to tell her, and she is cured!" "That is fine, what did you tell her that cured her?" "I told her everything you said."

Incredulously I asked, "But did you tell her everything at once?"

"Yes, just as you said I should. I told her about getting excited about being excited, and that makes her even more excited. She gets into a storm of emotion so that she cannot think very clearly, and the other things you told me to tell her. She is all better."

To my question, "Why?" the eager young doctor responded, "I don't know." He went on to tell me that when he had stated emotions are not dangers but are ways of helping us understand ourselves, she had in rapid order said, "If that is so, then such and such is so, and that means that this must be. It makes so much sense. I see what you mean." Clearly, the patient could observe emotion process within herself, think about her emotions, all the while absorbing knowledge about a new frame of reference about emotion and herself. Her descriptions of thinking about emotion suggests something quite different from a transference cure, and was not the result of persuasion by the therapist. It was clear that he did not understand the process of disorder and cure, although his patient did so almost immediately.

The second epiphanic cure via a "therapist" who did not understand occurred with a young woman who had episodes of panic for years. Her mother is my patient Freya, whose story is the subject of the next chapter.

One day the young woman called her mother and said she was in such a panic she did not know what to do. She did not want to call her psychiatrist, who in the past had consistently responded only "take more Mellaril." She was quite frantic. Freya, whose own panic episodes had disappeared on the basis of a rote adoption of the concept of emotion potentiation and storm, although she cannot fully observe her own emotion processes, told her daughter something she knew but did not yet understand: "It is all right to be afraid, but you do not have to be afraid about being afraid." This was a slight paraphrase of what I had often told her. The daughter responded almost instantly with, "Oh, I see. Of course that is right. I can just be afraid. . . . I feel better." From that time on (now a few years) she remained free of panic, although continuing with a psychiatrist who persisted in loading her with drugs. It was clear from what she said at the time and over the months following that she did have capacity to observe emotion process and that she continued to absorb meaning from what someone, who did not herself quite get the meaning, had offered to her.

The notion of a transference cure is the only answer that can come from those psychoanalysts who are incapable of observing emotion process. From their ability to sense, and from their indoctrination, that is the only possible answer. The notion is nonsense in each of these cases, for if Freya had that much persuasive power over her daughter whom she loved, the many comforting things she had said over the years would have had that effect long ago. The young doctor had not said anything persuasive to his patient. He had not in any way suggested that she would be better. He had only asked her if she could see that she was getting excited about getting excited. In so many other discussions, with those colleagues who have a ready capacity for self-observation, the process has been similar. There is a quick recognition of facts they have known, but not regarded as important. The facts had been there for a long time, but were never conceptually organized together nor to difficulties within themselves or their patients.

Rage Storms in a Preadolescent Boy: Morris

It was the grandmother who called me first. She had become familiar with my work and thought I might be the appropriate person to whom to turn. Her eleven-year-old grandson, Morris, had been subject to rages starting at an early age. He is bright, warm, friendly, energetic, playful, and is accomplishing well in school. Most of the time he is congenial with everyone. She finds him very enjoyable to be with. His angry episodes, however, were frequent enough to create problems in the family. He would scream, say nasty things to his parents, throw or break things, and when sent to his room would continue for a while. There were holes in his bedroom walls where he had kicked through the plasterboard in his rages. She described several episodes in detail that fit well with the process of potentiation of emotion. I informed her that from what I had heard, I thought these might be simple rage storms. If that proved to be so, he could be helped fairly rapidly. I told her I would be glad to speak with her daughter if she called me.

A few hours later the daughter phoned me to talk about the problem. She confirmed what her mother had said. Morris had rages, but somewhat more frequently than grandmother had described, starting before he was three years of age. He would usually be in great pain afterward and be "depressed" for several hours. Often he tried to make amends and would apologize, but that did not make him feel better or prevent another occurrence—sometimes only hours later.

My view from what I heard in the half hour conversation was that these were distraught states from unstructured emotion storms and therefore could be prevented by the kind of parental teaching that for forty years I have been urging parents to offer. No matter how dramatic distraught states are as one views them, they are quite simple disorders to understand and to cure. I suggested that she bring Morris to see me and, if possible, to have both parents there. We arranged the time around the father's work schedule and Morris' interschool participation in which he represented his school. My experience has been that for many problems, including distraught states, it is more productive to work with parents of preadolescents by helping them think about emotion as they experience their own responses while they work with their children to do the same. The aim is to produce a parent-child ambiance such as every child should have, dispelling affect phobia as a natural developmental stage that they must surmount. Symptom disorders evaporate within persons who evolve past that infantile view of emotion. This strategy of parents guiding their children never succeeds if the parent repels the concepts, and rarely succeeds if the parent and child are at war with each other. The strategy has worked well with many, and is especially indicated for instances like this.

Morris was a nice looking tow-headed little boy in schoolboy attire and wearing glasses. He was polite, alert, and responded to questions clearly and more easily than most at his age. His vocabulary and language usage showed that he is very bright. Most of the time while I was talking with the mother or the father, he played with an electronic math problem device, seeming to concentrate on the complex problems, but was clearly aware of the adult discussion.

I spoke of emotion and what it is and is not, how people flee, fight, or escalate emotion, how it is a natural part of all of us, not an illness or disruption, and described examples of why and how emotion is useful. The issue is always affect phobia. On this occasion I probably did more lecturing than tutoring (in the pattern I tend to follow when a patient or parent seems able to observe emotion in process), for the mother responded with statements such as, "I see what you mean. That seems so right. Of course, we waste much energy fighting emotion, why don't other people teach this?" She even concluded, "If we keep track of our emotions, they become useful information." It was clear to me that she was not hearing what I said as hypothetical constructs but could observe her own emotion processes and could listen to me in terms of actual process she experienced within herself. She seemed able to apply the concepts herself, for a couple times she declared, "If (such) is so, than (this) must be so, and that helps explain . . . ," and so on.

We parted with the agreement that the parents would make a special effort to think about emotion in themselves and teach Morris about emotion. They would contact me, and if he was not doing considerably better, we would work together on the problems.

I heard nothing more for about six weeks. Morris' mother phoned to tell me that they had worked on the problem with Morris. It had taken two days for Morris to become free of his rages. By the end of that first week, two of his teachers had commented to her that he suddenly was so much more at ease with himself and others that it was pleasing to them to see that change. He had lost his worried look and was performing even better intellectually.

If there was doubt about the effectiveness of his parents' teachings, an incident two weeks after their visit is persuasive. Mother and child were watching a television drama in which a little boy was in a rage at his father—yelling, physically assaulting, etc. The mother said that while she was watching the events on the screen she thought she would have to talk with Morris about the little boy in the drama. Even as she was thinking that, Morris turned to her and said, "That boy is the way I used to be." He clearly understood the rage portrayed, how it had been within himself, and that he would not have that kind of experience again.

On several other occasions I have been impressed by how readily children pick up my ideas about emotion and apply them to themselves. They do this much more quickly than most adults, perhaps because the common wisdom attitudes about emotion have not been fixed within them for as long a time. It seems probable that if we teach our youngsters about emotion we can comparatively easily create a much healthier population.

A reader might ask whether what happened with Morris is a matter of persuasion, as in transference cure, or simply compliance with parents' requests to stop behaving that way (which had not been successful with their requests for the years prior to visiting me). I believe it was a matter of his learning that emotion is a natural useful part of us that we need not try to manage, tolerate, fear, regulate, or fight, but can use as information and is separate from action. This vignette of change in a young boy is corroborative of what might be done with a prevention program with all children. This youngster with an unusually high intellect and many talents will no longer waste energy and time fussing with his emotions. That should allow him to use his intellect and talent in enjoyable, productive, and creative activity. Certainly he will be free of the various symptom disorders that are so common in this world. We have in this the knowledge to enable all children to be free of the burden of emotion phobia and make enhanced use of their intellect and talents to the betterment of all. The benefit of the new theory is not merely what it can do for treatment, but how it changes the experiencing of life.

Several ideas should be considered in thinking of what happened to Morris and quite a few others in their epiphanic cures. Those persons able to comprehend the theory outlined in this book, and to observe affect processes within themselves will therefore understand emotion storms as personal experience and most easily understand what had happened with this boy. Those who are introspective will not notice process. Those who understand affect process as hypothetic construct may be able to surmise what had happened in an "as if" way. Those who are rigidly tied to past theories will not open their minds to "outside" ideas enough to understand either the process or outcome even if they have the talents necessary to observe emotion process. They will not seriously consider the idea that the various previous theories of neurosis are invalid. These latter people will question whether cure was achieved, or if they concede it took place, will consider the basis or permanence of the improvement in terms of the limitations of their own tightly held theory instead of in terms of the new theory. Considered in those terms, they would have to reject that the cure was a cure, for no other theory seriously considers the possibility of an actual cure.

Beyond considering the treatment process as described, it may be worthwhile considering what other approaches might have done with this little boy over how long a time, and with what effects on the remainder of his life. The path taken depends to a great extent upon where a person turns when seeking guidance about mental health. He might have been guided to any of various kinds of treatment, in all of which his condition would have been regarded as a very serious problem needing immediate attention and having a guarded prognosis about the remainder of his life.

If the problem had been presented to a physician, the greater probability is that he would have been treated from the reductionist view that psychological disorders are brain disorders, to take care of the biological problem "that is at the base of the trouble" and given medication by the internist or referred to a practitioner of biopsychiatry. In either case it is likely that they would have given him psychotropic medications for any number of years to suppress the intensity of his emotions. It would fit with one phrase I have heard from biopsychiatrists: to make him "feel less," or even more commonly, to "correct a chemical imbalance." The influence of the approach would have been to make him more cautious of his emotions. That path would have settled him into a life of avoiding affective response, moved him toward affect muting, if not to the enormity of iatrogenic tension phobia.

Psychodynamic schools would have offered treatment in the belief that he had a serious character problem. He might have been seen a few times a week over the next few years to learn of infantile sources of personality patterns that "are at the base of his problems" as trigger mechanisms and caused his rages, with the result that he would have learned a great deal about his personality. This treatment approach would have removed some of the triggers of storms, and therefore reduced the frequency of storms, but would do nothing about either his tendency to storm or the intensity of his storms. His treatment would have enabled a richer awareness of his subjectivity that would have brought a greater awareness of interpersonal relations but would probably have brought a much more turbulent adolescence than otherwise.

If he had been advised by the family physician he may have been channeled to a Cognitive therapy. He might have been talked with to help him see the foolishness of reacting with rage to small matters and to recognize the interpersonal difficulties he was creating. He would have been encouraged to be sensible. There would have been an increased awareness of his already considerable guilt about the pain he caused those around him, and a likelihood that he would substitute other neurotic manifestations of his continuing storms.

Some school guidance departments would have sent him to a Behavioral therapist. He might have been subjected to behavioral therapy for a couple of years of discomfiting confrontations with his frustrations to "decondition his rage tendencies." Because deconditioning aims directly at simple processes of specific affects or simple behaviors, it would not have worked well with the more complex entity structure of emotion storms. He would have become more self-conscious about his actions and more guilt ridden. His storms would have continued.

If some friend of the family had guided him, they might have sent him to a Gestalt or other pop psychology affect ejection therapy. He might have been encouraged to pound on bean bags to "get out the rage stored within him since infancy." He might have worked to discover the "infant within" to coddle and protect it. He might have worked to build his self-esteem. None of these would have changed his tendency to storm, but would likely have done the disservice of increasing his tendency toward affect phobia by its encouragement to regard emotion as bad and disruptive, and thus increase the likelihood of his inner torment and increase the chances of developing multiple storm disorders over the years. He might have become psychologically addicted to treatment groups. Certainly affect phobia would have increased markedly so that he would likely have moved into a lifetime of symptom disorders and interferences with his life.

Interesting as epiphanic cure may be from a theoretical perspective, I hasten to assure readers that I do not view the future of psychotherapy as some form of televangelism. Until the use of this theory is disseminated so that prevention of the disorders is common, by and large, troubled patients will sit with sympathetic therapists and engage in the earnest endeavor that is one of modern psychology's enduring contributions. They will talk, and if the talk is useful, the troubles will be alleviated. The question is the nature of that talking. What will they talk about? How will they talk with each other?

Different Problems, Similar Conversations

If we can understand the nature of distraught states as based in faulty development of understanding about emotion process within oneself, the tutoring process becomes an obvious approach. Certainly it has been far more effective than previous sorts of attempts to cure.

To me, the frequency of four-to-five session cures that proved to have lasting effects was the most heartening support of the validity of the storm basis of symptom disorders. Although the epiphanic cures demonstrate cures in self-observing people who would not usually develop these disorders, those who were cured in a handful of sessions seemed to require expansion of self-observing function.

Fathering of Rage Storms—Consequences of Affect Muting: Kevin. About three months after my single session with Morris, his father Kevin phoned to say that he would like to talk with me about some problems he had with emotion and about the way his life, marital and family relationships were displeasing. We arranged an appointment for a few weeks later.

This man with a serious demeanor appeared thoughtful, and as I expected he was highly intelligent. He spoke of his difficulty in making decisions, his inability to refuse any of the never-ending projects presented to him by his employer, and of having a joyless life.

It turned out that Kevin had been in many therapies of various sorts over a few decades. These had included pastoral counseling, bean-bag pounding, joint marital counseling, and dynamic psychotherapies. None had brought changes of any significance to him.

I suggested to him that he might consider that decisions call for use of both intellect and emotion. To me he sounded as though he had suppressed his awareness of emotion, which would help account for both his indecisiveness and his joylessness. It is the gray state of people who function somewhere in the range between adequate affect awareness and depersonalization.

I continued with the tutoring that had taken place when he, his wife, and Morris were with me as a marital therapy. He declared that he must fit into the category of people who have little awareness of what goes on inside. I responded by telling him that neither he or anyone else was emotionless, for emotions are built-in for everyone, and that he is merely estranged from them, unaware of those emotions in some degree. We agreed to work on these problems because they were issues for his family relationships, and perhaps later bring his wife into our sessions.

He recounted his childhood experience with his mother frequently telling him that he did not feel whatever he said he felt. She never did tell him that he felt some particular emotion, but seemed to aim to blot out whatever emotion was noticed by him. In this she differed from some parents who not only worked to erase awareness of what was felt but also attempted to regulate their child's emotions by also declaring which emotions should be present. As with any autonomous function, neither erasure nor regulation of emotion is a possibility—the aim to accomplish either is an evidence of the pathology, affect phobia. Worse, those who promote regulation of affect infect others with the same pathology and set the stage for development of symptom disorders as well as blighting the lives of those they influence. The aim of affect regulation, even if suggested with kindly curative intention, destructively promotes psychopathology.

Fitting with the pattern that she had taught him, he said that he neither loved nor hated her, but was really indifferent to her. That indifference was a possibly unintended consequence of what she had taught him. However, his voice sounded more negative than his words. To me that hostility in his voice was encouraging, for any rift in affect muting gives greater likelihood of bringing more emotions into awareness.

Kevin seemed to think about emotion during the week between sessions. He realized that he has difficulty naming his feeling experiences, catching an emotion of the moment while he felt it, and connecting a feeling to the evocative situation. By taking on the task of being introspective, Kevin became alert to feeling experience that he has trouble naming and connecting to its evocative source. He also became more alert to issues of decision making.

His wife once had asked him why he was so reluctant to tell her of the good things that happened in his work day. She perceptively told him, "I won't steal your feelings." My comment to Kevin was, "She is right in what she said. Your mother did, in a sense, steal your feelings by telling you that you did not feel what you felt."

He became apprehensive about what it might be like to feel a lot of emotion. While, in part, this may relate to childhood fear of opposing mother, it is more likely to be the direct emotion phobia that has been encountered in so many patients. His comment about what it might be like to have a symphony of emotion is a clue to how grayed off his life experience is with emotions muted. Nevertheless he has taken on the task of persevering in seeking to notice the presence of emotion within himself. He considers it an assignment. I see no reason to change his opinion.

The problem seems to be that he has been unable to place a value of significance or meaningfulness of various tasks, relying completely on others to do that. It is the common result of the gray lives muted affect brings, without a process determining preferences or aversions, we cannot tell significance from insignificance. Commitment being essentially feeling, muted emotion makes for tenuous or intermittent commitment.

Later in treatment Kevin described a moment of awareness of a "strange" feeling. It was a swift experiencing of something that he could not name, could not connect with anything going on within or around him. He could recognize that it was emotion, was intrigued by it, and could not remember ever experiencing it before.

I suggested that he may have momentarily broken through a barrier (in his muting) and that he could keep trying as he has, because if he could do it once, even briefly, he could do it again. It seemed to me that this event may be a big start for his getting acquainted with his emotion experience. He has a long journey to travel.

The difficulties that Kevin brought are the sort that too often are judged as if they constitute depression rather than affect muting. The use of antidepressants or "mood adjusters" to enliven them makes such persons less able to become aware of their emotions, while temporarily seeming to bring improvement, but interfere with cure of the problem.

The Combination of Phobia and Depersonalization: Karen. Patients who have muted emotion disorders in combination with storm disorders have been slower to respond to treatment. When another approach has not been used in an attempt to treat depersonalization, treatment has usually been successful in producing a lasting cure in one to three sessions. For storm disorders that have not been otherwise treated, the successful cures usually appear after a dozen sessions. When these affect phobic disorders appear in combination even when not confounded by other treatment, the typical cure has required fifty or more sessions. The two disorders are mutually interfering.

The phone call from a former patient brought the information that her daughter was in great distress. The family had spent the weekend trying to comfort and reassure her, but the young woman was sure that she had "lost it." For some time she had been uncomfortable being alone at any great distance from home, but had bravely driven alone to work each day. The weekend episode of depersonalization-based panic left her with the usual "crazy fears" that are aroused by either panic or depersonalization.

Karen was trusting of me because her mother knew me. Bright, educated, thoughtful and motivated by the agony of her disorder, she was eager to do whatever it took to be well. I began the tutoring.

With the panic episode storms consuming the mental energy of this bright young woman, the affect education had to aim for the storms, but the depersonalization from the affect muting made the education more difficult. We needed the awareness of affect to disassemble the storms. The biopsychiatric approach of using anti-anxiety medications to "stabilize" the patient in such an agony of distress can be seen as antitherapeutic, for in some degree it anesthetizes consciousness of emotion and thus chemically mutes emotion and increases rather than reduces the disorder. Its implicit message is that feeling experience should be suppressed. That approach would have been a mistake. Because each panic episode is usually short-lived, there is ordinarily much quiescent time available. Reaching the patients' intellect for tutoring during those quiescent times is possible.

After listening to her story, I could tell her that despite the severity of the pain there was no evidence of a psychosis (she had not "lost it") and her troubles were of the sort that are usually completely cured. That knowledge was enough to reassure her and, in effect, "stabilize" her more quickly, thoroughly, and without the interference of mind-numbing drugs.

By the end of the week (three sessions) the panic episodes had disappeared, not to return. What was left to deal with therapeutically were the depersonalization and agoraphobia. The underlying issue was still affect phobia manifested dually in affect muting and affect storming. The solution had to lie in working at the affect phobia to undercut the manifestations. The process lasted almost one year, with the frequency of our meetings reduced to once per week.

The disturbing agoraphobia gradually diminished over the months. For her first couple weeks, she required her husband to bring her the fifty miles to my office, afterward drop her off at her work, and again pick her up from work at the end of the day. For another couple weeks she needed him to trail her in his car to my office and then to her job. From that time forward she drove her own car, unaccompanied, with reasonable but not total comfort, and improved steadily on that score.

The therapy consisted of tutoring, examination of specific emotions, and a gradual move from "situation equals panic" to recognition of the several steps in the sequence of feeling reaction to feeling reaction. She built a frame of reference of benign, transient, constructive affects. We mutually agreed that she needed no more treatment for the problems that had brought her to me.

That turned out not to be the end of it. Approximately six months later Karen called me while experiencing great distress. She was at a phone booth at the side of a road. "It's all back. None of what we did was any good. I am just as badly off as I ever was. What should I do?" I inquired about where she was and what had happened. She told me that she had been fine for months, and suddenly while driving to work on the highway she was terrified of being alone and needed to go home, but couldn't imagine driving there. She couldn't believe that she was in a healthy enough state to go to work, and could not reach her husband on the phone.

I said, "What is it that you have forgotten?" There was a period of silence that may have been a few seconds or may have been a couple minutes. I waited.

Karen then said, "Oh, it's OK. I remember. I'm all right now. Thanks." A decade later she continues to be functioning well. I am pleased to hear from her from time to time at holidays, on the births of her children, and other pieces of good news.

Conversations About a Bug Phobia: Celeste. Celeste said that being terrified of bugs of all sorts had hampered her life for about ten years. One result of that fear was being a spotless cleaner of her home. She used bug sprays that kept her home more than ordinarily clear of the crawling and flying creatures with whom we share this world. Each morning she would awaken to make breakfast for her husband and daughter. She looked carefully to see whether any bug occupied the floor or counter before stepping into the room. She would peer carefully into each pot, pan, and dish with trepidation that there might be some small living creature there. Each time she went to the door to bring in the newspaper, she would open it watchfully, carefully shake the paper in case something horrifying had crawled into it. She gave no clear description of what it is about bugs that was so disturbing, but did explain that they seemed dirty and probably covered with dangerous germs.

I suggested that most phobias seemed to be more related to concern with emotions than with the seemingly fearsome object to which people react. To most city dwellers, bugs seem dirty and an unwanted part of our lives. Most of us are perhaps a little squeamish about such creatures, but we do not turn to mush upon thinking of them or even when encountering them. The difference seems to be that our disliking them does not press us to get excited about not liking them.

"To find out if this is true of you I would like for you to focus on your reactions when you see a bug. You don't have to actually see one, but as you think now about doing so, what is the sequence in your thoughts and feelings?"

"I think bug, see one in my mind, and I am immediately terrified."

"Do you mean that it is an instant jump in a single step? That you think bug and you immediately become terrified?"

"Yes, that's the way it happens."

"My experience with other people with similar troubles is that when they set themselves the task of observing within themselves in great detail, carefully focusing to notice more of what goes on within their minds, they begin to notice some intervening thoughts and feelings. While I have no way of knowing what those steps are within you, my guess is that there are five or ten such events that you may eventually become able to observe. If you can, it will be well worth your effort to do so."

Over nine sessions, Celeste worked at observing, without deliberately putting herself into some disturbing situation. The confrontation with the object of the phobia that behavioral therapists suggest is experienced by many patients as torture and not helpful to them. That is why I tell patients not to force themselves to go into situations that disturb them. They can learn all they need to learn by using their memories of the events that had triggered disturbance within themselves and by working to observe even the most fleeting of mental content within themselves. As with so many people who have successfully done that, this woman, too, made the step of noticing that between visual awareness of a bug and the ensuing terror with much physiological involvement, there was a step of emotion response of disgust. To me that meant that she had broken the barrier to observation of process and that she could almost certainly become free of her disorder.

Seeing her twice a week to work on adding to her observations of herself, learning to comprehend the microsecond transience of emotion, learning a corrected comprehension, and sorting through of distinctions in language of emotion and para emotions brought acceptance of emotion as an ordinary useful function that is neither a trivial nor grand event. She built a new frame of reference for all emotion experience.

Celeste arrived at her ninth session with the news that the morning before she had walked into her kitchen and found two bugs on the floor. Her first reaction was to tighten up, with the squeamish reaction most people might have. But now able to observe her reactions in sequence, with her acceptance of feeling reactions that went into the squeamishness, she was able to tell herself, "Well, at least they are dead." She picked up the dead bugs in her fingers, threw them into the waste can, and went about her preparations of breakfast. What had been an agonizing experience for ten or more years was now within the range of normal experience. Two years later she remains free of any such problems. Experience with other patients persuades us that, as long as she can continue to notice what she feels about what inner and outer events and accept that her affects are a natural useful portion of her life, she will remain free of phobia and any other storm disorders.

The Common Storm Basis of Compulsion and Phobia: Barb and Ken. Two disorders, commonly thought of as very different, are therefore customarily treated as distinctly different problems. Both are considered treatable, but not truly curable. Both are the sorts of troubles treated by behaviorists as a kind of habit pattern disorder that can be corrected by conditioning. The treatment is painful, long-lasting, and, despite the touting of successes with these disorders, does not cure. Within psychology, the dynamic psychotherapy schools insist that the troubles are rooted in the personality and set about the quest for etiological sources of the troubles. They do not promise cures, but do promise amelioration, which they often produce. They work with a minor factor, which being relevant gives them some advantage over behaviorists, but does not produce the cures that their patients desire. Cognitivists believe that the problems are rooted in disordered ideation and work to produce greater clarity of thinking to change attitudes about situations, and thus dispel the disorders. Clearer thinking among the Cognitivists would enable them to see that the disorders have other causes and need other treatment to achieve cures. Biopsychiatrists prescribe medications to suppress some of the physiological consequences of the storm disorders and thus palliate, but call that a cure. If that were actual, cured patients would not be continued on medications for years.

Ken came to me at the urging of his wife, Barb, for their marital problems. She was threatening to divorce him if he did not cease his domineering control of their home life by insisting that every article had to be wiped, washed, rinsed, and cleansed almost endlessly. They, too, must be constantly cleaning themselves. He would return from his work at the end of the day and, as his first priority, wash his hands and arms in running water and much suds. If any water from the faucet splashed against the sink and then to his arms he would start the whole process again. He did not consider anyone, including his wife, to be clean. If they ate their evening meal in the kitchen and she decided to turn on the television without first washing her hands, he considered the TV switch to be contaminated so that both it and her hands needed to be washed. The impediments to easy living were many. For the wife it was nightmarish. Their sexual life was nearly nil, for he considered himself filthy, his wife filthy, and the bed filthy. While this man's behavior was offensive, it must be noted that his life was one of great pain. He was driven. It did not matter how much he told himself the activity was unnecessary, that neither he nor his wife was really dirty, and that his wife was in great distress from being hounded to keep everything cleaner, despite her every effort to do so.

The illness, which had driven him to such painful state, was now ruling him and his wife and distorting both their lives. I had told him it seemed to me it had to be painful to have his illness ruling his life, but if he continued to allow his illness to go beyond ruling him and just as tyrannically also rule the household and his wife, he was running some risk of losing her. He understood, but said, "I can't help myself, although I try." Ken had been in treatment previously for about two years, the treatment consisting almost entirely of the prescription Xanax, an anti-anxiety drug widely prescribed then for several psychological disorders.

I told him the disorder was completely curable in almost all instances, the cures coming from knowing and understanding what was going on inside his mind. He turned out to be a bright, somewhat introspective person. We soon came to the discovery that he was extremely frightened of contracting some horrible lethal disease. AIDS was a special threat, but other diseases also were sources of worry. He did recognize very early that his washing was a symbolic activity that would not kill or free him from bacteria except at the surface of the skin he washed.

The tutorial conversations began with the focus on the emotion he had noticed and its product—a fear-based emotion storm. He became much more aware of his fear, its long history as apprehension and terror, and the timidity it had instilled in him. He had worked out a way of attempting to compensate for his fear by a display of strength, very aggressive actions, strong voice, show of firm convictions, and by wearing the superficial robes of high self-esteem and confidence.

We moved from the two-position sequence of fear (of infection) leading to urgent washing activity, to the three-position sequence of fear (of infection) to guilt about being bacteria laden and dirty (symbolizing not a good person) leading to urgent washing. He had, by doing this, moved from the symbol to the subjective reality. That was when he could begin to reduce his obnoxious, driven behavior. The later addition of awareness of shame in the potentiation sequence brought him considerable ease in the washing process. The remainder of the cure could go on from there with any self-observing person working independently.

At this point, as he began to improve in the acceptability of his actions, his wife came to see me at his urging because the marital problems could now be discussed. Barb was relieved that the marital-home situation had become almost tolerable. But now that he was better, she planned to divorce him. She would not have left him while he was so ill.

Having told me that, she launched into her story of her own long-standing agoraphobia. She drove her car to her work, but as with so many agoraphobes, each additional increment of distance made her increasingly uncomfortable. I talked with her about affect phobia, about potentiation, about the move from the psychological processes leading to the physical reactions of adrenaline and other hormonal actions that created the disturbing physical symptoms that are consequences of the psychological troubles, but are erroneously assumed by biological psychiatry to be where the problems start. We spent eleven weekly sessions going through her potentiation of fear in a single affect straight line sequence (fear of fear of fear). She proved to be as bright as her husband, but more capable of real self-observation, whereas he was only introspective. The illness of many years duration, after a few current episodes were examined and disassembled by her, was dispelled.

During the several week span of the treatment she moved to her parents home, initiated a divorce, initiated contact with an old boyfriend, became able to travel freely—including a distant vacation with her new boyfriend, and was planning to marry this man (recklessly rushed, in my opinion) whom she found more suitable.

It seems to me of more than passing interest that a married couple, each spouse with fear triggered emotion storms, had different symptoms arising from those storms and were each cured by examination of the potentiation and storms. It seems a reasonable inference that the choice of symptom manifestations were related to the personality factors of each—the action orientation of the husband and the inner process of the wife—both starting from a previously unnoticed reaction to anathematized fear in which they each fought by potentiating it in their individual creative way and disabled themselves by that. The common attribute of severe emotion phobia may have been a part of the original attraction that got them into the marriage.

Conversion Disorders: Rene. Conversion disorders are not as popular currently as they once were. They were at one time a far more accepted diagnosis than current leaders such as depression, phobia, anxiety disorder, multiple personality, and the various anorexias. In the past, the conversion symptoms seen with some frequency were paralyses of limbs, visual or auditory sensory loss, and distorted movements of body, as in tics. Among conversion disorders, what seems to be more acceptable currently are conversion symptoms related to voice and throat and less frequently to leg anesthesia and movements.

The voice on the phone was hoarse. She told me her voice coach had referred her to me because for the past ten years she had continuous hoarseness rather than a clear voice. When she arrived for consultation, she was a poised, well-dressed woman who was quite intelligent. As a business executive she was in conferences and on the telephone much of the day. For many years she had been troubled by the lack of clarity in her speech, a condition such that people would frequently ask if she had a cold.

During those ten years she had tried many different professionals in unsuccessful attempts to become able to speak freely. None improved her situation at all. The first attempts included studies to learn what allergies she suffered. There were MRI and CAT scans to see if there were nerve fiber involvements. A throat surgeon could find no nodes on her larynx that might have caused the hoarseness. He advised her that sometimes nodes are invisible and therefore he recommended a surgical procedure "just in case"—so she underwent surgical scraping of the larynx to remove possible invisible nodes. She went through a series of speech pathologists to work at her speech vocalization patterns to attempt to help her speak clearly. She had tried psychiatric approaches with no success. She went to speech coaches, finally seeing the one who, knowing of my work, urged her to see me. It had taken a year of such urging before she accepted the idea.

The first session was mostly taken up by the dismal saga of futile attempts to satisfy her simple aim. I was able to tell her about the uses of emotion and the typical human response of fighting, fleeing, denying, and suppressing emotion instead of using it. She already had some preparation for this from the voice coach, so that what I told her filled some gaps in her knowledge.

On the second visit, the tutorial proceeded with some emphasis on the issues of observing mental content she may have glossed over in the past, and on some distinctions among emotions and para emotions. She explored her own emotion dynamics by using her good capacity for self-observation.

Her third visit was taken up with some issues of the sequence of mental content in situations in which she potentiated her emotions. The plan was to go through the material we had already covered and build on that for the next visit.

A few days later she called in what my secretary described as a remarkably clear voice, leaving a message canceling further appointments and thanking me for curing her difficulty. She was "very busy with her work and didn't want to devote any more time to her voice." She spoke glowingly of what had happened and said she would be forever grateful. She had finally gained what she wanted and needed to spend no more time on the problem. Although I would have liked to have heard that clear voice myself,

I never heard directly from her again. (Indirect information suggested that if she had further trouble she would have called me.)

What had happened is that after ten years of various kinds of activities to clear her voice, the three sessions with me, following the good preparation by the voice coach, had taken care of the conversion symptom. She had spent ten years of difficulty and about $50,000 to accomplish nothing. Because her capacity for self-observation was superb, despite the long-term disability and previous treatment, she had succeeded in her aim with three hours of tutorial therapy at a cost that for a highly paid executive was "pocket money."

The emotion storms in some people appear as rather quiet in comparison to the storms of the various distraught states. Why her problem was connected with voice rather than some other system must depend on her life experience, but learning about that was unimportant to her. Perhaps it should be unimportant to me as well. The choice of the throat, speech, neck, communication, etc., depends upon one's personal experience. I did not learn the story of such matters in her life sufficiently to suggest the rest of the story.

Agoraphobia: Samantha. Samantha was referred to me by a therapist with the splendid recommendation that, "Because you have a phobia there is only one person to see. He is the one to go to no matter how difficult getting there may be or how far it is." If there was a likelihood of a transference cure, this would be the introduction appropriate for it.

The woman was an educated, intellectually alert editor. It was clear in the first few minutes that she was wonderfully self-observing. She lived in a suburb and worked in the nearby city. While she could drive her car locally, she could not drive more than a few blocks from her home without becoming frantic. For that reason she used the train for commuting.

The difficulty with diagnoses based on superficial behavior is that we require ourselves to distinguish between being uncomfortable outside the home from being uncomfortable as this woman was: when driving herself in a car outside the home but comfortable in a train outside the home. The long list of phobias distinguished from one another by the dozens of different objects of discomfort has been compiled to fit with past theory and may be disregarded by those of us who have moved to the position that phobias all are the same at base. The cause—affect storm—and the particular triggering condition or situation is an incidental matter of minor importance for diagnosis or treatment. The choice of trigger is a matter of personal history.

This woman, having superb capacity for self-observation, learned about affect as transient, benign, constructive mental events within a few sessions and integrated that frame of reference into her life. She was free of her problem in three sessions, although we continued for a fourth session.

Paranoid Episodes: Henry. The psychological disturbance known as paranoia is often considered as if fused (if not confused) with paranoid psychosis and is regularly confused with paranoid schizophrenia. In recent years, the likelihood has been that paranoia almost automatically has meant the patient is routed to a psychiatrist. That may be either the cause or the effect of the lost distinctions. Paranoid episodes are consistently affect storms.

A therapist sent a patient he had seen twice. He described the patient as a thirty-five-year-old man with a violent temper, suspicious and challenging. In a rage the man had screamed at the therapist so loudly and so threateningly that the other doctor in the two-person suite came running into the office without knocking because he thought the patient was assaulting the therapist. Although he was wrong, he was right in supposing that the therapist was afraid.

Henry was a young businessman who was having a hard time with his co-workers, his family, and his few friends. He had always worried about whether others around him would treat him fairly, and indeed, from his story he had many experiences where he had been hurt when he mistakenly trusted others. He was often angry with himself for letting himself get hurt. He knew he frightened people but saw that as a kind of protection for himself.

"I think your life sounds very painful," I told him. "I hope we can work out a way that will give you both the protection you want and some kind of relationships that will be satisfying to you and not threatening to you or others around you."

That pleased him enough that his vocal decibel count came down several points, and we set about our work. "I think you are having a hard time accepting some of your own emotions," I told him. "You may be more excited about your emotions than you are about the events about which you complain. I wonder if you so much dislike being angry that you get angry about getting angry." I talked with him about the woman I had passed on the sidewalk who told her eighteen month old not to pick up a cigarette he was reaching for from the sidewalk. The cigarette so entranced the child that he disregarded her admonition and reached for it anyway. While he was reaching his angry mother said, "Don't pick that up or I will get angry." The child picked it up. She said, "Now you did it! You have made me angry." It seemed to me that her being angry was to her the most terrible thing that could happen. "I think you may have somewhat the same belief about your own anger as that woman had about hers."

It is hard to describe how relieved this man appeared to be that I understood some of what had been going on within him for years. Over six weeks, once per week, we talked about the distinction between feeling and action, the distinctions between emotions and pseudo emotions, and the processes of potentiation that got him so in trouble with himself and others.

He began to be free enough to talk about his paranoid fantasies, his suspicions that others as a group were against him, and his conviction that he was often in danger from such colluding opponents.

Both the rage storms and the paranoid suspiciousness of others diminished, although he remained somewhat distrusting. We came to the conclusion that his paranoid episodes occurred when rage depleted his intellect so much that he could not judge what was going on. His lifelong natural tendency to be suspicious and watchful produced automatic thought content he could not critique well enough to weigh the ideas—he automatically accepted the suspicions as verified truth.

Henry's financial situation determined that he did not continue further work on his pattern issues, and I do not know what happened to him after that. At the time of his departure he was very different from the screaming, threatening, frightened man of six weeks earlier. Without psychoanalytic study of the childhood basis of his lifelong patterns, he is unlikely to have changed from that pattern of protective suspiciousness.

Conversion Disorder: Helen. Helen had called me after approximately two and a quarter years of treatment for her limited ability to swallow. The difficulty had become so hampering that for all those months she could not swallow even very small pieces of food. She lived on liquids and mashed or ground foods. The severity of the difficulty was such that she was emaciated and worried about her survival.

When the difficulty first arose she had gone to her internist for help. He had her undergo many tests, but after six months could not find any physical basis for her difficulty. He referred her to a psychiatrist who listened to her story and misdiagnosing her difficulty said, "You have a phobia, and will have that the rest of your life. But that's all right, I can give you some medication that will make you feel less." He also sent her to a group therapy in which the patients pounded on bean bags to get out their held-in anger. She told me she felt silly doing that.

After many months of taking medication and pounding on bean bags, with no benefit that she could recognize, she decided to try something else. The prospect of endless medication was unsettling to her, for as a nurse she knew it to be physically risky. She found a magazine article about my work, and after studying it carefully came to see me.

Because that article was well written, Helen had a good basis for understanding what we were to do together. We were able to go to the issues of potentiation and storm, which because she was intelligent and self-observing she could absorb and apply to herself instantly. Noting this, I told her I did not believe she would have any problem in becoming completely free of the trouble, although I could not say how long it would take.

Because I was worried about Helen's physical fragility, I insisted she return the next day so that we could continue. The next day she told me she had gone home, prepared a dinner for her husband and son, sat with them, and ate the full meal without any difficulty. Her little boy said to her, "Mommy, I never saw you eat so much before."

The storm difficulty had been dissolved. She had quickly adopted the ideas of emotions as useful, benign, transient events and was free of the disorder she had been told "you will have the rest of your life." I was unsure in those first days of tutoring therapy that we could have accomplished as much so rapidly, so I milked the therapy by extending it to one more session to be sure it was real. Many years later I learned indirectly that there has been no further trouble.

In retrospect, I think the result was possible because she had done her homework before seeing me, she is a very intelligent woman with an open mind, and a superb talent for self-observation far beyond typical introspective capacities. The suggestion from her rapid response to treatment is that most people could become free of storm disorders with education that ideally should take place outside of psychotherapy. When that happens, the multibillion dollar industry that produces and dispenses drugs for psychological disorders can turn to dealing with medications for biologically based illness.

BARRIERS TO TREATMENT: IGNESCENT INTROSPECTIVE PERSONALITIES

Both of the ignescent persons described in the following paragraphs are Delta level characters. It was that factor that made them persist in trying to be in charge rather than participating in a peer discussion of what was happening with them. It is the Delta level concern with protection of weak ego boundaries. The form of self-protection taken by both was holding all at a distance. That stood in the way of developing even the rudiments of a healthy positive transference or even a working alliance. Interpersonal relationships at Delta level are usually partial (part object) and always temporary—lasting so long as ego boundaries are merged.

Two treatment failures in ignescent, introspective patients may help put this work in a clearer perspective. One was an ignescent writer sophisticated in psychological ideas through graduate work and through past treatment. The other was an ignescent artist who was psychologically sophisticated through twenty-some years with a therapist who claimed to be a psychoanalyst, but from the patient's reports practiced a sort of affect ejective psychotherapy.

These two patients, whom I saw briefly and unsuccessfully, were both highly intelligent and highly sophisticated people who were each, in their own ways, terribly disabled and miserable despite the fact that each worked in a chosen field. The barrier issues in each were not only their formal and informal education in varieties of psychotherapy, but also a fiery, aggressive, self-protective wariness of anything new. They had absorbed premises they could not leave. The latter attribute is one mark of the slow learner.

Both behaved in the manner of slow-learning students. They held new information at a distance from themselves, as if trying to observe every aspect of it to be sure it would not be harmful to them if they took it into their minds for even a moment. To them it was as if taking in an idea for a moment was an acceptance of the idea that would make it a permanent part of their set of beliefs—make them permanently stuck with it without later prerogative to reject it. The problem with such cautiousness is that one cannot comprehend experience without experiencing, never by viewing from a distance. The quick learners I have known seem to work with a greater perspective and are flexibly ready to adopt any intriguing new idea boldly *on a temporary basis* so that they first try out before accepting or rejecting anything. They appear free of fear that they will be captured and be without freedom to decide later what they believe.

Long-Term Agoraphobia (Introspection Is Not Enough): Sally

The man phoned to ask me if he could have a consultation about possible treatment for his wife who had been agoraphobic for many years. He wanted to learn what I might be able to do for her, how I would go about it, and the possibility of success of the treatment. That protective action as intercessor was itself a message well worth more consideration than I gave it at the time. We spent a full session talking about health and illness, and he decided to recommend to his wife that she work with me.

Sally was a forty-five-year-old woman, well dressed, intelligent, and read'ly communicative of the difficulties that had been part of her life for many years. She was a writer and worked from her home. Everything in her activities was arranged so that she rarely had to leave the house and never had to do so alone. Her phobia ruled her life. As happens with so many long-term symptom disorders, they not only rule patients' lives, but also rule their families' lives. Her husband could do nothing without making sure his presence, absence, schedule, and activities would not discommode or discomfort her. He subordinated his life to schedule his business about her comfort and would cancel trips, various engagements, or a day at the office if she were uncomfortable. He was loving toward her, obviously coddled her to the extent he could, and seemed fearful of her fragility and illness.

She recounted a series of experiences with various therapists and other professionals. She described them all as being remarkably insensitive, and they had evoked painful emotions in her by their hostility and callousness. Her anger at them and her contempt for them were intense. I could find no reason to suspect that this was anything but an unfortunate sequence of bad connections in the mental health and medical professions that justified the bitterness she manifested.

My initial optimism came from noticing her acquaintance with her own subjectivity, for she included a variety of specific emotion responses in her descriptions of her life experiences, and told me the writings she published were about her own experiencing, shared with others through those writings. My second reaction was pessimism that came from noticing that her highly developed introspective capacity was never augmented by the sorts of causative interconnections that self-observing people bring into their discussions. My further reservations were from her sophistication in mental health literature, from her previous therapies, and from postgraduate education in psychology. I told her such previous knowledge, very different from what I wanted her to understand, was often an interference such that it usually slowed the treatment but need not stop us. She demurred saying she was quite open-minded and could set aside her past learning. Unfortunately, she could not.

In our third meeting, as we continued in what I have found the most fruitful pattern, conversation about emotion and an attempt to enlist her mind in exploring her own emotion reactions in varieties of situations and the various emotion dynamics as they operated within her, she said to me, "Well, why don't we start and see if you can cure my problems." It was apparent that what she had heard from me was so different from all her knowledge and thinking about psychology it had not been considered even slightly by her, not allowed to touch anything going on within herself, not made a temporary part of her basis of viewing within herself to see if any of it fit with her inner experience. She seemed to have viewed what I had outlined about emotion to be irrelevant chatter. When I pointed out to her that what we had been doing was the way I tutored people in examining their own minds, she looked startled and said, "I don't know what you are talking about. Nothing you talked about goes on inside me."

It stopped us.

The problems encountered in attempting to guide people to use their self-observation, or even the slower task of helping people use what they have available from introspection, were exemplified in Sally. While she had claimed she could put aside her previous knowledge, she demonstrated that for her to accept treatment it had to fit the narrow pattern of her previous knowledge. She might have overcome that if she could have mustered some capacity for tolerance of new ideas, some willingness to learn without fear. Her ignescence was touched off by her fear that what she already knew was threatened by alien ideas.

My suggestion to Sally was that what we could do was go over what I had been talking about for two-and-a-half sessions and see if there was some resonance within her experience that could serve as a starting point for us. However, I insulted her inadvertently by also suggesting that she was holding the ideas outside herself thereby decreasing the possibility of her understanding them. She left at the end of the session quietly furious at me.

Long-Term Distraught State (Twenty Years of Catharsis Is Not Enough): Herbert

Someone in his former home town had referred Herbert to me. When the therapist he had seen for twenty years died, Herbert had moved to my geographic area and was, in effect, trying to find a replication of the therapist he had lost two years earlier. I believe I was the third local therapist he tried for several sessions each in this effort. Those rejections of the other locals did not mean to me they were inferior professionals although he implied that. He declared his past therapist to have been a wise, excellent analyst. I knew the probability that I or anyone else would fit the pattern of wisdom and excellence of his past treatment was nearly nil. The therapist's death had "fixed" the transference to make it almost immutable.

Herbert settled in for a long treatment, for treatment had become a way of life to him. He was in mourning for the lost therapist who had become a good surrogate for all his "bad" family members. Over a few weeks I began to know some of what happened in that interminable treatment series. They had declared the work psychoanalytic, but it had not been psychoanalytic in style or content. It sounded more like the pop psychologies that have taken on the idea of cathartic ejection of feelings—without much clarity of distinctions between affect and cognition.

It is important to understand that what had gone on for twenty years was a charade of affect discharge, based in the belief that feelings are unfortunate "stuff" that is generated and then held in storage as a disturbing substance. In such a belief, the stored affects continuingly cause troubles until they are somehow ejected—therefore the obvious cure is catharsis. With that belief nothing else had meaning, nothing else is as important. That is what the "thousand and one sessions" had been. Whatever counseling had gone on between "expelling" affects was inconsequential. He was an unlikely prospect for treatment. This highly sophisticated patient had been misled for decades and made a devout believer in catharsis. Despite having a better than average IQ, his poor social judgment and ignescence made him refractory to anything new. He forcefully took over the sessions to fit with the pattern to which he had been trained.

Herbert would walk into my office and usually tell me that he had been having a tough time since he last saw me. "Ken, you don't know how tough it is to be me!" He would then describe the problems he had with his lover, how unreasonable she was, how little she thought of what he wanted. (I never heard of anything she wanted.) He would tell me about the unreasonableness of the art agencies in the Midwest that could not understand his artistry and the advertising executives who were hopelessly behind their counterparts in his former workplace.

He showed me examples of his work. They were impressive and seemed to my unsophisticated judgment to be of high professional level. He was unsure whether he could make a living here because professionally he was too advanced for the local market—which may have been accurate. Of more importance, he was arguing with the people with whom he worked in most of the many jobs he contracted. From his reports, he was forcefully trying to teach others what they should want, what was artistic, what was eye-catching. With only one side of the stories, it was unclear who was being unreasonable, although he may very well have been consistently correct in his judgment while consistently wrong in tact.

The pattern of the treatment sessions was a demonstration of the travesty of virtual psychotherapy in which he had engaged for twenty years. As he warmed to the telling of each chronicle he would begin to grimace, turn his head, wring his hands, twist his body, and speak to me of his pain, hopelessness, and resentment toward the world—toward the people who could not appreciate him and the unfairness of his life. He would grunt and moan with the agony of his feelings. It was as a complaint to God (in the person of his former therapist) to change the world to make it more comfortable for him without any change on his part. It was a railing against fate for the fights and arguments he got himself into. If I attempted any intervention during such a demonstration he would hush me; telling me he needed to get out all the feelings.

If I did nothing, said nothing, he would often tell me at the end of our session, "Kenny, you are a super therapist. I feel much better." As a surrogate I was doing him a great service, perhaps as good as any barber or bartender might have done. He was merging ego boundaries with me and gaining great comfort thereby. That is not the same as transferring in ways that could give us something to work on analytically. My own reaction was that I was failing him egregiously as a therapist in a way similar to the failures of the twenty-year therapist before me. On the occasions when I attempted to let him know I could probably help him to a more satisfying life, he demurred, and reminded me he previously had the best analyst and knew this was what he should be doing—and supportively to me, laudatorily implied that I was a close second.

He was internally struggling to restore his mourned therapist by molding me to that model. There was no way I or anyone else could truly fit his requirement. The analytic problem was also that he was not turning any transference to me, merely verifying and continuing his existing transference to his dead therapist. I did not exist for him other than as a surrogate and so was excluded from a truly therapeutic role. He was not mourning—not able even to consider discussing his loss of the great man, not working through his loss. He was frozen in a pattern. Although there was no way I would be comfortable with that witless pattern, telling him he had never been in a real therapy would have been destructive at that point, although that is what he eventually must come to, after letting his past therapist be gone in order to proceed with a useful treatment. Month after month there was no way I could get his attention sufficiently for him to observe either his ritual of attempted symbolic restoration to life of his lost therapist or his wasted mock effort to get feelings (that were not stored) out (from the nonexistent storage space).

After months of the affect discharge charade, I began to push a little. My interventions, by commenting about the possibility of using me to help him work out his problems, only irritated him. Finally I enraged him by audaciously suggesting that I thought he could benefit from learning about some distinctions between feelings and beliefs that he seemed to consider identical—that some of the things that he was calling emotions are ideational rather than feelingful, and therefore need to be considered in different ways, and that there are some other things it might help him to learn about emotions. He told me, "What you are saying is unforgivable! You are telling me I don't know what I feel! I always know exactly what I feel." (I was telling him that he was not distinguishing between feeling and thought.) He would not continue.

We parted company. Herbert was so set into a pattern, so damaged by the fake therapy of twenty years, it would have taken years to build a relationship in which the transference would have turned to me, so that it might then have become possible to work with his introspectively known mental contents to bring him to realization that his ignescence was an unnecessary protection. It seems unlikely that any person with introspective—but without self-observing—capacities can get out of such a pickle by himself. Herbert was entangled in a pattern without inner resources that would help free him from the pattern. Sad to note, none of the current standard approaches would be likely to move him from his continuing long-term distraught state. My own reactions to him were of sadness and irritation about his easily curable condition that had been made impossible to cure by an inadequately educated, well-intentioned therapist, who turned an able but troubled young man into a middle-aged man with a wasting life. Herbert has been trapped so long in his unfortunate sophistication about stored emotion that he is unlikely to be persuaded to observe the emotion dynamics within himself.

10

The Story of Freya: A Tutoring Sample

The example of an affect tutoring analysis presented in this chapter is of a long-suffering patient who had become sophisticated about treatment by virtue of decades of treatment. The expectation she had was of an interminable process of lulling and comforting by either medicating or sheltering from situations that evoked displeasing emotions. It was long-standing indoctrination.

The patient had begun having panic episodes and phobic episodes starting at age twelve. She had various sorts of treatment off and on over the forty-eight years since then. The report of the work to this point describes the approach I used in a moderately successful treatment that for reasons described has already been of longer duration than is usually necessary. By being longer, it depicts more of what I do and how I am likely to talk with patients to help them become free of affect phobia. It is not a treatise on technique, but is an example of an approach to bring suffering people to healthy use of emotion and cognition as built-in mental processes. It does not call for rituals or standardized systematic activities.

CONVERSATIONS ABOUT PANIC AND PHOBIA

Panic and phobia over decades is an agonizing way of life. After consulting and being in treatment with various professionals over decades, this sixty-year-old woman suffering from a variety of storm disorders, of long standing, was referred to me. She had seen one psychiatrist for twenty years, several physicians for physical care (but only to one of them had she mentioned her psychological troubles), one social worker, and one psychologist for three years. For her it has been a lifetime of turning to people who set themselves forth as therapists, who sincerely use their knowledge and skills with an aim to cure, but who invariably fight mental health because their considerable knowledge and training about neurosis has a singular, unfortunate defect—being wrong! Despite all the years of treatment, she currently has the same severity of panic episodes and phobic avoidances. These are triggered by a now-generalized variety of situations, actual or contemplated: social events or entering busy restaurants (social phobia); being seated in a theater away from the aisle (claustrophobia); being in cars, airplanes, and boats (claustrophobia); and a fear of vomiting (losing control or being ashamed). None of the dreaded anticipations ever occurred. Physical manifestations have appeared from time to time, but diagnosing these as from physical causation or as psychologically based conversions is difficult to do in retrospect. Episodes of other troubles within the cluster of symptom disorders, including anorexia, have occurred. A mild degree of compulsive disorder has appeared as a symptom from time to time.

Freya is a pleasant appearing woman, well dressed in a suburban style of the season, wearing noticeable gold decoration, and displaying a superior sense of color combinations in her clothing. She speaks clearly and well, as is appropriate for a retired school teacher. She appears immediately comfortable with me, more trusting initially than most patients, probably because she had very positive recommendations about my work from someone she trusted. ("There is really only one person to see for the kind of troubles you have!")

She gave a brief overview of her symptoms, her previous therapies, and previous therapists. It was a motley group. Her wish was expressed as wanting "to be free of her fear," after nearly fifty years of discomfort, and the haunting concern that panic could occur at any moment, for she had no inkling of how the state was generated. She currently takes Xanax as prescribed by her internist to use whenever she starts to panic.[1] At present, she also takes a half pill before retiring most nights, as a sleep aid.

I told her that her difficulties are quite curable, but that her long experience in treatment will have given her a sophistication about psychotherapy that must have set up patterns of style and expectation that would be hampering treatment.[2] I suggested that this usually affected treatment so that a cure might take a bit longer than it would have if she had come to see me thirty or forty years ago, before so much other therapy. I did tell her also that in my personal experience (my own patients' results), her type of disorder had been completely cured in more than 95 percent of instances.

The crucial factor in determining how rapidly she could attain permanent freedom from the disturbing episodes is the degree of her ability to observe within her mind to apply the new knowledge she would gain from me. Also I told her the treatment with me would be quite different from what she had experienced in the past—that much of what I would do would be to:

Help her gain new understanding about her emotions and personality

Work in a tutoring way to provide knowledge that she would be unlikely to develop from associative exploration within herself, rather than my waiting to see what associations she had

Look to her to use her own observations to note a variety of mental processes, which she may have previously ignored, and to observe her specific mental content that we would need to help her come to an understanding of herself

I told her that "emotions are useful aspects of ourselves—always." It is our general misunderstanding of emotions that has made them seem enemies. As she becomes aware of the benign quality of emotion, she will gain increasing awareness of the varieties of emotion and how each helps to guide us.

She then told me her still vivid memory of her first experienced panic episode, which had occurred when she was in high school. Her father, while taking her to visit her friend, stopped at a bank. She first endured the agony of panic while in the bank. Although she wanted to go home, she bravely said nothing to him and went on to her friend's home. The episode passed in a short while. Over the years she had many episodes, but with the courage that is the mark of most sufferers of these disorders, she endured, hoped, and withstood.

Over the years there were also episodes of various phobias. I inferred occurrences of conversions and depersonalization, but did not ask then whether she noticed such. With storm disorder problems over such a length of time, patients typically run the gamut of varieties of diagnoses that are the consequences of affect phobia. (Reports in the literature that we can now understand as occurrences of emotion storm disorders start with Breuer's patient Anna O., with her multiple storm disorder manifestations. Thousands of articles in journals have demonstrated such clustering. While "fresh" patients are usually described with single symptom disorders, commonly such as a panic or social phobia, no theoretical restriction requires these to be first or sole manifestation of emotion storm disorder.)

I started by offering a further brief introduction. I suggested that all these difficulties came from the common misunderstanding of emotion experience. I pointed out that all of us have grown up in a world in which people are very uneasy with and cautious about at least some emotions. I conveyed the following ideas:

We seem to believe that emotions are interfering disruptions of our ordinary lives. That particular belief presses us to do something with or about emotions.

If emotions, which are biologically built-in, were somehow interferences with—instead of enhancements of—our lives, if they were
destructive in some way, those carriers of genes bringing the hampering tendencies toward having interfering emotions would likely drop
out of the gene pool over multiple generations. The reason that has
not happened is that emotions are very useful in our lives—if we use
instead of fight them. They tell us something of what is going on in
and around us. Fighting them causes your problems. If I can help you
understand how to use them, you can be permanently free of those
troubles.

What you are doing in those episodes is not simply being very
afraid but you are having emotion response to emotion response. It
may be that you become afraid about being afraid or create some other
sequence of emotion, afraid about being ashamed, or any of dozens
of possible sequences. We need to find exactly what your sequence is,
to help you.

"That sounds wonderful," Freya said. "I would so much like to be free
of fear."

"If you listen to what you just said, you want to be 'free of fear.' But fear
is a built-in response that is useful in telling us that we perceive danger or
risk. If we did not have that feeling experience we would be less protected
from actual dangers. What you need is to be able to have the feeling of fear
when you need it to help protect you, but become free of the storms of
emotion that are so painful and disabling. I hope you will always be able
to feel all emotions (including fear) and use them. Most emotions are
pleasant experiences, but no matter whether pleasant or unpleasant, they
are valuable to us."

"Oh, I see what you mean," she said. "I am afraid of being afraid."

"Your remark shows that you have embarked on the beginning of understanding what you need to learn about yourself to have a more comfortable
life. There are many details to learn, and as you begin to observe in this way,
noticing what you are feeling about what, and then what you feel about what
you feel, you are thereby on the path toward becoming free of storms. I hope
you will give us the time to add that knowledge to your frame of reference
so that you can automatically (without deliberation) consider your own
emotion experiences from this viewpoint and free your life from the terrible
episodes you have had for so many years."

I gave her some reading material so that during the intervening week
before our next meeting she would have some reference to the concepts that
we had started discussing.

Her descriptions of people, way of relating to me, and style of speaking
suggested that she was operating at a Gamma level and also was intelligent
enough to absorb concepts. That made me hopeful that there had been

sufficient personality evolution to work well in the treatment I planned for her, although the long span of years of various forms of treatment would be a formidable barrier slowing the progress of a cure.

The next week Freya arrived with her same enthusiasm about becoming free of her disorder. She had suffered two episodes of panic during the intervening week. Both were in crowded restaurants, one with her husband and nine-year-old grandchild, the other with her son.

"Did you notice what went on inside you?"

"Yes, I walked inside the restaurant and became panicked. I took a half Xanax and felt a little better. When we went into the first restaurant and I started to react, I asked my husband and grandson if they would not prefer to go across the street to another restaurant. Both agreed. My grandson said, 'It was so noisy in there I could hardly stand it.' I always knew that crowded places made me uncomfortable. I don't see how that helps."

"I don't think it helps very much either," I replied. "Let me tell you an anecdote that may help you understand what I am trying to convey."

A law of perversity rules that shoelaces break only when one is in a hurry. That's why it's always an annoyance when a shoelace breaks. Since most people believe that if you have an unpleasant feeling reaction that feeling reaction continues to exist inside you until you get it out. To them there is a burden imposed as a feeling of annoyance that must discharge. I have known many people who get irritated about the imposition of such a burden.

The trouble is, when they get irritated about being annoyed, they then consider that as imposing an increased burden. They get angry about being irritated about being annoyed, which instantly gives them a still bigger burden of emotion to get rid of, and that makes them furious about being angered about being irritated about being annoyed. The further step they take is to get enraged about being infuriated about being angered about being irritated about being annoyed that the shoelace broke. In that sequence, the shoelace is long gone as having continuing importance in the process. Its role was only as a trigger that activated an unaccepted feeling, and initiated the sequence of escalating emotion because of discomfiture about having displeasing emotion.

The purpose of that long story is to try to convey to you that the crowded restaurant was only a trigger—in that its function is like the shoelace—starting the sequence. What we need to find out from your observation within yourself is the sequence of feeling response to feeling response that gets you into the storms of emotion. Each person has his or her own sequence. I cannot know your sequence without your first noticing it and informing me. That's the task. In your past therapies, you probably spent much time trying to find why the equivalent of a shoelace became an important matter for you, why breaking it is so important to you, and thus why that shoelace triggered the slate. We can now see it is a foolish quest, wastefully diverting you from the more relevant issues. We will do far better for you by working at noting what emotions are evoked by the events that trigger the storms. The important search is for the sequence of feeling reaction to feeling reaction.

"I know the feeling. It's fear. I get afraid about the crowds. Next weekend I am going to a bat mitzvah, and I know it will be terrible."

"At worst that will be another opportunity to notice the sequence of emotion that occurs. At this point you are noticing that what goes on within you is not just the two-step sequence you had thought it to be—crowd equals panic—it has already expanded to a sequence of crowd, fear (of something), and panic. Please take it on faith that it is probably a sequence of several steps from beginning to end and try to find any intervening step. You do not have to put yourself in those situations to be able to note them; you can probably do that in retrospect because you have had so many episodes over forty years."

"It's more than forty years."

"We don't have to add to your agony by pushing you into the situations."

"Should I not go anywhere?"

"That would be a pity, but I leave it up to you. You know that you haven't done any of the things you feared you would do in those situations. You haven't fainted, screamed, wet your pants, or fled the room. Whatever you do, whether in new situations or in remembering past events, observe the emotions in great detail."

"It happens so fast, I don't think I can catch it."

"The wonderful thing about how our minds work is that they rely in great part on brain function that operates by electrical impulse traveling along nerve fiber at very high speed. We do a lot of thinking rapidly. We can do several things at once. That is why you can use one part of your mind working at high speed to observe the rest of your mind—and the observing part operates at the same speed as the rest of your mind. That is what will enable you to notice."

"I wish all this could happen right now."

"You have had this trouble for more than forty years. We need whatever time it takes to change that. You have already moved from "crowd equals panic" to "crowd equals fear of shame" (of contemptible behavior in response to panic) to panic."

"All my life I have always been worried about criticism from others. Worried that others might think I do not look right. I do not behave right. I do not say the right things."

"Let us take it a step at a time. Once we have the sequence of emotion response to emotion response you will start to change things. Until then, trying to understand those triggering aspects of your personality is a very difficult task."

The Affect Tutoring Analysis Goes Deeper

After a two-week interval, during which she went on a trip with her husband, Freya said it had been a better interval than she has experienced for a long time. Because there have been other good intervals over the years, I do not know that this qualifies as a meaningful improvement.

"Why were things better during this time? If we can understand what made them better, we can have a better chance to continue to make them better."

"I don't know. I am still afraid that the feeling will come. It starts sometimes, and then I think of your telling me that it comes and goes."

"When you say you are afraid the feeling will come you are declaring your discomfort with feeling. That is where the trouble starts. Let us start from the beginning again and keep in mind that each initial feeling you have is an accurate and precisely appropriate feeling to have. It gives you information about what is going on in and around you. It is the escalation, from feeling reactions against that initial feeling reaction, that brings trouble. Those initial feelings are never trouble."

"Yet I worry about the big feeling coming that makes me reluctant to go anywhere."

"The big feelings are the storms of emotion produced by your reactions against the useful initial feelings."

"Let me try to remember that. If I can write that down."

"Do whatever it takes to help you remember it."

"I would like to be free of this trouble for a long time."

"The way to do it is to become accepting of those initial feelings, which are never bad to have, whether they are pleasing or not. They always tell you something about what is going on in and around you. If you can see that you have feeling reactions against your feeling reactions, you can begin to be freer to notice what you feel and about what. That will allow you to notice the many feelings you have been skipping over. It will enrich your life."

"I would like to have less of this trouble."

"You can be totally free of all these troubles for the rest of your life, if you can start along the path of using instead of fighting the feelings. The later steps are easier."

"That will be wonderful."

Freya arrived at the next session declaring that she had been doing very well this last week. She talked about her lifelong friend Sam, whom she had always adored as the big brother she never had, and his wife, who both act as if they are superior beings. Now she notices they irritate her when they do that. Along with that discovery, she also has noticed irritation toward some other very close friends who repeatedly took advantage of her for years without her ever protesting.

Sam has prospered. While she and her husband are well off, they are not as prosperous as he has become. She has never felt envious of him. "I do not want to be envious," Freya said.

"If you remember a couple months ago," I reminded her, "when you told me you did not want to be afraid again, I said I hope that you will always be able to be afraid whenever there is danger. It is very important that you have as much emotion information as there is, about whatever is going on in and around you. I would like for you to be able to think in the same way about envy and all other emotions. They are each a kind of feeling experience information you can note. They may not always be pleasant, but often they may be of crucial importance in guiding you. You are noticing that Sam, who from all you have said is a very good person, is also condescending and a bit lordly toward you. He often seems to be patronizing toward you. You are probably also better off noticing that about him along with the many ways that he is wonderful to have as a friend."

"It is occasionally painful when you let yourself know what you feel. But with or without the pain, there is a large gain from the better grasp of the reality of the relationships that you have previously obscured with illusions about the perfection of the imperfect people around you."

"Why didn't I think of that?" Freya observed, "without you having to tell me!"

She arrived at the next session looking very comfortable, fashionably dressed, and pleased to see me. She said that everything is going so much better. She has not had a panic episode in several weeks. However, she said, "I have not tested myself by planning a long distance trip."

I pointed out to her that saying that meant she was still concerned with the triggering events (the shoelace) rather than the emotion potentiating factors. "When you accept and use emotions of all sorts for what they are—natural, useful, constructive, benign mental events—the trigger becomes much less important. Whether the trigger is a mosquito in the room or a threatening illness in someone you love, it is of less consequence than fighting feeling. You do not need to test yourself or put yourself through the agony of a panic episode to learn about protecting yourself from all sorts of psychological troubles."

"Am I getting better?"

"If you have to ask me, that may mean you cannot tell. If you cannot tell, then whatever changes may have occurred must be of little importance. What do you think?"

Freya told me she is changing quite a bit. She recounted what has been happening in her relationships with family and friends. When her husband misplaces his glasses, she does not have to throw herself into a search, unless she thinks she knows where they probably are. She can let him do it. She talked with Sam and his wife, who are estranged from their own children, and suggested how they could approach those estranged children, saying that a lot has happened that was displeasing, but that they still love them and that they are very important to them. She was able to do that, never previously daring to do so. Noticing her feelings more clearly makes it possible to notice that she, too, is a person. All this is happening in a way that the encounters estrange or offend no one, while cutting down on the way other people have used her. All this has occurred with no coaching on my part about her relationships, other than the idea that knowing her own feelings moment by moment could help guide herself in what she did in or with relationships.

The changes are like the superficial behavioral manifestations that occur in a successful psychoanalysis, based on central changes in the personality. Yet these have occurred without my directing her attention toward concern with behavior, to those personality patterns, or to their origins in childhood experience. The manifest changes are corroboration of the idea that when people begin to use their whole mind, instead of part of their mind, they can more easily deal with and solve questions about the early childhood resolutions of conflict, and do so without the long quest that such resolutions have usually required. Patterns that were previously noticed as unwanted ways of being become more meaningful because the related emotions are available and used. For the first time I see a considerable confidence in her about what we are doing and a firm belief that she will make the changes she wants in her personality: to be completely free of the psychological disorders.

As with so many patients going through an affect tutoring analysis, the few central changes in her frame of reference about emotion yield the manifest changes in behavior. These changes are what please patients, although knowledgeable psychologists aim directly for central function changes that will support the surface changes. In this patient, they are changes she had never expected to be able to make. Nor are they therapist-coached changes, for the tutoring has stayed close to the issues of adopting emotion experience as a natural, benign, transient experience of constructive function, and has increasingly brought it into conscious awareness. Thus, what most therapies directly aim to achieve is achieved as a by-product, an indirect consequence, in this therapy.

The insight patients gain comes from their ability to use an increasing proportion of their minds, so those with considerable intelligence paired with self-observing capacity work through much of the sorts of problems that are the long-term tasks of insight therapies. They do it on their own.

Despite any reservations I held at the beginning of the treatment because of the uncommonly lengthy duration of the disorder (forty-eight years), miscellaneous treatments used, and the varieties of medications, it appears that she may succeed in becoming free of her psychological disorder.

A week later, Freya is still free of symptoms. "But I have been too busy to have any troubles this last week," she said. "I know that before it did not matter how busy I was, whenever I went to a restaurant or planned a trip I would start again. It seems strange to me that I have seen you so few times and everything is better than it has ever been."

We have a discussion elaborating our previous discussion about shoelaces. I tell her that testing herself by a confrontation with threatening situations is completely unnecessary. It is not the object of the phobia that is important but the storm process that results from fighting emotion that is the important issue. *If she can preclude storms because she accepts and uses whatever emotions are aroused to inform her of what is going on in and around her, that will be the cure.* She will have no further storms in whatever situation she might encounter. Triggering circumstances may occur, but without her contending with feelings there is no storm. We spent our session going over the idea of using emotion as a natural benign event instead of emotion as something to fight.

Anyone who accepts and uses their emotions as a natural, benign, constructive function will never have any of the classic neuroses. The same idea may be stated obversely. Anyone who does not fight his own emotions will never have any of the classic neuroses. *It is contending with emotion, because it is considered something to deal with, that creates potentiation of emotion, creates emotion storms, and by doing that diminishes energy available for intellectual function. That is the cause of symptom disorders.*

The session revolved around this set of ideas. Tutoring to help a person build a frame of reference containing these ideas eventually gives permanent protection from all of the classic neuroses.

Freya has enjoyed another week of freedom from episodes. She is very busy with business and social activity and her times spent with her family. It is interesting that the focus of discussion has shifted from the episodes that, at least for now, have just "gone away." I spent time rephrasing and redescribing the uses of emotion, for we have moved our discussions from the pathologies—from emotion phobia and storm—to the positive values of emotion in our everyday lives. She mainly talked about how her life relationships have changed and that those changes are now more noticeable than the changes in freedom from symptoms. Her experience of relationships with family and friends is different. She is becoming more comfortable with herself and others, and that is somehow more important to her than her several weeks of freedom from symptoms.

With the new tone in her relationship with Sam, he notices that she has had a better life than he, despite all his professional accomplishments, his long successful career, and his considerable wealth. From her recounting of the conversations, he sounded envious of her relationships with her children and grandchildren. Because of his investments, he is rich enough to leave large bequests to various organizations, but he has no contact with any of his progeny, has dropped them from his will, and knows nothing of his grandchildren. Freya is now more comfortable being with him than in the past, for they have become more evenly on a peer level. He has noticed that she has some wisdom and asks for opinions, although for decades he had seemed superior, graciously condescending, and protective toward her.

Freya phoned to tell me that she had seen where someone had vomited in the street. She could not get it out of her mind. It is an unpleasant image to carry around. It had bothered her so much that she called me to find out if I could get rid of it for her. I told her that her reaction may be about something in her mind she is afraid she cannot hold in. I wondered also if she is potentiating. "We can talk about it when you come to my office."

During her session, I suggested that the unpleasant, obsessive thought was recurring in her mind because it was covering something else even less pleasant. I could imagine that because this occurred just before Sam's visit, it may be she did not want to "spill" out something she had refrained from saying over the years. Still, it could be almost anything. The issue was that she needed to cover something that seemed to her more unpleasant and was doing so with something that was quite obnoxious. It kept her from thinking about the other. She said she already knew she was somewhat worried that she might let Sam know of her newly recognized lifelong indignation at his condescension, and described more instances in this lifelong relationship with him as the "older brother" she did not really have.

"My experience suggests that when you have become a bit more accepting of your emotions in general you will notice more of the emotions you have, your personal symphony of emotion. At that point, you will solve obsessions more readily. Until then, doing so is very difficult."

Over the next two sessions the primary issue was coming to grips with the mortality of her father, now in his nineties. She did not want to be sad about his weakening and his recent shift toward inactivity. We talked about the necessity and usefulness of being sad. "What would it mean in your relationship to your father if you were not sad about the fact that he will not be around forever?" This is a repetition of the familiar theme. Although she has learned a great deal about the concept of emotions being useful, she has not yet generalized to the concept of all emotions being useful and then pondered about how each is useful. Apparently she will need to keep going through the same process repeatedly with each specific emotion to achieve conceptual generalization, and thus become free of illness.

Freya has been "upset" (feeling guilty) at the weeping of her daughter—eight months pregnant and having to go off Melleril for the delivery of her child. The daughter wept and did not want Freya to leave until she had gotten comfort from her. Again we go through the familiar sort of exercise. "Guilt is an important feeling. Its function is to tell something about your relationship with your daughter, that you want to protect, not harm that relationship. It is good information to have, even though it is painful to you."

Freya has had several bad days because of the pain from a back muscle. This has not triggered any panic or phobia intense enough to interfere with her activities. She tells about dining with a high school classmate. That woman, although a successful clothes model, has claustrophobic tendencies. She had to sit at the restaurant table facing out because it was so distressing for her to be facing the wall. Freya accommodated her friend by sitting facing the wall. This did not bother her much, although it would have in the past.

I pointed out that her daughter and her friend and many other persons also suffered from the same basic problem, emotion phobia. The manifestations for each are somewhat different, but the basic issue is identical. They each believe that emotions, or at least some of them, are big and dangerous events. We have gone through several specific emotions that have created problems in her life (fear, anger, resentment, sadness, guilt) and seen how they have created or activated her storm syndrome. In each instance she has obtained an increasing relief from the knowledge of what emotion is and is not. But she has yet to adopt the central principle I have reiterated, as a generality about affect phobia, which could have instantly relieved her of all storm tendencies. It is as though she has to be concrete about a formula without adopting the abstract concept as a generality: that use of emotion is a natural function. The concept of emotion transience has been part of each discussion although not yet absorbed.

She responded to my term "myth" with the idea of superstition. I used her term to try to explain why she has a hard time believing and adopting what I have said about emotion. She still clings to the idea that the problem may be that she is afraid of the phobia. Deeply ingrained in her is the idea that the situation or object of the phobia is the cause. She has not absorbed the principle that emotions are always useful, transient, and benign as fundamental, while fear of phobia is a secondary issue and a useless path. Focusing on it is a wasteful distraction from the helpful task of consistently using her emotion responses as helpful whether painful or not.

This is our problem to deal with for the future. I wish I could think of some way to free her from her concrete view of mental events to give her life the freedom that she needs so much.

We agreed to work at this next week. It may be a little easier when her back pain has gone.

"Does this kind of trouble go away for a while and then return from time to time?" Freya asked at the next session.

"Yes, it will do that until you accept all your emotions as a functioning part of you instead of fighting them. Once you accomplish that you will be free of all phobias, panic episodes, and other such troubles for the rest of your life."

"That would be wonderful. I would certainly want that. How can I do that?"

"Last week we talked about the superstition you and several billion other people seem to believe. The superstition is the belief that once a feeling is evoked it will remain inside you and store there until it is gotten out in some way. The truth is that emotions are microsecond events that may repeat rapidly for a while and therefore seem to be an enduring event. The truth is that all emotions are benign, constructive events that you can use instead of getting excited about them. Because they are benign, constructive, useful bits of information you do not have to try to fight, regulate, control, suppress, or tolerate, you do not need to act on whatever they urge you to do. Because they are so very brief and dissipate instantly, there is no real way of fighting or discharging them. They are gone before you could do anything with or about them. While several emotions are very obnoxious to experience, they are necessarily obnoxious to get your attention called to something going on around or within you. I think those are the emotions that people start getting excited about, then generalize to other emotions that they do not think of as distressing."

"That sounds so simple. Why don't I do that?"

"I don't know why you don't do it. You clearly do it sometimes and then do not at other times. You have not absorbed a general principle of usefulness of emotions, for each and every emotion that you have. You keep them separate. When you were a school teacher you must have taught some children to read, or taught them to do simple arithmetic."

"Yes, I did that with a lot of children."

"When you taught them these things you were teaching them so they would form concepts within their minds. You could not form the concepts in their minds for them, not directly teach them concepts. Concept formation occurs when there is sufficient information available for the student to make an inference about the meaning of the array of facts. Only then can a child adopt the principles involved in a five being two plus three, two plus two plus one, and so on. Until a child forms the concept, he can only learn by rote and repeat the sums. He has not gained the usefulness of the concept as a principle to apply to a great variety of sums.

What I am teaching is similar. We go through the idea on one occasion that fear is not something to get excited about. On another occasion we talk about how sadness is useful—not bad to have—and is not something to get excited about. Again we consider the meaning of guilt and how you are better off being able to feel guilt than you would without such an emotion. We have discussed that with anger and resentment. *You do not yet adopt the concept that each and every emotion is useful, part of a natural built-in system that is very valuable for guiding you.* That is what I am trying to lead you to, so you will not only have a built-in protection against the troubles you have had for so many years, but will be able to use many emotions you have not yet allowed yourself to notice."

"I hope I can do it."

"There is no reason not, except your natural tendency to cling to old beliefs of so many years. This will take whatever time it takes, and will be worth it in the end."

Freya Becomes Stronger

During an interim of several months, Freya was completely engrossed in the problems of her pregnant daughter, who was on a tranquilizer (Mellaril) and other drugs prescribed by a psychiatrist who had declared her "mildly schizophrenic." Although I was to rue it later, reminded of the advice to be careful what you wish for because you might get it, I suggested to Freya that what I had heard from her about her bright, vivacious, and highly social daughter, so feelingfully involved with many friends, busily organizing activities for her clubs, and busily active in and out of the family, did not seem to me to fit a diagnosis of schizophrenia. After the birth of her grandson, in response to my expressed doubt about the diagnosis, Freya got a referral from a counselor she had known for many years to have some kind of diagnostic study performed. That study turned out to be a consultation with a psychiatrist.

I had started an unfortunate chain of events. The psychiatrist they consulted did not reveal a diagnosis, but took her off Mellaril and put her on lithium. He then added other medications to the point that the young woman could not drive, could not organize her household, could not care for her new baby nor her four-year-old daughter. At this time, she began to manifest visual hallucinations that the physicians took to mean she was schizophrenic. She lost her natural initiative to do her ordinary activities and seemed to expect others to take care of her. That burden of daughter and two grandchildren fell on Freya. The daughter was placed in a state hospital because her HMO would not cover her costs. At the hospital they gave her high dosages of medications that further deprived her of capacity to function. Any question or complaint from her was met by the staff with, "That's all right, just take another Mellaril." The staff dealt with her patronizingly, as if she were not only schizophrenic but of dubious intelligence. With the multiple medications she became incapacitated.

My patient and I continued to meet, but it was understandable that Freya could not focus upon anything other than her family situation. We shifted from tutoring to a kind of supportive counseling process for the months that the patient was worrying about her daughter, taking care of babies, helping her husband with his business, caring for her ninety-four-year-old father, and carrying out her several service organization activities.

Freya's father, who had lived in an apartment with nursing care around the clock had weekly gone to restaurants with Freya's family. He was alert and attentive, although not vigorous. Suddenly he had a stroke, was hospitalized, briefly recovered somewhat, then died two days after being placed in a nursing home.

Later, when Freya's life settled down somewhat, we resumed our work. I suggested that the slowness of the progress was because she had forty-plus years of education that had told her that emotions were of no value and that she should ignore them. She reminded me that her mother had coached her about emotions all her life, often making remarks like, "You are not angry . . . , You are not sad . . . , You are not hungry . . . , You are not tired . . . , You are not afraid . . . , " and so forth. It was hardly surprising that she had paid so little attention to her own inner state. My suggestion was that she could take seriously that her emotions are a real and valuable part of her and always worth noticing, that she could push herself to try to notice what she was feeling, and about what, for twenty-four hours of each day. That would give us what we needed to know to help her.

Her response was of skepticism that she could ever learn what she needed to know, that she might not be bright enough to do it. I said, "You are bright enough to have been a good school teacher; you are bright enough to do this." We were ready to resume.

An exhausted and discouraged Freya arrived saying she was ready to give up. "I am depressed, I am filled with hopelessness, I am afraid about everything, I cannot sleep well, I cannot function. I would like a magic pill to make me better."

I said, "When you talk that way I worry about you."

"Do you mean that I might kill myself?"

"No, I did not think that. I thought that if you talk that dramatically to a general physician or psychiatrist you might be stuffed with medications or put in a hospital."

"Do you think I belong in a hospital?"

"No, that is not what I am saying. Anyone listening to you who does not know much about psychology might take what you are saying at face value and respond accordingly. Listen to what you are saying and think about it. Ask yourself whether you are really depressed or whether you are sad, grieving, mourning, and physically worn out with all your activities? If you are really depressed we ought to work on that. If you are not depressed we ought to deal with what is there. You do not look, act, or sound like a depressed person."

"I am not really depressed. You are right. I am mourning my father. I am worn out from emptying his apartment, cleaning it, managing the garage sale for the cancer society, and trying to help my daughter manage her home. She is taking so much medication, and I am trying to do these things while unable to go any distance from home without someone with me. I want not to be responsible for all these things I am doing for others."

"You sound as though you do not have the prerogative to shuck some of the many service organization tasks for which you have taken responsibility. You sound as though you couldn't take a minivacation of twelve or twenty-four hours just being free of all obligations."

"Well, when I leave here, I have to go to the store for my eleven-year-old granddaughter to get clothes for starting junior high school. In the morning I have to go to my daughter's house to help her. She cannot simply organize her day for herself and she cannot drive with all the drugs she takes."

I wanted to reduce the burden on her to allow energy to be available for her to work on her emotion issues. "I think you might consider begging out of whatever you can for now if you are overwhelmed. Figure out what you can drop, what you can postpone, what you can get someone else to do."

"I have always had to do whatever anyone tells me they need me to do."

"Maybe it is time to think about whether you always need to comply. Maybe it is time to observe what you feel about doing all these things you do. If you notice your emotions and consider the messages they give, you can better decide what to do and not run yourself into the ground."

At this point, my patient had come a long way. She was, however, in no condition to work intensively on the emotion potentiation issues. The death of her father, the birth of her grandchild, the incredible situation of her daughter being treated by physicians who seemed to understand nothing of psychology and too little about her, and the need to help her husband, in the process of relocating his business while working on a possible merger with another firm, all going on without any letup in her various service organization activities—it was too much. We continued to work together in a counseling relationship to help her function in the pressured life situation and await a somewhat more favorable time. The hope was that the groundwork for concept formation would continue to help her understand her emotion processes and that the progress would continue.

The interval grew to approximately a year, during which she tried to help her daughter, grieve for her father, and manage the responsibilities for multiple service organization activities. The continuing progress of concept formation was evident in the complete absence of panic episodes, the reduction in phobic self-protection against the various triggers in her life, and the steady improvement in her relationships in and out of the family.

We returned to work more intensively from this new basis, with the concept of the unnecessary fighting against emotion now a pervasive part of her frame of reference about emotion events. Even though her daughter was still taking heavy doses of medications for schizophrenia and depression, those illnesses did not fit at all with the descriptions of her personality, warmth, intense interest in life and other people, ability to organize her days, and even organize the activities of social groups. In one of those groups she was even voted the most sociable member of the group. She, too, appeared to be suffering primarily from emotion storms from potentiation of emotions. That is different from the "major depression" and "mild schizophrenia" she was medicated for currently.

Freya arrived saying she had something important to tell me. Her daughter had called, as she usually does several times each day, but this time to tell that she was in a panic, she was afraid, she did not know of what; she had taken several pills as the psychiatrist had instructed her to do whenever she was afraid. She knew that if she called him he would tell her to take more pills. My patient said to her, "There is nothing wrong with being afraid, but you don't have to be afraid about being afraid. Being afraid will not hurt you."

"I never thought of that," Freya's daughter said. "That is interesting." For the next two days, she called her mother several times a day, telling her how much better she felt realizing that fear is not something she has to be afraid of, that she did not have to be afraid about being afraid, and telling Freya how much that had helped her.

We spoke about the fact that she could tell her daughter more as time went on, and in so doing, could help her in ways the psychiatrist had not. Her daughter has had no panic episode in the several months since Freya helped her to understand the needless waste in contending with emotion. Two sentences of parroted information had been well absorbed by the young woman.

The treatment sessions continue following what is to me the minor achievement of having completely freed Freya from the painful panic episodes, freed her from the need for a planful caution in phobically protecting herself, and turned her into a far more comfortable person. Yet the overtone of apprehension in her life has not changed. Even so, the changes in her are significant as viewed by her husband who, for all the decades he had known her, had lovingly accommodated his life to limits imposed by her illness. He spontaneously commented, "I don't know what the two of you have been doing, but it is like some miracle."

To me, however, her continuing affect phobia leaves her susceptible to development of episodes of symptom disorder despite the current absence of episodes. To make her invulnerable to any further symptom disorder, she will need to be free of affect phobia. It remains our task to accomplish. As a by-product, her daughter has had no panic episodes in the year since Freya had helped her to understand the needless waste in fighting emotion. To Freya, the patterns of relationships that have been changing over these many months need to change more. She recounts many vignettes showing ways in which she is able to be different from her past. She wants more. It is a problem from the enduring "learning effects" of previous long-term treatment in therapies of all sorts, and her limits of introspective tendencies that are hurdles yet to be surmounted.

NOTES

1. Because Xanax takes one to two hours to reach blood levels sufficient to have its effect in suppressing awareness of an emotion state, while panic and phobia usually last about ten minutes and range in duration from one or two minutes to an hour, the prescription to use the drug at the start of an episode makes it helpful, if at all, as an attempt at suggestion, not as medication. Also, for this particular drug, the greatest dangers arise upon rapid reduction of the medication. Consequently, the use of this drug on an irregular basis is not only futile for the express aim of helping someone through an episode, but also brings physiological dangers from irregular usage.

2. At the time I did not tell her that in my experience patients who had any previous treatment had made the average length of treatment five times longer than for those without previous treatment.

PART III

THE BIOGRAPHY OF AN IDEA

11

Encounters with Mainstream Psychology

One sure way to irritate readers is to make statements they do not want to hear. Nevertheless, encounters with proponents of established concepts about health and illness point to several unpleasant truths that are important because understanding them brings eventual hope and promise of tremendous change:

The fundamental nature of psychological health and disorder is significantly different from what has been believed, taught, and applied. Highly trained professionals have erroneous knowledge about these matters.

Many professionals, including many who have spent a lifetime studying and working in the mental health field, have an insufficient degree of some talents necessary for effectiveness in the field.

The absence of those specific talents in mental health workers is the reason some fundamental aspects of the nature of mind, health, and illness were not discovered decades earlier and still are resisted today.

THE MYTH OF THE OPEN-MINDED PROFESSIONAL

The three statements above help explain the theoretic frames of reference used by mental health workers and also explains some difficulties in persuading those workers to open their minds to new ways of looking at some elements of their field. Technicians applying theory in practical applications consider whatever manifestations they discern in terms of the rules and techniques set forth by theoreticians as appropriate for presumably similar situations. The cognitive process used is rote memory. Theoreticians devise technical approaches by reflecting whatever manifestations they discern against the framework of whatever theory they have learned. Their theory offers an explanation of the phenomena and suggests what should be done. The cognitive process is deduction. Deductive process allows them to deal with the phenomena (compared with inductive attempts to understand the phenomena). It is a process that works with a partially open mind. A fully open mind works more slowly because it includes both the deductive process relating thought to existing theory and inductive process suggesting new theory. It is impeded or slowed by that consideration of "what else might be."

Deductive reasoning is a crucial part of useful everyday applications of theory and for scientifically embellishing and elaborating theory. Inductive reasoning (asking what else it might be), followed by thoughtful critique, is a crucial part of scientific advances.

The myth that "therapists are always open-minded people" more realistically stated is "therapists listen to anything, but they think about what they hear only after they have translated it to their own terms and concepts." Their listening to anything a person says means they abstract from or transform whatever a patient says into concepts in their own frame of reference, enabling them to understand phenomena in terms of their own theory. Whatever does not have a place in the frame of their theory is filtered out as irrelevant or unimportant. That means much is ignored.

We psychologists claim to be open-minded because we so willingly listen to everything our patients say. While we do so, we either force whatever we hear into our theoretic frame of reference or, if we cannot do that, we ignore the content. Our seeming open-mindedness is actually narrowly focused close-mindedness. No information is allowed to touch us until it is filtered through our theories and understood within those theories. Data that does not fit well within our theory is bent to fit, diminished in meaning, or disregarded. Patterns that are out of kilter with our theory are ignored. Any rigid theoretic frame kills artistic license by limiting thought to a constricted range. That is why even though theory helps us answer questions readily, by fitting many varieties of phenomena together or classifying them as different and in that way giving explanations for phenomena that may be very helpful, unproved theory taken to be ultimate knowledge invariably limits a field of study.

A second reason open-mindedness is limited in psychology is that whenever what is offered is strange, when it is about the unknown, it is unacceptable—it is incredible because it cannot be sensed, perceived, or even imagined as existing.

That the majority of professionals are incredulous is partly because apportionment of talents not found important for use within a field of study or practice can be distributed among workers in that field only in the same proportion as they exist in the general population. When fields change in ways that require new talents, there is disruption in the field until new workers with those newly required talents become members of the field.

This is a circular, self-perpetuating problem. Because those elements are not a part of past theory, there have been no factors related to them in selecting workers for the field. With few in the field having those talents, there has been little comprehension of the value and utility of emotion sensitivity and self-observation brought into the theory. Because the theories used previously did not demand that professionals be talented in emotion sensitivity and self-observation (for the theories did not even specify much about emotion sensitivity or have clarity about self-observation), people could study and become expert in the mental health field without any selection for those talents.

Comprehending the theory expounded in this book is enhanced by superior awareness of emotion. However, a problem in that is that most people believe they have just as much awareness of emotion as anyone else does. That belief exists because, when it comes to talents, none of us knows the experience of others who do not have the talents we have, nor the experience of those who have talents we do not have. How well can the color blind know what it is like to have color vision? How well can the color visioned know what it is like to be color blind? Perhaps this is more apparent to those who have a considerable but not a full amount of a talent. In a person who is partially color visioned trying to compare one's own experience with what it might be to have full color vision is tantalizing. Similarly, for those with a good but not perfect sense of pitch it is not possible to know another's experience in having perfect pitch. Within psychology, it is a difficult issue to resolve. Resolution of the issue must await study.

Previous views ignored the parsimony of nature. Inexorably all organs, systems, and processes yield either constructive functions enhancing survival to the point of reproduction or they drop out of the gene pool. Genes that serve destructive function operating before the point of reproduction drop from the gene pool rather rapidly. If emotion did not have constructive functions, it, too, probably would have disappeared long ago instead of remaining universally distributed in human and all animal life. Self-observation appears to be a talent with limited distribution among people.

A woman who had come to me because she was phobic and occasionally depressed, and who improved much without achieving a cure of her problems, serves as an example of limited self-observation. While I was sure that she did not comprehend what I had offered her about the subject of potentiation and storm, she insisted that she knew. It took a while for me to learn that even though she had listened seemingly carefully, had read some literature on the subject, had claimed to understand what I meant by storm, and had used my words it turned out she had repeatedly ignored what I wrote and spoke about concerning feeling reaction to feeling reaction and summarized it for herself to the narrower meaning of intense feeling. When I could finally point this out to her she was furious with me for "having never explained it to her." She berated me at great length, declaring that she was as able to observe within herself as well as anyone, and that the processes I described simply did not occur within her and a lot of other people. What she made clear, unknowingly, was that while she was introspective, she was not self-observing. While she could have a notion of emotion process as a construct, she was unwilling to use what I offered, for it was a narcissistic injury to admit that she did not have the particular talent to observe the processes I described. She had read and reread materials describing potentiation and storm, but repeatedly glossed over what I said by automatically translating both "potentiation" and "storm" as "strong emotion." Out of good will toward me (in positive transference) she had temporarily adopted my words but, because she was unable to perceive emotion process within herself, little of my meanings. The failure of communication between this patient and me is also a frequent occurrence when I speak to professionals. Those who do not observe emotion as process instantly reduce the complexity of the hidden process, which includes several steps, to consider it as a fictional unitary event that is, to them, merely a construct instead of a literal process. That makes it easy for them to mistakenly translate storm to intense emotion.

It has been thought that the several fields of study related to mental health are a ferment of activity with rapid progress in knowledge that makes the public increasingly better served by increasingly capable professionals. Hogwash! New ideas are not welcomed with open arms despite the popular belief that every professional in every field of study eagerly welcomes advances.

With each passing year of exploration, increasing numbers of concepts and implications were added. The theory became increasingly formidable for those trying to absorb it. It is not surprising that anyone would oppose a cascade of innovations: The following partial list of new ideas contrary to past teachings made it an ever more formidable, even overwhelming, task for students.

Emotion and cognition are equally important mental activities.

Each emotion event is of microsecond duration.

Any emotion may form lengthy emotion states by rapid repetition.

There is no physiological or psychological place or system for holding emotion.

All emotion is new emotion—never old emotion.

Every emotion is always benign.

Every emotion is always useful.

Each emotion experience informs us about what is going on in and around us, as a mental evaluation of sensory data.

The kind of emotion conveys information of the meaning an event has for us.

The intensity of an emotion conveys the importance of the event evoking the emotion.

Unease with emotion (affect phobia) is a near-universal problem—an infantile developmental stage that is rarely surmounted.

Affect phobia at an extreme can create an incurable tension phobia.

Affect phobia can lead to denial of feelings and serious consequent problems.

Affect phobia can foster suppression of emotion awareness (muting) with serious consequences.

Affect phobia can foster a sequence of feeling reactions about feeling reactions (potentiation) yielding painful distraught states.

Feeling reactions against feeling reactions create psychopathology.

Potentiation can create dangerous, transient distraught states.

Increased potentiation of affect can create self-sustaining emotion storms.

Emotion storms are briefly self-sustaining but are self-subsiding unless they become structured.

Repeated affect storms can become learned sets of reactions to some kinds of mental events. These have the quality of a structured (brain pattern) readiness to respond.

Specific types of symptom disorders are created by interactions of affect storms with character and personality patterns that are derived from genetics and personal history.

Although character neuroses and character disorders are rooted in personality patterns, symptom disorders are based in affect processes.

The classic neuroses are affect disorders.

Suppression of affect leads to "gray" lives because emotion experiencing is modulated.

Decisions can be made only with participation of both affect and cognition.

Valid knowledge of emotions sets people free of symptom disorders.

Some people (not all) can observe emotion in process.

People who use emotions can sort out pattern disorders.

Psychological disorders are, at base, different from what they have been thought to be.

Effective treatment process is different from past paradigms.

Taxonomic sorting clarifies explanations of psychological health and illness.

Implications of these and other ideas in this writing are viewed as an assault by some listeners or readers, as altogether too much to absorb easily. Also, there are good reasons why the more fundamental the new idea, the more vigorous its rejection is likely to be. In this world new ideas are treated harshly. Rejections of new ideas occur for any of several reasons. Those reasons are important to understand.

EARLY STRUGGLES

Twenty years ago I had made sufficient progress in understanding emotion process to concentrate more closely on the many important implications of emotion being benign, constructive, transient events. My progress over the twenty years preceding that stage of theory building had brought sufficient knowledge of emotion processes to bring cures regularly for many psychological disorders, especially those within the classification termed neuroses. Discussions with professionals about how this cure was accomplished called for descriptions of how the new ideas fitted with some ideas of the past and differed with others. Whenever it seemed relevant to a discussion, I began to tell colleagues of the expanding usefulness of the new explanations of health and illness and my thoughts on how personality developed and disorders generated. I described the visible unfolding of cures as patients absorbed the concepts of process and applied those to themselves. I usually included mention of the occasional epiphanic transformation as a kind of evidence that, for those who could observe the processes within themselves, the major issue in a cure is comprehension of affect phobia and its effects and application of that knowledge to oneself.

A Message that Could Not Be Heard

At first I was surprised by the almost complete absence of positive response to the promising concepts I offered. Could the high degree of success in treatment of the classic neuroses be simply ignored? Therapists are, after all, in the business of curing illnesses. Still, a high degree of success in applications could not only be ignored, it could be scoffed at and denigrated. Naively I had believed that, because therapists are in the business of curing, that had to mean they, too, would be interested in any knowledge that could help them cure their patients. Unpredicted restrictions on that general aim of professionals toward ever-better comprehension of their field of study became apparent.

No one seemed to know or even take seriously the idea that all emotions are always natural and useful parts of each of us. That omission is natural, for over the ages, from Aristotle on, that quality was omitted from past theories of mind. Some possible exceptions occurred, such as in David Hume's recognition that emotion played an important part in mind, and Adam Smith's recognition that emotion was an essential aspect of mind. Even though those philosophers perceived emotion as useful and not an interfering waste product of the mind, they did not come to the breadth of implications for the meaning of those two attributes of emotion, nor did they recognize that emotion is a microsecond event. Unfortunately, the truths they had about the value of emotion did not countervail the almost solid phalanx of authority against those truths. Additionally, since knowledge of modern science was not available to incorporate into their thinking, they were stymied.

An appalling eventuality is the bonanza of erroneous theory entangled in poor hypothetic constructs based on false premises from the fictions that support a general pattern of beliefs about mental processes. The impressive amount of careful expansion of false truths yielded a pretense of wisdom. Most such fictions are examples of metatheory about underlying processes with beautifully described internal coherence, but without significant connection with other empirical realities about fundamentals or applications. The current interest in intersubjectivity, self theories, object-relations theories, attachment theory, etc., are splendid examples of isolated theoretical constructions that are beautifully logical, unless you impose a requirement that they connect to and have meaningful effects in reality.

Besides the absence of backing by august authority, the reasons that few could take seriously what I presented are many and complex. Among those are natural mental hurdles and barriers that interfere with consideration and acceptance of new theory.

1. Conceptual learning is slow, difficult, and not automatic. It is far more difficult than rote learning that calls only for knowing, not for understanding. The steps call for building a body of facts through an integrating process, then individually abstracting meaning for those facts. A process of building knowledge by assembling many facts into a meaningful cluster can allow us to deal with any data that comes to us by using the guidance for understanding in such a frame of reference. That enhancement of useful function by having a conceptual framework offers great advantage in understanding what goes on in and around us. Its existence also forms a hurdle that slows acceptance of new ideas that controvert anything we have already placed in that frame of reference. People have to consider, ponder, compare, and try out aspects of new ideas to comprehend fully the concepts they meet. The same process is repeated in each individual as a part of their learning. That commonality of experience does not make the process different or easier for those who have yet to learn. When any new learning is counter to our previous learning, the old and the new have to be compared, but are compared only if we are flexible enough to make such a comparison instead of out-of-hand rejecting the new.

2. An important additional interrelating factor—the built-in human tendency to maintain attitudinal stability—sometimes creates a nearly impenetrable barrier. Few would take the cynical view that professionals do not want to cure patients. All therapists with whom I have spoken about therapy displayed a sincere desire to cure their patients, but invariably that aim carried the tacit restriction that a cure must result from use of their current indoctrination, not from ideas that controverted any significant portion of that indoctrination. There was little

readiness to modify their understanding of technique and, with few exceptions, no flexibility for making a major shift in fundamental beliefs.

3. Changing people's attitudes from their existing indoctrination is slow and difficult. Any belief system that has developed through a long-term learning process creates a loyalty that, in intensity, compares with religious adherence.

4. The long human history of diffidence about emotion created obfuscating language for emotion and made communication about it difficult. Imprecision and slipperiness of definitions allow professionals to pretend to themselves that what they are stating is the same as what their fellows say.

5. Long acceptance of diagnostic study that ignores underlying processes of mental function makes it difficult to draw attention to crucial aspects of those processes. The surface manifestations or observable signs are generally accepted as sufficient to understand and diagnose.

6. Disregard of underlying processes of mental function resulted in use of psychotherapeutic technique bridging that incognizance. The consideration of surface manifestations of mental process as of greater value than the actual mental processes nudged the field away from building a science of mind—psychology—and toward building a science of surface manifestations.

7. Muddled theories of mental function in cognition and affect make it difficult to draw upon neuroscience support for descriptions of mental processes.

8. Religious devotion to authority-theorists makes a theory untouchable and devout minds inflexible. Contesting the sayings of Aristotle, Freud, Skinner, et al., is a sacrilege to the devout believers of offerings from the past. That gives rise to vigorous defenses of important illusions.

9. Individual differences in the capacity to notice and comprehend emotion processes within self and others limited professionals in the work they did. For instance, self-observation (narrowly defined) occurs as a variable capacity, is described by the same sorts of curves of distribution as all human attributes, and has not been a significant part of psychological studies. There are many other capacities held by limited numbers of people that also are not seriously explored.

10. Most mental health practitioners function as high-level technicians applying systems and rules derived by theoreticians from theories of their school of psychology. They rely on operations (techniques) and operational definitions considering those to be sufficient explanations instead of merely descriptions. They rely on systematic rules rather than being concerned with how and why applications work or fail to work in particular instances. They typically look to others for how to apply theory and may flounder unless they obtain supervision to find the appropriate rules of technique.

A smaller portion of mental health practitioners are comfortable absorbing a theory to use as a frame of reference so that they can deductively infer explanations by moving back and forth from theory to the events they are studying. Thus patient content is reflected against the theory to provide an explanation that enables them to devise applications appropriate for the moment. They do not ask for or need rules of operation.

Impediments to Understanding

My results from applications of the new approach were clearly effective beyond anything any of the commonly accepted theories of psychology could produce. The message of those results and how they were obtained had an effect comparable to that of a tree's fall in an empty woods: no human eyes, ears, or minds could register it, therefore it did not meaningfully exist. Few minds could seriously consider the implications. Few were ready to consider alternatives to fundamentals of their past learning. Most people who have developed even a modicum of sophistication in psychology hold the description of the fundamental nature of psychological health and illness with religious devotion not to be considered a candidate for modification. If I could persuade those at institutions to test the theory— even with simple comparative outcome studies—and the results were at all comparable to past achievements, denying the advantages should be harder for them. I approached those in position to arrange that in every institution with which I had acquaintance. Occasionally a few professionals were interested enough to adopt some parts of the theory, but developed no interest in testing the "radical" approaches. The only study reports available remain the simple, annual outcome studies of treatment by a few of us. They continue at approximately 95 percent of all who stick with the process for the several necessary sessions. That does not qualify for scientific purposes as a controlled study with random selection of patients, numbers of therapists, externally verified diagnosis, process, outcome, and objectified record keeping. However, it is an indisputable indication that patients with symptom disorders are curable and are cured in the sense of remaining invulnerable to such disorders for many years.

Improving communication to professionals might bring better reception. Perhaps I had been less informative than desirable; maybe I had not placed the important issues in the proper order for listeners or readers to absorb new concepts. Perhaps my manner of presentation put off people who could otherwise absorb the ideas. I worked out increasingly precise ways to describe each bit of my message. I began to cushion each step in words less likely to jar the listeners. I learned that whatever descriptions I used, communication was impaired because widespread common usage of cloudy definitions, confused diagnostic categories, and vagueness about underlying processes meant that each listener was hearing something quite different. A confusion of tongues! The problem was not so simple as my being incoherent; it was not the offering, it was a general language problem that gave people great difficulty in seriously considering the message.

I also continued to grow in awareness of ever further ramifications of transient, benign emotion. I added observations. With each added observation I could bring to others, hoping that it would help convey the theory, the whole theory became even more complicated for others and more difficult for them to absorb. The paradox was that each increase in usefulness made the theory less agreeable to hear because it was a step more complex.

As I learned more about affect and cognition, our two significant mental functions, the implications of the new knowledge seemed almost endless. Of immediate relevance for troubled patients, the new understanding of the part emotions play in health and illness helps us understand what therapy can become. Several therapists who adopted my theory were able to cure patients who had troubles generally thought of as therapeutically refractory problems and did so more surely and easily. We cured patients who had failed to be cured or even temporarily relieved in past treatment. Affect theory changed my understanding of diagnoses. It was not just the weakness of concrete, superficial definitions by "signs" in the official diagnostic manuals, but also the unconnectible metatheory that had stifled and, worse for the field, stultified the diagnostic process. The entire system of psychological diagnosis currently in use is insufficiently related to the underlying processes involved in the various disorders to move them from "mysterious" to "comprehensible." Therefore, the disorders remain incomprehensible; the diagnoses inaccurate, the illnesses treatable but incurable. Through comprehension of fundamental process that connected theory to people, it became obvious that the disorders that I was curing were preventable. Those illnesses did not have to continue as a scourge of humanity. That should be good news to everyone—but it was not so for the incredulous.

I perceived that the cloudy misuse of the language employed to describe feelings was a natural consequence of attitudes toward emotion. Those attitudes encouraged cloudy meanings and obscuring of meaning through euphemisms for feelings in our everyday language. They protected the inert state of mind that helped people avoid energized thought on the subject.

Few colleagues with whom I spoke could comprehend what I was saying. Most of those who heard me at all missed the main point. A frequent response took the tangential general form previously mentioned: "I agree with you. I too think affect is important. I pay a lot of attention to that in my work. Everyone should pay more attention to affects. I notice when my patients smile or frown and I talk with them about that." In that sort of response, people tended to connect the new ideas they heard from me with their old ideas that are related remotely, if at all. Unfortunately, in the process of simplifying by connecting new with old ideas, they obscured the novel aspects of the ideas. Such partial acceptance itself became a barrier to learning, for paradoxically those partial acceptances became more refractory barriers to the new ideas than might have come from direct opposition. In a way, those who agreed that affect is important, but equated my suggestions with those of psychologists who suggested therapeutic attention to affects without the clearer delineations of each specific affect that I suggested, and without attention to the seemingly invisible processes, were the least likely to learn anything new. They presumed that they already knew all there was to know about affect, including what I offered. Their barrier to learning anything new came from the common protective incredulity that there could be anything important about fundamentals previously unknown to them. Their minds remained inert.

Infallibility of Past Authority

Most of my psychoanalytic colleagues seemed to assume that all of Freud's ideas were pearls of wisdom. They were as susceptible to being fooled as any who may have been enticed by the jewelry store's newspaper ad offering "genuine faux pearls." Few could comprehend that most of what Freud had said about affects were also "genuine faux pearls" distorting understanding, creating false paths and blind alleys. Why Freud blundered by accepting common wisdom ideas about emotion, erred about emotion as discharge, and emotion as anxiety is described with the new theory. That, in itself, enlightens us about a personal limitation in Freud (emotion muting), despite the marvels of his illumination of many mysteries. It also helps us understand the common limitations of the multitude of therapists who were content to follow along on the same path in complete ignorance of that limitation in Freud and themselves.

The reality and importance of memories, events, and reactions that served in the formation of personality patterns gave unwarranted credence to other aspects of Freud's theories that were not as well grounded or testable as these. The aura from the apparent verifiability of the psychodynamic patterns produced an illusion of knowledge about unrelated matters that we should have called into question long ago. The whole theory was used even for purposes for which it was not useful.

Whatever knowledge we have of any subject matter is the only knowledge we can use. Danger to any field of study arises when we come to believe that our particular state of knowledge has achieved the ultimate set of facts for a subject matter: that we have all the significant facts and they are all true. We could find this same kind of problem in any field of study. Physics, chemistry, biology, and geology all suffer the same impediments to advancement. Psychoanalysis, behaviorism, and cognitivism suffer from the weight of misguided "authority." Eminent people, the authorities in a field, if they assume theirs is the final knowledge of fundamentals, ignore anything that does not fit within what they already believe. Nevertheless, if they cannot achieve reasonably appropriate aims with their explanations or applications, the theory is not yet competent. *Insufficient effectiveness of applications of a theory should always be a scientist's cue that something remains to be learned. Rationalizing failures is folly!*

It is unlikely that any theory will be perfect. As scientists, we work with what we believe to be the best explanations contrived to describe phenomena of interest to us. Our allegiance is to logic and fact, not to particular explanations. That is why when we find a theory that appears more useful, we move the focus of our thought and activity to work with that theory. The defect in sciences is not the imperfections of theories, for all theories are imperfect. The trouble is that the authority of dominant figures in each field restrains freedom of thought, and that, when combined with the human tendency to stick with one's indoctrination, fosters persistence of inadequate theories much longer than is appropriate. If it were not for that, we would have noticed past theories for what they are, we would have brought forward any value from them to new theory and incorporated that in the next step of theory building. In studies of emotion, we would have noticed that some theories are impaired by being partial theories, or by being special theories that relate to special conditions and ignore important relevant observations, or by faulty inclusions or exclusions due to defective taxonomy so that they failed to give us an adequate basis for providing some order in our accumulation of ideas to study phenomena of our field. Thus, attempting to study mind by restricting our study to tangential elements as in behaviorism, attempting to study affects by concentrating on a single emotion as in psychoanalysis, attempting to study mind by concentrating on intellective processes as in cognitivism, attempting to study illness by concentrating on symptom manifestations as in biopsychiatry, etc.—all fail to place the explorations and tests in sufficient perspective to provide the help we need in understanding health or enabling healing of illness. The impaired theories deliver small value for the sufferers of psychological disorders. Far too often impaired theories spawned nearly useless therapies, and some have spawned damaging therapies. Of far more importance, those dominant theories have had little value for parents and teachers of the young. They offered insufficient knowledge of underlying processes as basis for their efforts to support health in their youthful charges.

One problem of impaired theory is that the metacomponents relied upon, being only indirectly testable, must spawn testable hypotheses to study the theory. Yet the unclarities and defects in the metatheories used meant that the attempts to formulate testable hypotheses could produce little that was helpful to the theory. The therapies in their derivation from metatheory should have led to testable hypotheses that yielded knowledge of use in applications. Any valid metatheory should lead seamlessly from that through scientific tests to bring useful applications. Whenever there is a gap in that path it is likely that we have an improper derivative hypothesis or a failed fiction (metatheory). Typically the psychotherapies resulting from such jumps to practical applications have been ineffective, at best. For instance, the behavioral therapies have had minor benefits for the patients because their fictional metatheory is weak rather than false, while the applications of the emotion ejection theories have been useless because their metatheory is false rather than a fictional truth.

Impaired theory often inspires religious devotion to sets of unprovable (metatheory) beliefs. Priest authorities in the mental health field over decades have arrogantly claimed valuable arcane knowledge although what they patronizingly offered was only elaboration of weak metatheory. As pretenders of knowledge they influenced others by claiming access to and comprehension of valuable knowledge that when examined turns out to be merely cloudy thinking.

Various special theories had been devised to deal with small portions of affect theory, such as discharge or signal, or some particular emotion such as anxiety or anger. The differing premises of these several special theories precluded construction of coherent general theory of affect from combined pieces of past theories. The internal incoherence of premises in attempts at such combinations assured that no matter how complex the aggregation of special and partial theories became, they provided little helpful information about human life.

A theoretical frame of reference is a ready-made set of explanations of phenomena from which we can deduce the meaning of any observed event. However, when the theory does not cover some of the observations, professionals may try to stretch the theory to make it seem to cover the phenomena and thereby risk being very wrong. As an alternative, when theory does not explain well what processes underlie the observed phenomena, it is more appropriate to use inductive inference to try to develop a law that gives an explanation.

Self-Consciousness

One test of a person's capacity for work with the uses of emotion is whether he or she can become aware of potentiation (on occasion getting angry about being angry or sad about being ashamed or in some way have one feeling reaction contend against another feeling reaction).

A commonplace example is that of being ashamed about oneself, or about one's activities, and having a feeling reaction about the feeling reaction. Customarily prostitutes become ashamed about being ashamed. It makes them comfortably brazen and able to conduct their vocational activities in relative psychic comfort. The sequence is exactly the same in clowns, or in some unrestrained comics who do or say outrageous things that most of us would never openly do or say. Those people who can observe, rather than unknowingly go through such a sequence, have the easiest time comprehending the theory being presented.

If professionals could retain perspective and a sense of humor about limitations in their knowledge and the struggle to learn bits about the world, they would be less smugly complacent, less closed. They could accomplish that only by abandoning false pride in being authorities about a field in which expertise of the most widely recognized authorities is more limited than they seem to have noticed. When their comprehension of the matters they deal with is so vague as to offer only imprecise explanations, treatment that gives some comfort, small hope, and no cure, it does not justify pride or complacency.

By twenty years ago, I had a fairly complete theory of affect that explained more aspects of personality more usefully than previous theory, benefited my patients, and often markedly shortened the time needed to provide them what they wanted from treatment, with lasting results usually more thorough than those I heard about from other therapists. Some, upon learning that I had expeditiously taken care of their former patients' problems, thought the rapidity was a serious defect on my part, that it meant that I had not taken care of important underlying factors rooted in etiology. They fooled themselves by believing that I was fooling myself.

I persisted in believing that my esteemed colleagues were simply resistive to new ideas. The unpleasant fact is that most are actually unaware of emotion processes that few among colleagues and patients could observe and discuss. Eventually it became undeniable, despite my resistance to the idea, that the largest part of the problem in this is that some actual processes are invisible to many people. The insensive can respond only with what they have available to them. When we tell them of variables unsensed by them, they can regard them only as mere hypothetic constructs with no recognized advantage over other hypothetic constructs.

By 1970 I knew that the classic neuroses that had drawn the first attention in psychoanalysis, and had occupied so much time for thousands of therapists and millions of patients, were really not much of an illness—despite the terrible agony and disablement they cause. These turn out to be simple affective disorders—not mysteries, not chemical imbalances, not unfortunate habit patterns, not poor quality thinking, not a surplus of old feelings causing trouble within, and not brain disorder. To be understood they require a different definition and description from what in the past has been considered affective disorder.

Closed Theories, Closed Minds

Commonly, however, my presentations to my colleagues were unabsorbed by them. Repeatedly my attention was drawn away from theory construction by that difficulty and forced to the problems of obtaining colleagues' serious attention to theory, to rethinking about processes, and communicating ideas to them. Each person encountered some points in this complex theory that they did not comprehend, and most used those as a basis to reject the whole theory. They often imputed things to me that I had neither said (nor believed) as a basis for disagreement with me. For example, some thought that for my view that emotion cannot store to be correct I must mean therefore that neuronic functions for cognition and affect are different.

Their stance was that memory of an idea brought that idea to consciousness. Therefore, memory of an emotion must bring that emotion to consciousness. They had convicted me without a hearing. But they also maintained that bringing an emotion to consciousness created an abreaction and ridded one of (or at least reduced) that stored emotion. The parallel gets twisted to an inconsistency, for it is generally accepted by them that bringing an idea to consciousness strengthens rather than rids one of the memory of that idea. In fact, their stance that neuronic function for cognition and affect must be the same is proper, but their criticism should be aimed toward their own position, which means something quite different from what they think. Human physiology is consistent. That is why the brain processes for both cognition and affect must be expected to be comparable.

Both mental functions seem to operate in the same way. Remembering an idea means we know the idea we had at some previous time. When we remember an emotion we know the emotion we had at some previous time. Each memory has been electrochemically stored in brain cells. However, remembering does not remove whatever is remembered from those brain cells as the catharsis theories would have us believe about emotion—as in "get out your feelings" to rid oneself of those feelings—but not about cognition—as in "review the poem, formula, dates so that you will remember them"—for the comparable process helps fix the memory of ideas. Remembering does not remove or even lessen the engram in either. When the coded bit of memory of an idea is activated, we have the memory of that idea—moved to consciousness. Comparably, when the coded bit of memory of an emotion is activated, we have the memory of that emotion—moved to consciousness. The memory of an emotion is different from experiencing that emotion. We can all remember past feelings of anger, sadness, hope, fear, surprise—but in that remembering of past feeling, we do not necessarily feel the experience of those emotions. It takes something more to do that. The strong suggestion is that memory function in thought and feeling are comparable activities. Thus memory of either emotion or cognition is similar in that they can produce the abstraction. In neither does reawakening of engrams erase the engrams. "Getting out feelings" is an exact equivalent of "getting out thoughts." Neither is a truth as description of mental process. How difficult it seems for so many psychologists to comprehend this!

The re-experiencing of emotions seems more likely to occur by replication through a new evocation of similar emotion (not through recovery or repeated presentation of an old emotion). For emotion experience to recur we need to have a repetition of the evocative situation to serve as a basis of an evaluation in emotion terms. The replication is not memory of the emotion in its usual sense but memory of the situation that then evokes anew the same sort of emotion as the original situation. That difference in explanations is crucial for understanding emotion processes.

Corrected by My Colleagues

Another professional who reviewed an article I wrote for a journal was so disturbed by the theory that he declared the whole thing "preposterous." He listed examples of preposterous statements in the article. Indeed the examples he gave were foolish. However, none of the statements that he declared foolish were in the article, nor were they ideas I had implied or even believed. Apparently he was so offended by the article's implications—but at the same time was unable to dispute or muster criticisms of the actual contents—that he repressed what was there and made up distorted elements, declared them mine, and having done that, appropriately shot them down. He did not notice that they wore his uniform, not mine. It is a problem that recurs in trying to find peers to review work that controverts fundamental aspects of their own work. My work has sometimes been unsettling in some other ways.

On several occasions similar criticisms were made when I gave drafts of my writings to others and occasionally when I submitted papers for peer review. Some of the ideas were found interesting, but a frequent comment was that some word or words I used were not really words or were good words not used properly. After such responses I would always recheck the words in the dictionary to make sure what was correct. Never was it necessary to correct the manuscript. The problem seemed to be that the ideas were unsettling, but because they were persuasive, the impelled criticism was deflected to word usage.

The most common reason for the impenetrability of the closed minds of professionals in psychology started with the beginnings of psychoanalysis. Freud, with all his genius and creativity, suffered from a passionate drive for fame. That is part of what led him, despite his stated scientific aims, to turn his nascent science away from the open inquiry favored in science into making psychoanalysis mimic a religion. This was supported in part because so much of what he had discovered and devised were of merit while so much of what others had suggested was foolish. He became jealously intolerant of any serious doubt about any part of the theory he presented. He rejected suggestions made and was chary of anything that did not come from him. He also tended to reject the people who persisted in differing with him. Properly enthusiastic, submissive, adoring priests were acceptable. Because he had so much to offer, there were many faith-filled acolytes. Some who differed about fundamentals were excommunicated. The effect was that contributions to fundamental theory finally came only from Freud.

The devout still believe that all of psychoanalysis that could be important is contained in Freud's writings and that other writers have contributed only minor embellishments. Fortunately for humanity, there is both the psychology of Freud and psychology beyond Freud. Outside of psychoanalysis, the influence of Freud's endorsement of common wisdom about affect as science hampered examination of some important fundamental premises. Other attempts at theory construction incorporated his views, or worse, ignored affect as if it were not fully one-half of the human mind.

When I spoke of emotions to my psychoanalytic colleagues, what they heard was filtered through an "article of faith in Freud" that his premises were "writ in stone" and not to be questioned. What could have led to fruitful discussions with some bright people, and advances in the field, were inadmissible. In that ambiance the following seminal, enlightening, and useful assertions I offered for discussion were dismissed:

Affect is a fractional-second event rather than an enduring event

Affect discharge is a nonevent

Affect is not capable of "strangulation"

Anxiety is just another affect—neither more nor less important than any other affect

Psychodynamic patterns of resolutions of infantile conflicts are only a minor factor in symptom disorders, not the entire basis, not the major factor, and not the cause

Affect phobia is a universal human problem

When a colleague expressed interest in my work, I suggested to her that by substituting a new broader use of affects in a theory of affect, after dropping Freud's entire anxiety theory, we could achieve an astonishingly valuable theory of personality. Her only reply was to ask, "Do you mean Freud's 1916 or his 1926 views?"

She had been too incredulous to believe I meant what I said, and had no capacity to open her mind to comprehend the fatal limitation of Freud's ideas about emotion. She showed that her own emotion awareness was seriously limited. Her apparent opinion, however, was that I had not read or understood Freud.

These sorts of troubles came from talking to priests of psychoanalysis who were more devoted to psychoanalytic process rather than to cure of their patients. Their faith was in the metatheory and its related technique. These were not scientists eager to learn more about facts of their science. They were "followers" of a guru, only eager to learn more about the "truths" within the set of ideas they espoused. They believed in the infallibility of Freud. Anything I said that differed from his original text meant to them that I did not comprehend the "truth." They sought to pin down my errors. They immediately classed what I said as due to my deficient comprehension of psychoanalysis. Their assumption was that I was ignorant (or not quite bright enough) while they were bright and knowledgeable. However, to their credit, their condescension was usually gracious as they kindheartedly attempted to help me and "correct" me within the terms of their own dogma.

Another eminent psychoanalyst in response to my theorizing kindly lectured me, "The material of psychoanalysis is the flow of association of the patient on the couch." This tunnel vision notion is far too narrow for it is comparable to saying that the material of biology is what is observed with the microscope. In both instances, restricting the definition of a field of study to a currently available device used to obtain data, instead of the field of study itself (mind or life respectively), stifles growth of the field. Those limitations would constrict any science from a free ranging study of related phenomena within a subject matter to use of an exploratory device.

When I insisted that adding a theory of the broad span of emotions to classic psychodynamic theory, after erasing the classic theory of anxiety, enabled us to understand more, to cure expeditiously, prevent neuroses, and cure problems that previously had only been ameliorated, they knew it could not be true. They searched within their theory to find how I was wrong. What they did was comparable to searching under the street light for the key that had been dropped fifty feet away in the dark alley—but not searched for there because it was not illuminated for them. They were optimistically searching within the light of old theory they knew for a desired value where it did not exist.

Resistance Is Only Natural

Our curing of 80 percent of dozens of patients, within a shorter time than most therapists took for history-taking and over a longer time curing an additional 15 percent of patients with neuroses that usually took therapists three to ten years merely to ameliorate, was ludicrously turned into a deficiency on our part. In effect they were declaring that the enduring cures with 95 percent of symptom disorder patients, which astonished them, could not be true. Without information to support their doubts, they were asserting that my patients' and my own belief that they were cured was due to my patients' misunderstanding and my ignorance and incompetence. They were declaring, "Good is bad."

My surprise at the patronizing condescension by colleagues toward an advance that brought results they could sometimes acknowledge but not comprehend helped me realize that such resistance is a natural human attribute. It occurs even with good minds, if they have acquired a barrier to new knowledge. It is self-protective assumed confidence of educated and indoctrinated people (in any field) whose minds might be fully capable of comprehending more if they could remain open. At some point they regard their accumulation of knowledge as sufficient for their careers. They decide they do not need new ideas. They do not notice anything "outside the box." Those closed minds are like closed eyes; they detect nothing but afterimage.

Procrustes set the pattern. Such translations allow them to run data through their theory. But this is a necessary part of each profession. As in all translations, distortions are inevitable. But worse, data not noticed or encompassed in a theory, even if important, is omitted. Data translated to erroneous theory yields only error. Data omitted narrowly circumscribes a theory. Distortions from omissions appear in all sciences. Certainly they appear in applications within every school of psychology. There is no flexibility of framework and little room for new or unnoticed events and new knowledge. Petrified theory gives solid comfort to therapists who want to treat patients as they have been taught to do, unfettered by the tasks of learning new fundamentals and perhaps free of the need to understand why they do what they do. But this makes it hard for patients with any variation on a theme and impossible for those with any issues not encompassed in theory.

It was perplexing to me. I spoke to colleagues whenever I had the chance. I accepted every speaking engagement offered. My shyness was outweighed by my wish to reach enough people to be sure that these useful discoveries were used to help people, not lost. The public deserved to know of the far greater hope for their lives than they could obtain from the established authorities in various institutions. Soon I found that some bits of the theory were being taught in some schools, mingled within various courses. Here and there around the country a few professionals in various disciplines were adopting parts of the knowledge of transient, benign, constructive emotion in health and illness. They helped people to more satisfying lives. This brings assurance that the human race eventually will be free of what has been called neurosis, and free of the awkwardness of incompetent theories that are insufficient to help people suffering from such disorders. But that cadre still is a tiny minority. In a limited circle, I occasionally became the therapist suggested for people who had not improved in previous therapies and still wanted a cure.

My attendance at meetings of psychological theoreticians and practitioners however, sometimes made me impatient.

My mind wandered as I sat in a conference listening to some eminent psychologists discuss facets of an issue I considered relevant but immaterial in the light of new knowledge. I imagined a comparable conference of practitioners taking place two hundred years ago. I compared the current presentations that earned my inattention to a fantasy of presentations that might have been made many years ago. The participants in that earlier conference were similar in their seriousness about their subject matter though they differed in clothing, manner of speaking, and topics. Discussions of their field and the details of their work were as carefully described as those of present day professionals. In that imagined meeting, the seven men were barbers become physicians. What they authoritatively spoke about was the difference in handling blood flow in veins and arteries, of bleeding process, stanching the flow, and of the improved equipment they designed and used. The devotion to their science and their seriousness about their work was easily evident to onlookers. Their logical approach to disease was indisputable.

I imagined they also described technology to each other, discussed variations in specific techniques used. They, too, discussed their manner and style in relation to clients or with families after their patients died. There were honors, awards, and recognition for scientific contributions and for lifetime services to their profession.

They showed considerable concern with the high failure (death) rate of their patients. They were aware of how difficult it is to cure people with some disorders even by intense treatment. One man thought that removing all the blood would be most efficacious. By doing that he could extract all the "bad" humours and give the body a better chance to recover. He reported trying that a few times, but unfortunately even that heroic measure had not saved the lives of his patients. He offered his considered opinion that some disorders were simply incurable, but believed they would usually be ameliorable by copious bloodletting.

Those professionals were sure their theory and technique were correct despite being vague about what they regarded as a minor matter, the details of explanations of how its underlying processes influence health and illness. They were confident that blood-letting was the most assured path to health based on the soundest premises of their profession. From our view, two hundred years later, there is only the one small problem about their knowledge—it is entirely wrong. Sadly, too many professionals today also sincerely profess invalid, partially correct, ineffective, and uncertain ideas as if all were valuable certainties. The examples are legion.

A SCIENCE IN NEED OF A PARADIGM SHIFT

It is hard to imagine how a purportedly technical-scientific field that has a few hundred thousand licensed professionals in various specialties could have operated for more than a hundred years using loose definitions, imprecise formulae, cloudy concepts, and vague allusive descriptions of the functions of its elements, and still grow into the multibillion dollar a year industry that enriches practitioners while prolonging and even worsening the condition of patients. Even the gross outlines describing mental health and illness have no distinct, clear, communicable definitions. The treatment processes used by professionals are unclear, difficult to convey, and disputed. The measures of effectiveness of their work are mostly without substantial scientific demonstration, other than those about minimal and minor changes in functioning, attitude, or relationships.

Some of those working at the edge of psychology, in behavioral science, have worked out careful studies of peripheral aspects of mind. With these, they devised painstaking treatments that are highly touted as state of the art, but when tested are of limited effectiveness as psychotherapy. Although panic episodes and phobias have responded to such approaches, treatment of other varieties of symptom disorders, such as conversions, obsessions, paranoia, multiple personality, heterophobia, anorexia, reactive depression, etc., have not succeeded with that approach. Their confrontational approach is often a painful, torturous activity with questionable theory and a very modest success rate. Those touted claims for successful cures are mingled with their declarations that the illnesses are mysteries because we cannot see into mind and that complete cure is impossible. Use of the word cure needs to be reconsidered carefully and thoughtfully.

Biological psychiatry presents many studies supporting the idea that neuroses are the results of chemical imbalances and neurological dysfunction. Those studies are confounded by poorly contrived hypotheses, murky definitions, poor research design, loose definitions of terms, and questionable diagnostic validity for subjects, all making the results of uncertain value. In an alarming number of these studies, cause and effect appear to have been reversed. Their successes in manipulating moods are taken by them to be the same as doing something curative in personality patterns or (because they do not discriminate between mood and emotion) with specific emotions. Despite glaring defects in research and effectiveness, they have promoted biological treatments of psychological problems. These studies have spawned and supported symptom suppressive treatment. But it is stretching truth to consider symptom suppression as a cure of the disorders. Nevertheless, such temporary suppression of symptoms has been described as if that is a cure. It never is. Worse, the approach by chemically suppressing symptoms too often iatrogenically causes illness (tardive dyskinesia is a troubling example). This and some other illnesses, notably tension phobia, appear to be irreversible.

Because there are millions of troubled people, we need a mental health field. What we have contains a Babel-like unclarity of jargon. There are not accepted standard definitions for even the most basic elements of the field, descriptions of syndromes and diagnostic categories are cloudy, and often they are superficial. There is dispute about which of various mental processes are the more relevant functions.

Unfortunately, some people are being treated to cure their responses to untoward events. Such responses as sadness, fear, grief, anxiety, or anger are healthy responses to untoward events. The attempts to cure patients of such discomfiting healthy responses is an unfortunate travesty that has turned healthy people into patients with chronic disablement.

Despite every effort I made within psychology to publicize the reasonableness, advantage, and efficacy of recasting fundamental beliefs about emotion and the consequent reformulation of descriptions of health and illness, these ideas have remained essentially secret. Journal editors and their professional reviewers are rarely prepared to comprehend papers about alternative fundamental views in their field. Book editors often turn to academia for peer review opinions about new theory from those most tightly ensconced in past theory. Program committees may declare interest in innovations, but are mainly interested in innovations in applications and select papers about details or embellishments of applications of existing knowledge, sometimes having interest in underlying process but rarely accepting something that would change foundations. This is a problem in every field of knowledge.

Mental health workers' incredulity toward new ideas is a defense that protects the existing, structured frame of reference on which they base their work. Truths are not necessarily readily recognized nor automatically accepted. The slowness with which new ideas permeate the field is also a matter of politics of the profession. Sheer numbers of professionals have to be persuaded, despite all the sorts of resistances described, to think about unsettling ideas. Many more have to comprehend new theory before a stage of controversy about it can develop. Only after a conflictful discussion takes place among many people are new concepts absorbed by a field of knowledge. That makes it necessary to publicize ideas to create discussion and also, unfortunately, controversy. Strangely, no fundamental shift gets considered without that. But it is additionally delayed because priest authorities disdain whatever they do not know, for any new idea in their field is automatically defined as unimportant error or unfortunate misunderstanding.

In contrast to reactions of professionals, the public has been slightly more open. Whatever recognition by the public that has come resulted from recognition that pragmatic applications of our new understanding often frees people of disorders that had crippled their lives for years. Most have persevered in trying a sequence of one kind of therapist after another. From across the country a few people come for "cure" instead of "treatment." From across the world come letters of inquiry.

However, those facts of greater efficacy of applications of the theory, even including the promise of prevention programs that can permanently eradicate many psychological disorders, are unimpressive to those ensconced in past erroneous learning. We do not easily dislodge past indoctrination, even when it is error.

OTHER HURDLES FOR A NEW THEORY

Another difficulty in developing and disseminating the new theory has been the absence of funding. There is a great deal of funding for theoreticians working in institutions. There is a more limited amount of funding for theorists working in universities. There is no funding to support the work of theorists in independent practice. The cost for a private theorist supporting his own work is far greater than most people can imagine. It forced the work described in this book to be a part-time endeavor so that what might otherwise have been accomplished in a decade took several.

Usually students in each field accept premises as if they are "final truths." Those are not to be disturbed. However, the advances that transform any field come only when a more valid premise replaces an existing fundamental premise. Any change in fundamentals touches everything in the field and makes at least a little change in everything.

The move from theory of enduring emotion to the more valid theory of transient emotion has already taken forty years to gain minimal acceptance. Understanding implications of its meaning will take more time. The evidence from applications of the theory tells us that as the idea and its implications are increasingly absorbed, psychology will leap forward.

The defense of status quo has often been deprecating. One colleague brushed aside the whole carefully delineated set of ideas and applications by saying, "Maybe it is a theory that will work well for you, but not for others." That statement was intended to please me by granting that my success was real, for he admittedly knew about my therapeutic successes with some of his former patients with whom he had long been unsuccessful. His faulty logic produced a bogus compliment that was too belittling of the theory to cheer me. Without a meaningful set of explanations, my successes would have been possible only by attributing to me an artistic use of charisma to create transference cures. Even if he had been correct that no other therapists had duplicated my successes, my own successes could not have come, as he asserted, from a peculiarly personal theory. In what earthly realm could scientific laws differ from person to person? That could occur only in a magical kingdom.

Another analyst said to me, in response to my mentioning the fact of cures making my patient roster turnover more rapid, "I do not have that problem because I never do brief psychotherapy, only long-term therapy." I thought (but refrained from saying), "Even when it is not what the patient needs?" She could not comprehend that I was working with major factors in psychological disorder to effect cures. Because work with major factors has vastly greater advantage over work with minor factors, the cure can be more effective and often more rapid. I knew that in contrast to what I do, she worked slowly with minor factors that she sincerely believed to be the major elements in psychological disorders (although using a great deal of sophistication skillfully and sensitively) to achieve minimal benefit in amelioration of the same sorts of disorders that I had described as cured in a relatively short time. Theories with weak validity, if they produce any successes at all, can do so only slowly.

My treatment was not in any way aimed toward brevity. That is, the brevity that I frequently (but not always) achieved was not a central aim, but was a natural product of the greater validity of my approach. That is very different from the transparent, somewhat cynical implications in brief psychotherapy fostered by insurance companies, that "little can be accomplished in any psychotherapy, so why not do that 'little' more briefly, to save time and money."

I told another analyst of my theory and described helping thirty-six out of a series of forty patients achieve what they and I agreed was cure of their disorders. "I would have to see the progress notes of each therapy session," he said in a condescending put-down, "to judge whether it was transference cure!" All of the patients in that series had suffered classic disorders (phobia, conversion, etc.) that are generally refractory. This eminent analyst, whom I think is rather bright, had temporarily lost his capacity to think clearly. It was as if his mind had temporarily locked down. The notion that I could create a transference cure (by virtue of the forcefully persuasive personality that I do not have) is a plausible possibility with any therapist over a year, for no more than one or two patients at most. That anyone could do that with a half-dozen patients is highly improbable. For him to think that I or anyone else could create transference cures in thirty-six out of a sequence of forty patients was utterly illogical, if not delusional. Because he had considered my descriptions of the sorts of storm processes in these patients immaterial, I knew he had never noticed such processes within himself or others. To him I was speaking of imaginary events in a personal fictional account from which I had devised a hypothetical construct to answer some questions for a metatheory. If he had sufficient talent for self-observation, he might have noticed what I and a number of others (patients and colleagues) have noticed: that these processes are observable actual process. His emotion blindness keeps him from understanding some crucial facts about personality processes. He is left with only his classic theoretical ideas from which what I described must be seen as nonsense.

If that eminent analyst had the sense of humor that a greater mental perspective would have allowed him, he would have been on the floor rolling in laughter at his preposterous suggestion that I or anyone could produce transference cures in such proportion. Such extraordinary results, if he had been correct in his myopic view that they had occurred without my having a comprehensive theoretic basis, should have at least brought thoughtful reconsideration about the nature and value of transference cures that could be brought about by new methods. As a high priest of psychoanalysis with vast knowledge in the field, he was unfortunately limited by the premisal circumscription created by his overload of indoctrination in that field. The cures I described were achieved using a carefully delineated set of explanations, including descriptions of the process of illness (unfortunately invisible to him) and the therapeutic progress, and earned thought and study from open minds—unless they believed I was lying about the process and results.

The sources of incredulity of various sorts are of interest. The important source of incredulity in the eminent analyst just described relates to the individual variations in capacity for observing inside to notice emotion and its processes. A very high percentage of people are as emotion blind as he is, whatever their ability to discourse lengthily about Freud's description of anxiety, its processes, and its implications. In part, emotion sensiveness appears to be a talent that is probably distributed as variably as any other human talent. Because it has never been a factor in selection for entry into the field, that distribution of talents must vary among mental health workers in the same way as it does among the public.

Some people notice very naturally that they first have a feeling reaction, and then often a feeling reaction to that reaction, with associations to the other times, places, and persons related to those. Others seem to know only that they experience emotion. Some of them, the more introspective, identify what particular emotion it is that they feel and the surface features of the evocative event ("You made me mad doing that").

Psychotherapists rarely consider that they themselves may have some psychological deficiency—a limitation to their ability to observe within themselves. Many who have introspective but not self-observing capacity are confident that they have all the functions that anyone could have.

Those who are able at least to notice the continuing sequence of feeling reaction to feeling reaction within themselves are far more ready to consider the ideas presented in this book than those unaware of those processes going on within themselves. It seems quite unlikely that the analyst who suggested my results might be "transference cures" would have made that suggestion if he had been capable of observing his own emotion processes, for with that, he could have followed my discussion of the complexities of the dynamics of emotion response sequences as applied within himself. Without such awareness, he automatically deprecated the process to meaninglessness, perhaps with some thought that it might be a sub-process to the cognitive processes to which he had comfortable access. His response illuminated the fact that many are currently able to function in the mental health field while being relatively unaware of some areas of their own inner life. The well-accepted fact of individual differences in all human factors was not considered as real in relation to himself and his own awareness of his internal processes. Incredulity in that particular analyst is bolstered also by his previously stated belief that "psychoanalysis is essentially a completed science." That means that he believes that psychoanalysis is so near perfection that at most it might only need to be touched up here and there. My suggestions of events that controvert what a "completed science" defines as the realm of the possible, meant to him that my observations of occurrence of the events were faulty, not that his "perfect science" is imperfect. Perhaps he meant, as some nonobserving patients have suggested, that my observations were of nonexistent mental content.

All these people, like thousands of other indoctrinated professionals, dare not leave their premises. To abandon premises is frightening, for it puts one on unsure ground. For them it is not as it is for some of us—an exciting adventure, a risk worthwhile in seeking useful truths and gaining a clearer perception of reality.

Friends Like These

Often those professionals who are unable to absorb and integrate the breadth of meaning of concepts of transient, benign emotion attempted to trivialize that which they did not understand. They followed a familiar pattern of reaction to new ideas within any field. As a first reaction, because the ideas differ from their knowledge, they react with denial: "That is not true." After a period of absorption of portions of new ideas brings some comprehension to them, the response is accepting, but denigrating: "Yes, the ideas are true, but they are unimportant." Finally, when the new ideas become generally accepted, the reaction is condescending: "They are true and important ideas, but these are things we always knew."

Sometimes when I lecture, a member of the audience will comment, "[the writer, . . .] also said . . . , " and then offer a minor element of similarity, as if that were the essence of what I had presented, thus diminishing the contribution to something they already understand. Doing so means that they do not grasp the breadth of meaning of the new theory. For example, I have heard, "You are saying what Freud also said, 'emotions are to be felt . . . , " which I do say but that falls far short of the totality of what I am describing. "Buddhism has the same ideas as you," I have been told. "It also has the concept of accepting emotions." This is true in some Buddhist writings and not in others, but far short of what I am saying of what emotions are and of their processes and implications for health, productivity, or creativity.

I often hear something like, "[Doctor . . .] said we should accept and work with emotions." Again, my reaction is always mixed. On the one hand, I am cheered knowing they have moved as far as the second of those three stages (in which they have a glimmer that what I say is true), but believe those truths are unimportant, subsumed by a series of partial ideas. At the same time, I am saddened, for I know that the commentator, having found a single point of congruence, erroneously believes they have a grasp of the whole theory and therefore may make no further effort to understand. Those who believe they can encompass an extensive theory under a single item of commonality with another theory usually use that commonality to close themselves off from the effort to grapple with the entire set of ideas needed to use the theory effectively. Those who tell me that they agree with each statement of theory because it fits with what they had learned from past theory never seem to be able to answer why that past theory did not answer questions and bring cures such as are enabled by the new theory. It usually turns out to be that they have glossed over a great number of significant parts of the newly offered theory and often also parts of the past theory.

Several uncomprehending professionals have said, with only slight variation in the wording, "I understand the theory, but I do not see how it can (would, could) cure." Because the theory is essentially an explanation of processes of health, illness, and cure, they are innocently disclosing they have not grasped the theory, while narcissistically defending their past indoctrination.

Scholarly studies within each school have centered on how better to apply those theories to explain or change important phenomena. Unfortunately, premisal circumscription, the inability to leave premises of past theory, is a serious scientific trap. The efforts to understand phenomena of their field of study are locked within a conceptual radius inadequate to provide sufficient answers—or worse, perhaps too small even to generate important questions.

Another difficulty encountered in psychological theory has unduly burdened the field. When a theory provides coherent structure, but that structure fails to mesh with either the realities of mental processes or the realities of human experience, that theory belongs in the category of metatheory. Such a theory may be viewed as a step toward either scientific theory or entertaining science fiction; never should it be seriously considered as anything more than a starting point as a set of ideas worthy of study.

Many tests of personality theory have been inadequate because its metatheory has been asserted by pseudo scientists to be part of a different kind of science requiring different rules—and that it is not testable in usual ways. The true problem in the mental health field has been the necessity to move from science fiction of metatheory through scientific logic and testable hypotheses to corroborative scientific statements, before including knowledge in the category of established scientific fact. Wrong or improperly stated questions have in the past brought many uncertain answers and a confused field of study. They have not brought health to the needful public.

By 1980, I had a fairly complete theory of affect that explained more about personality than past theory, benefited my patients, often markedly shortened the time needed to help them to what they wanted from treatment, and did so more completely than I was hearing from other therapists. I had corrected error in past theory and filled in some places where there had been omissions. Some colleagues began to realize that I was highly effective in my work. Some sent patients to me and learned that the patients prospered. Even when colleagues were complimentary, they still could not listen when I tried to tell them how the patients were helped. At best, they regarded my remarkable success as the result of skillful or more likely fortunate applications of the same knowledge they possessed. At worst they believed I had fallen in with the abomination of virtual treatment as "brief psychotherapy." They could not comprehend that by correcting errors and omissions in the various therapies available it becomes possible to cure. Because the new path is more direct, that cure is usually more rapid than the amelioration from past approaches. As one analyst who had from time to time sent me his unsuccessful patients said, "It's good you could help her so quickly. I brought her as far as I could, and you topped it off!" He could not comprehend that I had shifted from his approach with her and taken an entirely different tack in my conversations with her, despite my telling him exactly what I had done.

In that ambiance, enlightening and useful statements were dismissed. Apparently acceptance of these concepts would be a narcissistic blow to some therapists. Paradigms of treatment are based in fundamental premises about theory of health and illness. Treatment approaches in the past have been of limited effectiveness, but lauded because they create some change. Studies of treatment results have usually been of measurements of tiny, sometimes obscure, shifts in attitude, comfort, or relationship, or a minor degree of subsidence of symptoms. Painfully slow improvement has come to be regarded as a necessary "given" in mental health treatment. Rapidity has to mean significant underlying faults remain as danger and will increase the chances of recurrence. That is another reason that this new theory, which supports highly effective therapies, is viewed with doubt—precisely because it is so effective. Therapeutic changes from applications of the new theory are often complete, lasting cures, not just the minimal amelioration produced by past theories. Many patients cured ten to fifteen years ago remain cured. None has surfaced as ill again. Once one has adopted the new view, with its more useful explanations of mental functioning, our listening to discussions based in old theory, seems to us comparable to a modern astronomer listening to a pre-Copernican system scientist discussing the universe. The central fundamental premises are different. The mixtures of sound truths and garbled erroneous theory applied to problem solving are always inadequate to the task.

12

Unfamiliar Truths and Familiar Fallacies: Reflections on Science

In a better world theories would not have a biography. New theory would arise, be tested and then accepted, rejected, or modified. If it passed the tests, it would be used. If it failed the tests, it would be dropped. That would be the story.

In this world it is different. Proponents of established theories tenaciously preserve their theoretical positions so well that more competent new theories have great difficulty gaining a foothold. The decades-long struggle to discover the series of hidden truths to formulate the new theory presented in this book required tremendous effort and perseverance. Nevertheless, that was less effort than is required to persuade professionals to open their minds to discoveries of fundamental premises that are more useful for explaining psychological development, health, and illness and achieving actual cure of psychological disorders.

However, shifts in fundamental premises confront the two following difficulties.

1. *The fixity with which scientists hold to whatever fundamental premises they already believe (they cling to these as if they were final truth)*[1]

2. *The personal limitations of individuals in observation of phenomena (we differ in talents and sensory capacities)*[2]

Individuals may have either or both of these difficulties—few persons are unaffected.

DARING TO LEAVE THE PREMISES

The most common enslavement to existing fundamental premises comes unknowingly from our indoctrinated premises. This is a serious complication that, along with other factors, impedes the advance of science. That occurs because our premises, once in place, become unobserved frames of reference for autonomous selection of our responses to sensory data. Yet those premises also participate in the determination of what is even allowed to be perceived or noticed among a multitude of sensory receptions.

Such changes as the shift from mechanistic to quantum physics is an excellent example of how slow-going a move it is for new fundamental theory to reach acceptance—seventy years later the absorption by physicists of these new, helpful ideas has only begun. The fact that quantum-based answers to old and new questions are helpful has disturbed scientists even while intriguing and amazing them. The process of adaptation to new fundamental premises creates an immense intellectual task that may be beyond the energy of many people.

One major difficulty stemming from the mental health field being in the hands of practitioners untrained in science is *ignoring the crucial distinction between use of variables in observable actual process and use of hypothetic constructs as if the latter were observable actual variables.* For technicians this does not matter because their job is to apply techniques they have been taught without thinking deeply about the theoretic underlay explaining why and how those techniques are supposed to have the desired effects. But when technicians also consider themselves theoreticians and try to act like theoreticians, as is typical in the mental health field, theory building is a seriously presented travesty. Fantasy is presented as if it is a developed fictional construct. Constructs are presented as if they are confirmed processes. Untested hypotheses are presented as if they are scientific findings. Some practitioners have naively rationalized that "mind-science is different from other sciences in ways that make usual scientific tests inappropriate." Some have declared that each treatment session is a research study, reducing the idea of research to mere exploration. Presentation of such fatuities is a defense offered because of ignorance of the systems of formulating meaningful questions in testable form and the imperative need to make such tests. But technicians acting as theoreticians rarely focus on fundamental premises. Instead, their interest centers on operations in the arena of their work.

Theory building, taken to mean constructing a "best explanation" of a cluster of related phenomena, is the business of science. Each study is an attempt to corroborate or modify the current theory. In every science we have to build a meta theory containing as many actual variables as we can bring to bear upon the phenomena we study. We fill the gaps with hypothetic constructs that are the best fictions we can devise for the purpose. Theory building involves persevering in study to accrue actual variables as replacements for hypothetic constructs to make our theories increasingly solid. Ultimately the hope is to free us from the need for support from hypothetic constructs. However, reliance upon constructs is all we can have until we find actual variables or verify that our fictional constructs are actuality. To forget that constructs are constructs is to stray from science. In various fields of science, hypothetic constructs have too often attained long-term status that reifies and so exempts them from the requirement of reexamination. They become spurious ultimate truths stifling better truths.

We ignore some of what exists because our theories declare it unimportant or irrelevant. That is part of why emancipations from learned beliefs about fundamental premises are rare occurrences and are hard won when they do occur. The difficulties in creating such changes in premises were noticed and entertainingly described by philosopher of science Charles Fort in 1919 in *The Book of the Damned*.[3] Much later Thomas Kuhn covered part of that same ground in a more generally acceptable scholarly fashion in *The Structure of Scientific Revolutions*.[4]

Charles Fort recorded many unaccepted facts and protested the difficulties encountered by new or deviant ideas or events unable to fit with existing theory and therefore excluded from sciences: "A PROCESSION of the damned. By the damned, I mean the excluded. We shall have a procession of data that Science has excluded. . . . The power that has said to all these things that they are damned, is Dogmatic Science" (3).

Thomas Kuhn more recently brought together and organized examples of such difficulties in the development of sciences. From his organization of incidents he described patterns in the seemingly necessary processes, including obstacles, in the development of sciences. These accurately depict the same sorts of difficulties I had encountered when I offered discoveries to my field. I refer to some of his statements for they help place that "ignoring" of useful advanced knowledge in psychology within the general framework of sciences, explaining how and why comparable sets of ideas are typically ignored for a generation or so. Kuhn said, "Normal science, for example, often suppresses fundamental novelties because they are necessarily subversive of its basic commitments" (5). And he added, "The commitments that govern normal science specify not only what sorts of entities the universe does contain but also, by implication, those that it does not" (7).

In that light, because a true cure of psychological disorders can be neither described nor expected from therapies based on any of the mainstream psychological theories, a certitude develops that no theory could ever enable cure. This is reflected in the pattern Kuhn found in "the activity in which most scientists inevitably spend most of their time [activity which] is predicated on the assumption that the scientific community knows what the world is like." The important consequence of this confidence is that "No part of the aim of normal science is to call forth new sorts of phenomena; indeed those that will not fit the box are often not seen at all."[5]

However, neither Kuhn nor Fort dealt with the issues of distinctions between hypothetic and actual variables, which have become of crucial importance in the current chaotic state of psychology as a science and surely are just as important in all sciences. The general assumption appears to be that hypothetic constructs inevitably become proved. Freud naively considered that we rely on descriptions of processes we cannot observe and eventually they are established as true, even though in his own experience he had tried and rejected a series of alternative sets of fictions before settling on those he preferred. He implied that all his concluding fictions must turn out to be provable actual processes. In that he was wrong. If he had been far wrong in most of his fictions, his whole edifice of theory would have failed. By being right in many of his fictions although wrong in several fictions, but insisting he would eventually prove them all, he forestalled full examination of the theories and set his followers on the path of trying to discover how to apply them, instead of the more scientifically valuable first task of establishing whether or how they work. Omitting recognition of the difference between the actual and the hypothetical serves to maintain the integrity of an existing theory by discouraging examination. The purely hypothetical becomes a creed so that it is protected by a priesthood that punishes acceptance of controvertive truths even if they are observable and more useful than what they replace. However, all theory is interim theory and all practice is interim practice.

All Theory Is Interim Theory

One reason for ignoring the important new discoveries presented in this book is that psychology, as a science, has remained at a rudimentary stage busily exploring and attempting to extend its first discoveries. To anyone cognizant of scientific requirements for theory of a field of study, it is dismaying to encounter the superfluity of volumes of incogitant current writings about affects. A circular interreferencing appears to close in the horizons of thought so that there is little, if any, consideration of whatever is outside that small circle.

Additionally, each current fad about subjects in underlying but not fundamental elements in psychology seems to those involved to be both more important than the processes of the illnesses they seek to understand and more important than cure of those disorders. Current examples are the faddish concentration on intersubjectivity as a refinement of transference and countertransference process, object relations theory and self-psychology, and attachment—all valuable vehicles for treatment process in pattern disorders, but none appear to be fundamental psychological issues nor demonstrably curative. It is precisely this crucial point of empirical tying to externals that must yet be done for each of these. Some discussions by proponents of each fad that arises seem to vie in significance or relevance with theological arguments about numbers of angels dancing on a pin.

Part of the slowness in growth of the mental health field is from volume after volume of books on psychology that fail to build from a base in scientific logic, examine fundamentals, clarify definitions, or measure the value of ideas in terms of anything other than the elegance of internal coherence without regard for ties to outer reality. They fail to discern the distinction between actual process and hypothetic construct of process. Their invalidity makes them fail to produce what every patient seeks—cure. A general theory of psychology must encompass what may, at first glance, seem to be disparate bits of fact as legitimate working pieces of the multi-dimensional puzzle in a way that offers explanations of their relationship.

Another reason for ignoring new ideas about fundamentals is that unlike some other sciences, clinical psychology, and indeed perhaps the whole mental health field, is largely in the hands of its technician-practitioners (not scientists and not scientist-practitioners) instead of being shared with basic scientists working at the forefront of knowledge. Their concentration on applications may be why so many seem not to have a perspective that allows them to know how weak, primitive, and inadequate their science is in comparison to what it needs to be and eventually will become. That innocent ignorance fosters an unquestioning acceptance of previous indoctrination as being both accurate and complete enough knowledge for all practical purposes, and therefore creates a readiness to ignore anything new. It makes people ready to fight whatever is counter to indoctrinated fundamental premises. Independent thought that takes anyone outside the established premises is anathema. To many professionals, a true cure of psychological disorders is too good to be true. Their certitude, which may appear to be cynical, is more likely based in pessimism from our past theories that give little basis for optimism about cures.

If professionals never doubt, never allow questioning of their existing premises, they cannot move to new fundamentals. Such intellectual inertia in relation to premises has effectively stalled progress in psychology for decades. For some professionals, there is comfort in believing they know all that is important about a subject matter. That assurance enables them to assume the stance of authority, proceed confidently along a path indicated by their accepted truths, and be patronizingly condescending toward any questioning of premises in their science.

This has been the case with past theories of emotion. They each contain untenable premises that their stalwart protagonists are unlikely to examine or even notice. But asking the protagonists of an existing theory to evaluate and compare their own with a new theory is like asking Druid priests to evaluate Christianity. These are touchy matters because those indoctrinated in some past theory hear my suggestion for the proper solution for evaluation of new theory as ignorant arrogance. Only those who understand the intricacies of finding the necessary perspective for evaluating theories can turn to objective solutions.

The standard in publication, conference program committees, and faculty recognition is the use of peer reviewers who are active in the same field of study to consider the value or acceptability of each contribution within each science. However, outside of normal science, when a contribution to science is new theory that controverts old fundamental theory, mainstream scientists may be considered peers, *but they are not peers in that new science*. Regardless of their standing as knowledgeable authorities in comprehension of past theory, no matter how intelligent they are, regardless of how open-mindedly objective they seem, for them the new has little chance of being considered as seriously as old entrenched beliefs, nor is the new easily understood by them regardless of merit. That is why the first presentations at the forefront of leaps in sciences can have no meaningful peer review—simply because they are new ideas.

For instance, confrontation with recent neuroscience findings that emotions are concomitantly generated independent of cognition, which I had suggested as logical years before neuroscience support arrived, is still not taken seriously by those in the mental health field as having the profound implication it has for theory of personality functioning. Additionally, the implications of now venerable neurophysiological knowledge of processes involved in nerve fiber mediation of all that moves, as impulse from synapse to synapse and there regenerating, is rarely given serious consideration for its implications in psychological functioning. Further, most psychologists have refused to let themselves realize that units of emotion events (as different from emotion states) can have a maximum duration of only microseconds, a fact that mandates a vast transformation in personality theory. The useful applications of the new theory that derive directly from those and other truths are typically judged by peer reviewers from the frame of reference of their old theory, and therefore consistently have been deemed illogical (or simply dumb) because they do not fit the premises and restrictions of their earlier frame.

On the other hand, the normal scientific advances I suggest, such as the clarifying of definitions of terms and concepts, are usually accepted by professionals as sensible and true. But they consider them not important enough to adopt and integrate with other knowledge, although all existing theories of emotion founder on the omission of such taxonomy. Careful description and discussion of the basic elements of emotion usually are not even recognized as fundamental. While the task of integrating definitions with theory will be considerable, the advantage from doing it will be immense. However, the even more important innovative truths in fundamental theory are usually rejected outright as preposterous, derided as absurd, or declared unimportant, untrue, or useless. These reactions are remindful of Ambrose Bierce's wry definition of absurdity: "A statement of belief manifestly inconsistent with one's own opinion."

When, additionally, professionals are personally blind to actual proc-esses included in the new theory, and because they are blind to them consider those literal processes as merely additional competing constructs, they are naturally doubly skeptical.

Built-in Sensive Restrictions

This second basis of our enslavement to existing fundamental premises is that unknowingly built-in restrictions to our personal abilities also irrevo-cably limit our ability to sense various aspects of the reality in which we exist. Some of what exists is ignored because, to many people, it is simply not observable and even when described by others is not comprehended as actually existing. How strange that all humans do not see infrared, sense radio waves, hear ultra high frequencies (sensed by none), or observe some emotion processes (sensed by a few). The rarity (such as observing emotion in process) is cast into the category of the nonexistent (such as sensing radio waves). To me, the most startling of my discoveries was the recognition of the breadth of individual variation in self-observing capacity and the severe limitations in such observational capacity in the vast majority of people, including professionals! It explains why some very bright, knowledgeable professionals were utterly uncomprehending when offered descriptions of processes observable to some of my colleagues, patients, and me. Encounters with professionals were often comparable to debating about color with the color blind, for they regarded my suggestions as mere hypothetic constructs. My original assumption had been that observation of emotion in process was universal—that everyone else also observed emotion in process.

One sensive colleague, after adopting my theory, urged that we should "Emphasize potentiation of emotion. Since everyone can observe emotion responses to emotion responses, even though they don't think it is impor-tant, you can lead them into the rest of the theory." At first I agreed, but experience led me reluctantly to the conclusion that he and I were wrong. Not everyone is aware of such a process. Very few people are. Repeated confrontations over years with people who had no idea of what I was talking about finally convinced me that emotion dynamics are invisible to many (and possibly most) people—a portion of their own mental processes hidden from themselves. The limited capacity for self-observation explains much of why psychological theory remains what it is today. In the hands of the relatively affect blind it has advanced as if trapped in a highly viscous fluid—bogged down, restrained, and with view obscured. In such an arena, fact has had no advantage over fiction. That ineluctable reality of personal limitation affects what gets built into theory, for theories are structures based only upon what can be known or imagined by theorists.

We rarely get more than a glimpse of the range of individual variations in sensation and perception. A common first reaction to recognition that we are insensive in some way is to experience it as a narcissistic blow. The realization that we can, at most, only vaguely comprehend what many others can easily know well—that it is immutably beyond our sensory capacity—may be too incredible for us to comprehend. We cannot know whatever our personal limitations keep us from knowing. It is humbling to realize that there are such unfair limitations. When we first come to realization of a limitation, compared to others, we may be admiring but often angrily envious. We want it not to be.

Unfair differences exist. For the deaf there is effectively no consideration of use of sound in recognizing and understanding reality. For the hard of hearing there is a strain in attempting to make sense from partial perceptions. To the congenitally blind there is effectively no comprehension of what vision is or its use in relating to the world. For the visually impaired there is a considerable strain in even minimally gauging one's surroundings with partial perceptions. They may vaguely understand what it might be like to see clearly. For those among us who are oblivious of subjectivity, there is effectively no comprehension of use of internal mental process for understanding oneself or other people. They have little comprehension of what it might be like to have fuller access to emotion or even of the fact of their own limitation.

Even for various capacities we all have in some degree, individual variations of abilities and talents that are difficult for each of us to comprehend. The extent of individual variations in perception of the realities in which we live is not often enough taken into account in attempts to understand our sciences, ourselves, others, our world, or the cosmos. How difficult it is to do so! Additionally, the study of individual differences has been very different when conducted by behavioral scientists concerned with surface manifestations of mind compared with studies conducted by psychologists concerned with subjectivity.

We can fantasize about but have no way to stretch our minds to comprehend whatever is for us beyond the reach of our senses. The commonly held belief is that others perceive and experience what we ourselves perceive and experience. That is why we often dismiss as nonexistent whatever is described that is beyond our sensorium, or if persuaded by others that it is real, we wish it to be inconsequential. We have no direct way to consider it in our understanding of the world. Thus we reduce a real and useful phenomenon to the equivalent of one more fiction in competition with other fictions. That is how it is with the concept of color to the color blind—a hypothetic construct, although it is a usable actual variable to the color sensing. Affect processes as outlined in this book are hypothetic constructs to the affect blind although actual events to the more sensive among us. Theories constructed by the affect blind can only struggle to explain phenomena by use of those factors of which they are aware. In the long run, however, those limited theories do not compete well with more encompassing theories. Any actual variable is always vastly more useful in transforming theory to surer explanations, transforming applications to far greater usefulness. The length of time needed to accomplish this is unpredictable.

One of the earlier attempts to point out such a problem was Edwin Abbott's description, in his satiric 1884 novel *Flatland*, of dwellers in a two-dimensional universe trying to imagine and finally rejecting the concept of existence of a three-dimensional world. *Flatland* provides a satirical view of the limitations of human capacities for comprehension, and the consequent resistances to even considering the possibility of existence of elements of reality unsensed by them.

The intellectual gyrations employed by the inhabitants of *Flatland* in their attempts to rationalize descriptions of phenomena that did not register with their own sensorium is similar to what occurs in our world. It was echoed frequently in my encounters with eminent, brilliant, knowledgeable, affect-blind theoreticians who had no way to deal seriously with what they regarded as my fanciful ideas. They had no awareness of the ludicrousness of their own fight against acceptance of actual processes observable to others but invisible to them.

The implied story in *Flatland* is that there is much to the universe that we do not or cannot ever know because of our own sensory limitations. In a very real sense we are forever, in that way, all Flatlanders denying that realities beyond our sensorium do exist and insisting false and limited truths are full reality.

SCIENCE BY LEAPS AND STUMBLES

The pattern of rejection encountered by the ideas contained in this book is clear in its fit with the difficulty of progress for revolutions (meaning shifts in fundamental premises) in all fields of study. The pattern of resistance to new ideas always creates a lag of decades before acceptance and use of beneficial knowledge. In no field of study is there a readiness among workers to make a leap to new fundamental premises. This is not a problem solely in psychology, for it occurs in all fields of science, causing similar delays in advances.

In contrast, a minority whose loyalty is more to scientific logic than to the dogma of their school, and who favor the clarification of definitions, concepts, and processes, have considered and benefited from the ideas presented here about fundamentals of psychological health and illness for use in relation to themselves, their patients, or future generations. This includes many who, having limited self-observing capacities, can use the processes as only hypothetical rather than actual. The professionals who have mastered the distinctions that are crucial underpinnings of this new theory, and use whatever they have of capacities for self-observation to follow within themselves and their patients how the explanations fit with actual mental processes, have begun to use the ideas with increasing effect.

They find order in aspects of theory that had been chaotic. They find new and more helpful answers to old questions about phenomena in their field. They find new questions and answer those questions. Adding knowledge of processes not previously included in old dogma has transformed their science, and it is changed further by viewing old problems in different and more comprehensible ways.

Many professionals who, for various reasons, do not keep the whole set of ideas in this complex theory together in their minds, or who do not at least consider a new idea on an "as if" basis to try it out on its own terms, and especially those with limitations in their own self-observing capacities who are therefore unable to comprehend the ideas as actual process continue to find the new theory a puzzle. In the past such persons (especially those with insufficient talent for self-observation) often have defensively attempted to trivialize the set of ideas in various ways. In the previous chapter, I described some of these resistances, because understanding the sticking points that people clutch to defend their past indoctrination and my answers to those doubts may help you better understand the usefulness and validity of this new theory.

Incredulity about innovative descriptions of fundamentals often comes from the belief that psychology is a completed science—that the scientific community fully knows the reality of psychological matters. That belief promotes clinging to a portion of truth circumscribed by existing theory. When events consistently appear that controvert what is considered the realm of the possible within a "completed science," those events are considered "wild" or classed as "error variance," and it is the occurrence of the events, not the "science," that is likely to be doubted. To those whose devotion to comfort from their theory is greater than their devotion to reality, leaving their premises is frightening. To those whose devotion is to fact and logic, acquisition of useful new truths and ever clearer knowledge of reality is more alluring than comfort in orthodoxy.[6]

Scientific explanations of psychological health and illness offered to us over the last century are well off the mark. Because most of those theories contained some validity, an aura from the valid portions brought to the credulous the comfortable illusion of the theories being wholly unassailable ultimate truth. It is, however, in the nature of theory to be an imperfect explanation and always incomplete. Such incompleteness should be expected and regarded as a persisting condition tantalizing us to seek further in all sciences. But the unfortunate illusion of knowledge, as always, has been detrimental, for it has supported the longevity of some unfortunate errors and worse, supported proclaiming those errors to be ultimate fundamental fact. With our new discoveries, it is possible to understand how some of those errors were made. This makes an interesting historical note, but more important, the ability of the new theory to explain and also correct past error further corroborates the validity of the new theory.

Historians of science have noted that revolutionary shifts in fundamental premises and paradigms occur when a field confronts questions that its past theory cannot answer. Kuhn speaks of such a condition as a crisis that brings forth new theory. His description is not as clear as it could be, for he also recognizes that the advanced theories have often been available for a long period, unacknowledged and awaiting recognition. Therefore the better statement is that new theory appears when an individual theorist finds a puzzle (perhaps that is an individual recognition of a crisis) that he can solve through observation, tests, and inductive reasoning leading to new premises, paradigms, and further tests. It is only later, after enough practitioners in the field "take notice" that the problems exist and that a better basis for solutions of problems is available and assimilable, that the changes get adopted. Thus, to the question of whether the revolution occurs when a theorist devises new theory or when the bulk of scientists in the field adopt the new ideas, I suggest that the important revolution in knowledge occurs with the creation of an idea rather than with its adoption.

A revolution in activity occurs with the noticing of ideas that had been hanging around and beginning their use. Thus for many revolutions in science, the ideas have been "hanging around for a long time, waiting for the field to notice them." So it is with many ideas presented in this book that were stated even before the first draft in 1980—some of them had been hanging around for two, twenty, or forty years, awaiting usage that will revolutionize the field and ultimately change the lives of most, if not all, people.

Studies within each school of psychology, as is usual in any science, have centered on how better to apply the existing theories to explain important phenomena, usually with the aim to support, expand, and embellish the theories. It is a long phase in each science and continues only until the elaborations do not answer questions well enough. The naive belief about any theory that "It is all true" portrays religious rather than scientific devotion. That devotion (welcomed by colleagues as a comfort) forms a barrier to healthy, skeptical examination of the theory. Unfortunately, regardless of basis for its existence, the inability of psychologists to leave or even question the underlying elements of their past theory and correct its errors is what creates a premisal circumscription of their efforts to understand phenomena of their field.

That circumscription is a self-constructed dead end. A difficulty related to such premisal circumscription is perhaps too obvious to be a formalized scientific law, *but elaborations of error always yield error.* The error component in extensions of a theory will at least equal and may exceed the proportion of error component at the base of a theory. This is not a new idea. At approximately 350 B.C., Aristotle understood the conceptual generality, but made the point by imputing undeserved precision: "The least initial deviation from the truth is multiplied later a thousandfold." What we all can recognize is that nothing substantial could be secure on a foundation of faulty premise. Comprehensive psychological explanations based in errors may be nearly useless and are often worse than useless because they sponsor damage. Even when they provide clear, internally coherent structure, if those neat structures fail to mesh well with either the internal realities of mental processes or the outer realities of human experience, they exist as false truths.

False truths are encumbrances that are often worse than a dead weight to a theory for they block consideration of more useful alternative ideas. Henry Adams declared, "Nothing in education is so astonishing as the amount of ignorance it accumulates in the form of inert facts." That is why, pitifully for suffering people, some defective theoretical foundations in psychology based on untested or poorly tested conjecture have been built into an accumulated mass of inert fact forming false knowledge. That invalid knowledge fails the test of enabling true cure, scattering effort in useless, digressive activity. Foggy comprehension of health and illness has led to ineffective treatment practices, which is what left space for "wild psychologies" to develop and seem as credible as the more accepted psychologies. The fact that any palliation of symptoms or real but very limited successes such as (not cure, but) "improvement after seven or twenty years" could make practitioners proud of their accomplishments should alert anyone to the puerile inadequacy of the current stage of the science.

A scanning of a random selection of books in psychology will quickly demonstrate how the typical practitioner-theoretician's untested and untestable musings fall short of the mark for scientific approach. Much is asserted with the authority of priests unwilling to concede value to scientific logic.

The seminal phase in advancing knowledge in a field of science is that of devising theory that generates testable hypotheses. The first step in that theory building consists of a pondering about the insufficiency and incompetence of current explanations of phenomena in a field of study and contemplating and even fantasizing possible alternatives. The next intellectual activity is that of contriving fictional explanations that may offer more satisfactory understanding of those phenomena. Although many scientists dislike the term fiction in relation to their work, in truth each theory starts as devised fictional explanations that either acquire corroboration to qualify as "truth" or fail in attempts to do so. They become true or untrue fictions. Those fictions supportable as truths are used by theorists as metatheory. Metatheory, as a general explanation, by its nature is not directly testable because it includes abstract constructs that are explanations describing processes that may or may not exist as actual process. These are corroborated, temporary explanations that are a necessary supportive aspect in every field of science. The metatheory has the function, as a general abstract explanation, of spawning coherent clusters of operations and testable hypotheses that bring results corroborating, modifying, or refuting the metatheory. Thus it is the metatheory that enables scientists to formulate explorations of the phenomena of their field from a network of interconnecting ideas. However, it must be remembered that when metatheory is anointed as "all true" and inspires religious devotion instead of a series of tests the science has become a religion.

In psychology much of the theory relied upon is metatheory and therefore not directly tested. The testable theory is clinical theory. The simplest of tests is that of outcome studies that display the adequacy, although not the processes, of applications. This sort of study gives confidence to technicians about the theory they apply and helps them improve technique. Studies that examine the processes described by the theory are more difficult, but these are what move us from mystery to more satisfactory fundamental understanding with the hope of ever more effective applications. The theory presented on these pages suggests many testable hypotheses that will provide scientific tasks for the future.

What is presented in this book of understanding and explanations of health and illness is a sufficient advance beyond currently accepted knowledge to turn some mysterious, agonizing, refractory, chronic illnesses into minor treatment problems, easy to understand and completely, although not always, easily cured. That can be satisfying as an accomplishment, and it reassures us of the rightness of the path that tells us: Neuroses are not what they have been thought to be in any of the existing mainstream schools of thought. Patients who hear about the new ideas increasingly turn to those of us who cure instead of merely treat, unless they have been indoctrinated to see cures as "too good to be true" and stay with the presumed "safety" of ministrations by mainstream practitioners.

It is simple logic that when we increase the clarity of definitions of terms and concepts, increase differentiation in observation of processes (as part of normal science), or discover processes previously unknown (as part of leaps in science), we will invariably advance the field. Still, that the first reaction of "authorities" in a field will be deprecating disparagement of such clarifications is also just as logical, no matter how restricting of progress that is.

The typical reception that occurs when you tell somebody something about matters they believe they already understand is their automatic translation of whatever you tell them into concepts and terms familiar to them, which they substitute for the new concepts and terms. Having made substitutions that distort the new ideas to identity with old ideas, they may even concur that the theory makes sense (because they have translated it to something they already thought made sense, which therefore changes nothing in their minds and does not alter their understanding), and that although they understand it, they find it adds nothing for them. The applicable aphorism is, "Minds are like parachutes. They only function when open." Thomas Kuhn observed that science is a dynamic process. "[A discovery] does not simply add one more item to the population of the scientist's world. Ultimately it has that effect, but not until the professional community has reevaluated traditional experimental procedures, altered its conception of entities with which it has long been familiar, and in the process, shifted the network of theory through which it deals with the world."[7]

The discoveries about affect and its processes change the view of psychological health and illness, treatment, and what occurs in psychological development. Consequently, human experience will become different; we will advance human potential. In one, or two, or surely within three decades psychologists of that day will scoff at what the mainstream now believes (and does) in the same way we now scoff at bloodletting, high colonics, and other exorcising therapies of the previous century. To our great grandchildren, twentieth-century psychological approaches will seem pathetic.

Fundamentals must be reexamined occasionally to consider how well they fit with new knowledge in and around a field of study, but too often they have been revered because hallowed beliefs are invoked by authority as proved by the "test of time." Amusing, apocryphal stories of tests of time make the point of time being a poor test.[8] But time is not a scientific test. The statement more correctly would be, "Over time there is opportunity for making tests." Unfortunately, in the mental health field, whether psychological, behavioral, psychiatric, or biological, those tests have not been sufficient and too often when attempted have not been well carried out. When we are engrossed in our field of study, we work from premises acceptable to us. It is difficult to keep in mind that our premises are in turn based on other premises so that our comfortable grounding on accepted premises that seem so solid to work from may actually be a morass. Sciences are refreshed by reviewing not only their premises but, from time to time, the premises of those premises. Denigrating or avoiding that reexamination (as if pointless obsessiveness) may be temporarily comforting, but does not make the scientific grounding any more solid.

FUNDAMENTAL CHANGES CHANGE EVERYTHING

This book offers new fundamental concepts of emotion and personality, clearer definitions of terms and concepts, and discussion of processes previously unnoticed or disregarded. The information offered, because it is fundamental, is usable as underpinning for all schools of psychology. Its suggested approaches will improve the understanding of health and illness in all schools of psychology. It has already brought full cure and prevention for some disorders. Suggestions promise other beneficial consequences. As with any changes in fundamental theory, predictions of ultimate effects cannot take into account possible collateral changes that alter effects of the new theory. Among other things, this book will serve as a source of many testable hypotheses. Beyond bringing eradication of some illnesses, the more important effect of the knowledge will be the enhancing of quality of life and the freeing of humanity for greater creativity and productivity, and allowing increasing numbers of people to achieve greater potential. Some of those who read this book carefully will become more effective therapists, some will free themselves of psychological disorders by using the new knowledge as *a frame of reference*[9] for considering what they observe inside themselves. Some others will need consultation with teachers who have mastered the knowledge. The book is offered for those who want to understand psychological theory of health and illness, professionals who want to know how to cure instead of treat patients, educators or parents who want to prevent illnesses in the children they guide, and theoreticians who want to advance their field. There is room for a great deal of research on the varieties of human talents and capacities and how they vary from person to person.

This book contributes discoveries and new explanations of a single basic mental factor—emotion—and delineates its relation to past understanding of psychological health and illness. Comprehension of that single additional factor and its many implications significantly increases our understanding of health and illness and helps the field move from the nineteenth to the twenty-first century. As this new understanding comes into use, it will be especially helpful to those with psychological problems, but also to most other people, for the common misunderstanding of emotion has narrowed the lives of everyone on earth.

NOTES

1. While the efficiency of human mental function depends in part on the construction of ready to apply patterned frames of reference, flexibility and openness are lost when these patterns become crystalline.

2. There is room for a great deal of research on the varieties of human talents and capacities and how they vary from person to person.

3. C. Fort, *The Books of Charles Fort* (New York: Henry Holt & Company, 1941).

4. T. Kuhn, *The Structure of Scientific Revolutions* (Chicago: The University of Chicago Press, 1970).

5. Ibid., 5, 24.

6. There are many reasons why illogicalities and even what may later be recognized as folly retain the allegiance of bright people. In addition to the limitations from incapacity (e.g., affect blindness), there is the effect of having been indoctrinated by statements of authorities (such as respected professors or recognized leaders in a field), as happened with the imposition of "organ neuroses" (as a conceptualizing of psychosomatic disorders) on a gullible group of professionals and much of the public. Finally, the tendencies for consistency that are built into people as a natural part of personality produce reluctance to drop an old idea and adopt a new one.

7. Kuhn, *Structure of Scientific Revolutions*, 7.

8. Anthropologists visiting a Stone Age tribe in its first contact with modern societies and technology soon learned that a group of six elders were the most revered of all in the tribe. It turned out that these six had the awesome responsibility of beating drums and chanting perfectly each morning and evening to ensure the sun would rise and set. That process had been carried out for generations by the most carefully selected of elders. The sun had never failed to rise in the morning and set in the evening. Thus it was clear to all the tribe that the elders had always been effective in their chanting and drumming. They were rightly revered. How often do psychotherapists perform similarly important tasks just as effectively?

9. I prefer this functional expression to Kuhn's static term "network of theory."

Epilogue: The Work Continues

Existing premises are accepted by workers in each field as if divine revelation—not to be disturbed. However, the advances that transform any field come only when an existing fundamental premise is replaced by a more valid premise. Such a change in fundamentals makes at least a little change in everything in the field. That presents the field with an immense task.

Affect and cognition are basic processes of mind. Everything in psychology relates to the nature of affect and cognition. Changing our view of either changes everything in psychology. What I have proposed and explored involves a profound change in view of the *nature* of emotion and its processes and functions to recognize it as *the equal partner in mind* that it is. The result so far is a new theory of development, health, and illness—a way of life.

Without use of an extensive, coherent, fundamental theoretical frame of reference, surface manifestations serve as surrogate to understanding the troubles for which people consult experts.

In the absence of clear understanding of the mental processes involved, two issues that are starkly visible are: (1) Diagnoses used follow current popularity in professional and media exposure, and (2) both the public and professionals understand diagnoses in terms of surface rather than underlying manifestations of conditions. Because the repertoire of surface manifestations is limited, the symptom manifestations described by patients are applied to diagnostic choices made plastic enough to be appropriate for almost any symptom. The professional's choice is often whatever is currently popular among the public or therapists. By working as technicians, therapists do not need to think about theory and deduce illness process, but instead use a check list of surface manifestations. Possibilities for error abound.

Therapists, only a few years ago, found such disorders as "multiple personality" exotic, and phobia and "panic disorder" along with major depression (both painful and dramatic) to be interesting—treatable but incurable. Multiple personality has fallen off the popularity list, while the others continue. All became overused diagnoses because they were much discussed in the media. A few decades ago a very common choice was psychosomatic (organ) neuroses. We know now and should have known then that these are not psychological disorders. Treatment for these is waning, but still continues despite the clarity of the literature. A hundred years ago, hysteric ritualistic dramatizations ("grand hysteria") were quite common. Currently, no patient with any sophistication would appear with such a disorder. However, anorexia, which has similar underlying processes, is very popular currently. All of these are dealt with as great mysteries, but treated with little effect using an array of medications.

New understanding supports a new theory of treatment. It is the theory of treatment that has attracted the first interest in my work. But this book is not really about treatment. However, because the theory also provides the potential for prevention of those very illnesses requiring treatment, there has been interest aroused in prevention of disorders. But this book is not really about prevention. The biography of the ideas offers some conceptual understanding about philosophy of science, and has brought some interest about the implications for science in general. But this book is not really about philosophy of science. The major theme of this book is that of the *uses of emotion* as one of our built-in mental functions. The changes that brings mean that quality of life for everyone can be improved, but only after there is much modification in the field of psychology and other mental health fields.

The move from theory of enduring affect to theory of transient affect has already taken forty years to gain minimal acceptance. The evidence from applications of the theory to guidance for everyday life as well as use in psychotherapy until now tells us that, as the theory and its implications are increasingly absorbed, psychology will leap forward—and then await further changes in fundamentals.

Thus these simple fundamental concepts necessitate the complex and lengthy task of forming a new relation to every aspect of mental function and every aspect of human experience. Many professionals have found this enormous task boggling. However, those who have bothered to struggle to comprehend, step-by-step, soon found they have a very pleasing, useful understanding of themselves and others. It is worth the effort because using the concepts makes chronic, "incurable" troubles such as phobias, conversions, panic, and multiple personality lose their mystery and become curable. The change in experiencing of life is even more important.

The amount of retraining of therapists required to develop the newly possible curative effectiveness is formidable. It is such a tremendous task of retraining that a common reaction of trained therapists is to notice the drastic differences compared with what has been considered "knowledge" and retreat from the new knowledge to leave it for future generations of practitioners, most often defensively castigating the new ideas as "not very important."

When I conducted a workshop on emotion theory for a group of psychoanalysts, there was great resistance from many in the group. At the end of the meeting, one participant privately summed it up to me with refreshing candor. "I don't care whether in twenty years everyone is using your ideas. I am not going to go to all the trouble it will take to learn them. It has taken me too many years to learn what I now use. The next generation can change."

At his official recantation, Galileo is said to have muttered under his breath, "But still it moves!" Emotion continues to move us, too, and Nature to offer us its use. Ultimately we learn from Nature. Our task is the rewriting of psychology.

Relatability

You and I and every other person on earth are unique in personality. Our uniqueness as whole personalities is from singular combinations of qualities we share with some other people. It is that sharing of traits that enables us to group people according to characteristics and ways of being. Because some attributes form natural clusters that we can place in a sequential hierarchy, we can describe portions of personality development in those terms.

When we consider clusters of characteristics that belong together as steps of maturation in a category of personality evolution, it enables us to know more about people within each cluster. These are not miscellaneous accumulations. They are integrated aspects of personality changes that make each step a shift as if to a new world in which axioms of life are unique to that world. Each of these clusters, as a developmental stage, is a psychological matrix that determines patterns of reactions and creates styles of personality.

Fixation at a stage of development below the predominant stage of our society is estimated to occur in approximately 25 percent of our population. Such persons may be stopped at a lesser evolved state due to genetically based limitations, from constitutionally set tendencies or restrictions, or from early experiences. No studies convincingly support any one of these sources over the others as the basis for failure of a personality to evolve. Regardless of how they got to be that way, they are, from the societal point of view, interpersonally subhuman. One way or another, as will be described, they create special problems for society. They do not quite fit in because they do not regard anything interpersonal in the common ways of the culture.

THE VALUE OF TYPOLOGIES

Attempts to define various types of personality by use of categories and clusters of characteristics have been a part of psychology for many decades. The aim is to establish similarities of patterns among people in order to understand them. Various workers have used sequences in different paths to define some aspects of the developmental processes. Some have attempted to do so by declaring each stage as having central elements different from other stages. Others have attempted to follow changes in a single characteristic as it evolves. Some have produced what they can see as a partial range of development rather than the full path of development to maturity. Omissions are consistently a pollarding that cuts off the mature range of the various scales.

Various sequences offered in the past have defects as diagnostic referents for clinical use. Relatability has proved useful clinically and for understanding social structures and how people adapt to those depending upon their degree of maturity. Relatability, as the sequence of steps in perception and understanding of complexity of interpersonal relationships, allows increasing comprehension of self and others. The clearly delineated steps of increasing awareness, with their internal coherence, are graphically described in the accompanying chart and the logic of the steps outlined. The clusters of attributes that fit within a stage appear to be so coherent that if one of the attributes is present we can be confident the remainder of the attributes of the stage are also present.[1]

The Concept of Relatability

I chose the term Relatability[2] to describe a construct defining distinct developmental stages of transformation in qualities for interpersonal relationships. The portion of personality development defined in this way gives precision to what psychoanalysts have loosely spoken of as object-relations differentiation.[3] Perceptual capacity is the central determinant of a potential for types of relationships.[4] Relatability describes evolving steps in capacity for comprehension and perception of complexity in interpersonal relations. The sequence of the stages is such that each stage is a necessary precursor of the next, and the move from each to the next occurs as a complex epigenetic step simultaneously involving several tightly related aspects of personality. Each step generates a new orientation toward people for each configuration not only enables, but compels its own kind of view of self and other. The highest level of development an individual displays designates that person's marker level. An individual may operate at that level most of the time, but more likely will ordinarily function at an operating level somewhat lower (never higher) than optimal and retain the possibility of descending to the lowest level under some circumstances.[5]

Among the advantages Relatability has as a theoretical and clinical tool is the clarity of simple, distinct, sequential steps in perception of interpersonal complexity. The steps in perception of complexity are object-relations differentiation seen as internal process. Steps in changes in behavior are surface manifestations and are consequences of those internal processes.[6] Behavior yields descriptions and possibly predictions of future behavior, but not understanding. Central processes give explanations needed for understanding people. The psychological arena in which we work is the inner life—subjectivity. A skeletal outline of object-relations steps in that inner life is graphically depicted as a structure in the following pages, and the logic of the changes is described. These serve as structural framework for each of several personality types. The clusters of attributes that fit within each stage belong together with such cohesiveness that if we find one attribute of a stage present, we can be confident all the remainder of the attributes of that stage are also present.

Another of the significant advantages of Relatability over competing approaches to differentiation is that the internal coherence of the characteristics of each stage is such that one only needs to find any kind of manifestation of any single characteristic of a stage to be assured that the other components of that stage are also present. Additionally, Relatability is not encumbered with an overambitious attempt to describe multifarious aspects of ego development. Instead it focuses narrowly on interpersonal matters. Therefore, it frees one of the necessity of using any particular test devices, because, for knowledgeable clinicians, any expressive material is appropriate basis for deductive reasoning.

The term Relatability denotes a hierarchy of six distinct levels of development in object-relations differentiation that determines a repertoire of subjective qualities of interpersonal capacity. The advances occur as epigenetis steps.[7] Thus it is not an accretion of miscellaneous items of personality attributes that accrue randomly or haphazardly, but a tightly related set of characteristics. Although the change is subjective for each person, it is as a step into a new world with new axioms about human nature and new paradigms. In this evolving sequence, a person's view of relationships and qualities of other persons shifts with the arrival of capacity for new affects and affective attitudes beyond those from past stages, and brings a new repertoire of relationship qualities at each step of the sequence.

The differences in the axioms of each stage make expectations and views of people at one stage jarring to those at another. Sometimes people are contemptuous, sometimes pitying, sometimes irritated from the disappointments about the "ways" of others. Some aspects of the experiencing of a situation are different enough from stage to stage that there is a natural attraction and compatability between those people at each stage. They see each other as being more realistically comprehending of the world than those at other stages. This makes for a kind of kinship of people at each level of development and an estrangement from those at another stage, who are viewed as "not with it."

The Process of Relatability in Ego Development

Ego development, as a generality, consists of a broad path of several aspects of personality function, such as qualities, abilities, skills, understanding, mechanisms, competencies, integrations of experiences, and personality pattern tendencies that serve adaptive aims. The specific threads within that large group of attributes have individual developments correlated simply because they are all aspects of development. Yet because they are independent threads they are correlated only loosely. Relatability is one such thread within ego development. It is one that serves as a pivotal aspect of an individual's life for his ways of fitting into a society. Indeed, the type of society and social institutions that people form seem to depend crucially on the predominant level of Relatability of its members. Social structures, types of law, religion, and group interrelationships are consequences of the predominant level of Relatability and, once in place, attract other people of that level. Determining who is to be in or out of the societies follows according to the predominant level, which thus defines humanness for a particular society.

At Delta level, another person is not recognized as a person and does not exist as a person in the eye of the beholder. Instead there is a concern with rules, man-made laws, aims, coveting, self-protection, etc., rather than person. At Gamma level, there is a concern for other persons' lives as if oneself. It is the attitude, "We are all brothers and sisters." At Beta level, there is a concern for another person as that person. Thus the social potential is greatly different from level to level. (The societies that are constructed by people at different levels are quite different. The societies may be business, club, athletic, marriage, etc.) Marriages across Relatability levels have a hard time because the two persons, in effect, are in different interpersonal worlds. Marriages (and other partnerships) work out better, but not infallibly, when the participants are of the same Relatability level. The importance of similarity in Relatability level is greater for marriage than is similarity in culture, race, education, personality, talents, or personal interests.

The shift to a next stage occurs with simultaneous transformation in several aspects of personality. Because of the complexity, we do not yet have a clear understanding of the key cause of the transformation. Because the transformations are singularities, happening only once in each person's life, it is improbable that we will witness the change as it occurs in others.[8] Because much of what goes on in each shift is outside of awareness, we are more likely to notice the manifestations resulting from the change in others, rather than the change itself. The cognitive element in the leap is that of adding perception of another step in complexity of relationships among people. It is a leap in psychic organization not easily sensed or noticed at the time by other persons. Of the various elements in a cluster of personality attributes, it is the appearance of manifestations of a new affective capacity at the move to a new stage of Relatability that may be observed most readily by oneself or others.

SIX STAGES OF RELATABILITY

The stages range from the neonate's initial limited awareness to the most mature awareness of complex interactions. A rough description of the categories with the clear cut distinctions of perceptions are diagramed in the graphic representation (see Figure 1) to follow along with the words in this section and can be used as a guide to the content of each cluster. It is as follows:

First Stage: ζ Zeta

This is the commonly imputed level of functioning of neonates. Typically it is passed through within the first few weeks of life. Surely the first responsive smiles at four to six weeks signal its passage. The importance of the stage is as a beginning. Adults rarely operate at this level other than during illness, emotion storm, and drug use. It is a state in which self/nonself are unbounded. Thus there are not meaningful relationships with others or even with self. Because existence and cognizance of self is only at the most rudimentary level, neither intra- nor interpersonal relation is conceptually possible.

Second Stage: ε Epsilon

This stage brings a hazy awareness of self/nonself, without awareness of meanings of the interpersonal actions that occur or a sense of meaning of the other's existence. The axiom is, "Stick with the crowd." It fits with the typical adolescent conformity to rebellious peer standardization of costume, music, and other fads, but without either the rebelliousness or sense of kinship. There is perception of one's own needs and gratifications, but not of the participation of others in the process of gratification, for these are seen as entirely within the self rather than from, to, with, or between persons. Part-object relations connote the beginning of object relations, but that new perception of others, because it is limited to part-object relations, advances people from the *obliviousness* of others at the previous stage to an *indifferent insensitivity* to perceived others. Their distinctions between animate and inanimate objects, or between humans and other living creatures, continue

Figure 1
Object Relations Differentation in Relatability

Z – Zeta

ε – Epsilon

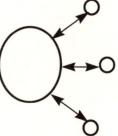

δ – Delta

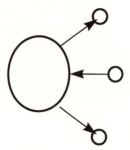

Γ – Gamma

β – Beta

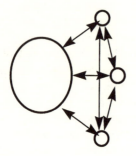

α – Alpha

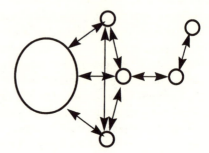

to be murky. Societal compliance is sometimes in a sheep-like following of leaders or in avoidance of that by the solitary existence they live even when in groups. Neither cruelty nor tenderness is personal or particularly pleasurable; it is merely interesting. At this level people tend to be blind, incogitant followers, like the unperceiving followers of authoritarian leadership (Nazis, Communists, and their counterparts over the ages, but even with those blindly following political parties). They are the mainstay of the marchers, the picketers, the rallies to push for political correctness or "causes." To them, all other individuals, because different, are considered not quite as human as themselves. They live among, but not with, others. Some people at this level participate in group activities and movements, but without the qualms that finer moral distinctions bring to the more evolved participating in those same activities. Examples are antiabortionists who kill and animal rights activists who destroy laboratories with animals inside or who harm humans in "defense" of animals or trees.

Third Stage: δ Delta

This stage brings a beginning recognition of one-way transactions, in which one person can affect another. It is the start of a process of recognition of others as somewhat meaningful. Recognition that one person can affect another can occur only if there is some separation between them. The concern at this stage is to build a firmly held, clearly delineated boundary dividing self and other. Because the primitive boundary is a fragile, uncertain separation of self and other, it brings concern about possible encroachments and infringements and makes the Delta level people particularly self-protective. An uneasiness about safety and vulnerability makes people at this level always ready to "man the ramparts" and instantly ready to fight to be in control. It makes them bossy, directly or subtly, with an undertone of competition. The view of increased interpersonal possibility being—"I can have an effect upon others and they can have an effect upon me"— makes for the axiomatic master/slave relationship (or law of the jungle), and yields distrust, untrustworthiness, suspiciousness, insincerity, pity, competitiveness, wariness, and righteousness that occur as natural byproducts. Interpersonal kindliness takes the form of pity (containing hostile superior scorn) and establishes transactions between people rather than interactions. There is the tendency to love by looping ego boundaries around the other, a kind of merging into one, and then treating the merged other as one would treat oneself, or alternatively treating others as objects separate from self but as owned.

There is a further tendency, whenever offended, to eject the other from the ego boundaries and instantly make the once loved now an enemy. There is a common use of projection as an ego mechanism that goes with the assurance that others must feel what I feel, believe what I believe, know what I know. Or they may have assurance that the other is an opponent.

That makes them tend to leap to conclusions and believe that they know what another is thinking and impute their own ideas to the other. This makes them able to consider themselves in complete accord with the other in a kind of merging, or argue with the other against whatever they have imputed to that other. When confronted with that, most of us are startled that we seem to be considered in close alliance with the Delta level person or suddenly in the midst of an argument that we did not see coming. Commonly the Delta level concern with ego boundary process is paired with limited spans of horizons for such individuals. For them the close-in reality to which they are bound may obscure a hazily understood greater reality. They are thus more readily susceptible to mastery by others. The readiness to relate by merging (to make a "we" a solidarity with groups instead of among a group as occurs with the Epsilon groupies) makes persons at this level of development more ready to affiliate to narrowly focused life as groupies, cult members, or to enter a folie-a-deux.

Somehow with development beyond Delta, the awareness of a broader reality decreases susceptibility to presumptuousness by others. Compliance and conformity at this stage stem from rules and enforcement based on whatever rules have been laid down. That makes for beginnings of cognizance of others sufficient for civilizations to form. However, emphasis is on conformity to the rules rather than to the principle. They view codified law as justice. They view compliance with authority primarily without consideration of the reasons or principles generating the laws unless they separate merged boundaries and become rebellious. Transient (virtual) identifications are based on merging of boundaries with other persons and sometimes with organizations. Sensitivity to another's plight takes the form of pity. This is the stage of enforcers, litigation lawyers, and bill collectors whose morality is derived from rules. Their assumption is everyone is out for himself—the law of the jungle. Marriages, partnerships, and other interactions at this level, whether with others at the same or different level, are more stormy than at other levels. These are the people who live with others in a negotiating style of relating. The weaker boundaries compel ego activities in terms of the fragility of the boundaries and to protect those boundaries—looping boundaries around another and loving that person as oneself, perceived by them as merged. But ejecting them when offended thereby instantly making them the enemy is often a serious problem in relating. In all these manifestations, loyalty and commitment are subordinate to self-interest. They are unreliable and as inconstant (perfidious) as are the boundaries. Social structure is authoritarian, for one can be either submissive/compliant or master/dominant.

Fourth Stage: γ Gamma

This is the operating level of the preponderance of our population. Its axioms therefore define humanness in our culture. Societal structures and institutions derive from the axioms of this level. The laws we have in current societies are designed to require what most people at this level would do most of the time anyway, even without laws. Conformity is based on awareness of others as others, and a concern for them as persons like oneself. People at earlier levels are constrained to fit in with this level of development. Because this level is the most common operating level, attributes of any other level are considered more primitive, even if they are from more advanced levels. It is the beginning of awareness of interpersonal mutuality and comprehension of meaning of two-way interactions. Trust and trustworthiness, sympathy, and cooperativeness appear, supplanting wariness, pity, and forced compliance, respectively. Consideration for another takes the form of "what I might think or feel if I were in that other person's situation," as an advance over callous indifference. Sympathy for another supplants pity as the basis of interpersonal concern. Gamma level people internally generate justice and fairness because they see equality with others. Love is based on the person as equal, separate, and worthy of consideration as equal. Compliance occurs by virtue of consideration and sympathy. There is a consistent expectation of trustworthiness in self and others. The life axiom is the Golden Rule, putting oneself in another's position. "Bread upon the waters" is cast with expectation of eventual return, in all fairness. "I will do my part. You do yours." Thus there is a kind of rigidity to the niceness, a limitation to the generosity. I will do my share, but demand that you do equally.

Fifth Stage: ß Beta

The development of Beta level is a shift to shared multiple interactions. Empathy supplants sympathy as a means of awareness of the subjectivity of others. There is a move from capacity for cooperation (as recognition of doing one's fair share) to capacity for collaboration (as recognition of doing all one can in each situation). Love for others now occurs in terms of those others rather than in terms of self. Misidentifications and partial identifications (this is different from part-object relations) allow for the formation of an intra-psychic separation from the object as person to object as representation. By integrating the various partial identifications that have accumulated with attributes from other sources, the Beta personality constructs a unique personality. Empathy has the meaning of temporarily adopting the other's views, ideas, interests, etc., by experiencing what another feels, in his actual position, instead of the Gamma level "what I believe I would feel if I were in that position."

The Beta level life axiom is "live and let live," but from the Gamma viewpoint, Beta level tendencies are not understood, and are indistinguishable from Delta level. Thus Gamma level efforts are to constrain both Delta and Beta tendencies as if identical roots to the similar manifestations.

Sixth Stage: α Alpha

Arrival at comprehension of meaning of shared and unshared indirect multiple interactions enables one to participate psychically with those with whom one has no direct contact. There can be meaningful personal under-standing of those. With this advance in perspective on relationships exopathy becomes possible. The assembly of aspects of various identifica-tions of the past combined with other elements of personality form a unique assemblage of characteristics. Individuation with freedom from the energy demands of the process of forming individuality of personality at Delta, and of forming identity at Beta, energy is available for relating. This shows in the capacity for meeting the "other" unobscured by the screen between self and other. Where Beta warmth may go overly far in taking on the other's problems to solve self problems, at the Alpha level there is a modulation from continuing awareness of the changing feeling reactions of the other. Constructiveness is a principle at Alpha level, rather than compensatory as at earlier levels. This may be an idealized, rarely attained level for continu-ing operation of personality, but is one that some people attain for at least some periods of time. It may be a distant future of humanity.

RELATABILITY AND AFFECT

These developmental levels are steps of acquisition of new affects. It is this capacity for a greater repertoire of specific emotion that enables types of relating to others, but also of importance, relation to self.

NOTES

1. Freud's systematization of psychosexual levels, posited that each child se-quentially moves through a focus on oral, anal, and then phallic-genital stages of development and that, according to the experience during each phase, there are consequent derivatives as characteristics found in the adult personality. It ap-peared reasonable to consider it as a basis for viewing certain personality charac-teristics. Freud's complex fiction has been used as a metatheory since its invention. Tests of its validity have not been well designed because two aspects of the theory have been confounded. While the internal coherence of the clusters of attributes within each declared psychosexual stage appears very strong, and in that sense, valid, it is the connection of these to the development process that failed to be confirmed. The relation of the typology of psychosexual level to developmental stages is questionable—despite face validity. The more likely ultimate finding is that the tightly bound clusters of characteristics are biologic—built-in genetically as a part of given temperament. Some neuroscience studies appear corroborative of this.

2. K. S. Isaacs, "Relatability: A Proposed Construct and an Approach to Its Validation" (unpublished doctoral dissertation, The University of Chicago, 1956).

3. In psychoanalysis, the general term "object relations differentiation" used to describe such distinctions, had been so loosely defined that it has not proved

clinically useful. Various workers have made attempts to demonstrate increased differentiation, but these turn out to be awkard attempts that do not fit with other studies because the definitions either lack precision or are different from those of other workers.

4. J. Loevinger (*Ego Development* [San Francisco: Jossey-Bass, 1976]) used the descriptions by Sullivan, Grant, and Grant, who had formulated their behavioral developmental sequence from test results in work with delinquents at the same time (1950) as I was formulating Relatability from my recognition of the mental/psychological changes that would fit with the clear-cut steps in evolving perception of complexity of interpersonal relations. Sullivan, Grant, and Grant (and Loevinger following them) restricted themselves to the behavioral manifestations. In doing so, they missed the value of subjectivity and affectivity, which are so informative in Relatability. But they, too, found six distinct steps, with most of the characteristics in each step similar to a parallel stage in Relatability. It is a kind of corroboration of the concept of development through a series of stages, and most important, a beginning of validation of the sequence and content of the stages developed in my own work and in the work of Sullivan, Grant, and Grant. Loevinger's statistical approach brought corroboration of truth of the clustering of the attributes and the sequence of the stages of development. Her use of signs in incomplete sentence tests misses the value of the demonstrations (samples) of mental content I used. The careful scientific observations failed to include the central elements. That limited her comprehension of the inner processes at the stages. It also interfered with her perceiving that object relations differentiation is only a part of ego development, not the whole of it, and from understanding the sequence as an integrated process as a whole. That is why it did not contribute explanations of why the elements in each cluster belong together or why they can only follow in the order they do. It is the contribution of Relatability theory that it includes issues of affects and the basis for understanding the organization of stages of development that makes the sequence and the cohesion of elements at each stage useful in understanding people. Behavioral approaches must necessarily omit such understanding.

5. This is not different in concept from what happens in the operating level of intelligence. We each have an optimal level to which we can stretch, but generally we do not use that full capacity for most of the activities throughout our days. Thus the actual use of our abilities fluctuates within a range, falling well below optimal much of the time. Just as we do in relation to intelligence, we can consider the person's marker level to be his best score on our measuring device.

6. Behaviorists consider internal (subjective) processes to be unverifiable, therefore of secondary importance and unworthy of serious study. Others of us as subjectivists consider those processes central as the determining basis that engenders the behavioral manifestations and therefore most worthy of study. Behaviorists think "observable phenomena" and subjectivists think "inner process." This appears to be a difference between concentrating on factors viewed as relevant and significant no matter how difficult they are to observe and quantify versus concentrating on those factors amenable to ease of observation and measurement that are hoped to be established as somehow relevant and important.

7. Epigenesis is the key to shifts that come about through concept learning and is very different from shifts that come about through increases in acquisitions by

rote learning. Rote learning occurs with bits of knowledge acquired from outside being added piece by piece to a mass of knowledge. It is a process of adding to the volume of knowledge of an individual. Construct learning differs in that it does not add a small piece of knowledge but instead is an internally created abstract conceptualization or interpretation of meaning of some group of rote "pieces" of information. It is a form of learning that produces a principle for understanding clusters of a person's knowledge. It is a bit of wisdom.

8. In a rare exception I once witnessed such a change as it occurred in a person. A man whom I had seen for a few years who had been alcoholic, jack-roller, and burglar who was solidly ensconced in the attributes of the Delta level responded to my comment that he did not trust people. His answer was a surprise to me. He said,"I don't trust anyone, except you, sometimes, a little bit." He had moved from Delta to Gamma level as he spoke. It was his first consideration of trusting as a possibility. Over the next several weeks he evidenced the various manifestations of Gamma level function in several ways. He stopped his criminal activity, joined a Gamma level fraternal organization devoted to good works, found employment, and in many ways found he could be cooperative with others, and demonstrated that he was sympathic and considerate. All that was new to him. In a few others I have noticed changes, but never at the moment of change.

Glossary of Emotion Terms

The following material is offered as a tentative rather than definitive listing that may be useful in helping to sort out aspects of mental processes. It is intended to indicate distinctions among varieties of emotion experience and processes. To understand our emotions, we need to have a careful use of taxonomy. That is necessary to enable us to think, communicate, and talk clearly about the subject. One reason the processes of emotions have been a puzzle is because past theorists have mixed emotion, external condition, idea, opinion, belief, attitude, and pseudo emotions with a fusion of physiological experience, mental experience, and behavior. The potpourri also includes various subjectivities, situations, combinations, and conditions. Because there are many differences among these, attempts to find regularity among them has been frustrated. Each of the entities that has been carelessly lumped together with emotion, as if all were essential emotions, has importance as a mental entity in its own ways, but not as emotion. These do not have the same processes as emotions nor serve us in the same way. They also are different from each other. When these entities are considered separately, rather than carelessly lumped together, we find an emerging comprehension of the usefulness of each.

AFFECT: A category that includes all mental and physical feelings. Psychologists have used the term as a wastebasket category to include anything that has a feeling component regardless of whether it is a simple or complex entity. Thus such distinct elements as resentment, lust, hunger, and placidity and the physical sensations of hunger, thirst, lust, fatigue, satiety, etc., have been classified in this group. Wrongly included also have been depression, mania, phobia, and other complex mental states.

APPETITES: A physical feeling category that includes driving motivations such as hunger, thirst, lust, fatigue, satiation, chill, hot, etc.

EMOTIONS: A mental feeling category that includes specific evaluations of internal and external conditions offered to us in the form of specific feeling experiences. Offered to us in attributes of quality and intensity, the information tells us of meaning and significance of sensed data.

EXIGENT (POWERFULLY URGING) EMOTIONS

ANGER: The feeling experience for perception of a situation as extremely unacceptable, disturbing, or possibly damaging to oneself. It urges us to harm or destroy in service of self-protection.

FEAR: The feeling experience for perception of danger or risk. The feeling urges us to flee to protection and safety, or submit.

SHAME: The feeling experience for perception of self as failing one's own and others' standards. It urges us to hide or disappear from the situation.

SURPRISE: The feeling experience for perception of unexpected events. It is a mental disequilibrium that urges us to recover a previous state or to put things in order again.

IMPASSIONED EMOTION

ENVY: The feeling experience that goes with a desire *to have something equivalent to what another person has*. That may be a possession, situation, relationship, esteem, etc., like those of the other. It is an emulation of the other.

FALSE PRIDE: The feeling experience that goes with the avoidance of shame.

GLOATING: The feeling experience that goes with hostile pleasure in the perception of surpassing another in a competitive comparison that places self one up and the other one down. It may be through succeeding in some task or without direct competition a pleasurable sense that another has descended to a less favorable situation.

GUILT: The feeling that goes with a sense of having disrupted an interpersonal or object relationship, including those with self and internalized objects. Includes an urge to make amends.

JEALOUSY: The feeling experience that goes with a desire *to have what another person has*—whether it is their possession, situation, relationship, esteem, etc. It is a desire to take the specific away from another.

JOY: The feeling experience to an extremely favorable, wished for event—an excited pleasure about the occurrence of something satisfying.

LONELINESS: The feeling experience that goes with an urgent requirement for companionship.

PRIDE: The feeling experience that goes with recognition that one has accomplished (or has obtained or possesses) something of considerable value.

SUSPICION: The feeling experience that goes with a belief that some person or persons are likely to do something untoward.

MILDLY URGING EMOTIONS

CONTENTMENT: The feeling experience of having reasonable desires supplied.

CURIOSITY: The feeling experience of desire to know or understand some matter.

SATIATION: The feeling experience that one has received or gained that which was wanted.

SATISFACTION: The feeling experience that goes with the sense of sufficiency; a relaxation of drive.

GENERAL REACTIONS TO SPECIFIC EMOTIONS

DISTRAUGHT: Distressed to the point of emotional and intellectual disarray.

DISTURBED: A reaction to feeling experience that is uncomfortable and unsettling.

HAPPY/UNHAPPY: A summative judgment of positives and negatives about the array of specific feeling experiences.

UPSET: A negative reaction to some particular emotions.

PARA EMOTIONS

BEWILDERED

CONFUSED

LOST

PSEUDO EMOTIONS

For each of the following judgments, situations, conditions, and beliefs, people wrongly say, "I feel . . . "

Abandoned/Deserted

Accepted/Rejected

Alone

Bewildered

Bright/Stupid

Crowded

Depressed

Devastated/Decimated

Distracted

Fat

Hurt

Late/Early

Left out

Literate

Lost

Loved

Nice

Okay
Pretty/Ugly
Punished
Put down
Scorned
Taunted/Mocked
Unappreciated
Welcomed

APPETITES

Hunger
Lust
Thirst

Bibliography

Alexander, Franz. *The Medical Value of Psychoanalysis*. 1936. New York: International Universities Press, 1984.

Alexander, J., and K. S. Isaacs. "The Function of Affect." *British Journal of Medical Psychology* 37 (1964): 231–37.

Arnold, M. *Emotion and Personality*. Vol. 1. New York: Columbia University Press, 1960.

Basch, M. "Toward a Theory that Encompasses Depression: A Revision of Existing Causal Hypotheses in Psychoanalysis." In *Depression and Human Existence*, edited by E. J. Anthony and T. Benedek, 485–534. Boston: Little Brown, 1975.

Benedek, T. "Adaptation to Reality in Early Infancy." *Psychoanalytic Quarterly* 7 (1938).

Brenner, C. "Depression, Anxiety and Affect Theory." *International Journal of Psychoanalysis* 55:1 (1974): 25–36.

_____ . "A Psychoanalytic Theory of Affects." In *Emotion, Theory, Research, and Experience*. Vol. 1, *Theories of Emotion*, edited by R. Plutchik and H. Kellerman, 345–48. New York: Academic Press, 1980.

Darwin, C. R. *The Expression of Emotion in Man and Animals*. 1872. Chicago: University of Chicago Press, 1965.

Dunbar, F. *Psychosomatic Diagnosis*. New York: Hoeber, 1944.

_____ . *Mind and Body: Psychosomatic Medicine*. New York: Random House, 1947.

Federn, P. *Ego Psychology and the Psychoses*. New York: Basic Books, 1952.

Fenichel, Otto. *The Psychoanalytic Theory of Neurosis*. New York: Norton, 1945.

Finney, B. C. "Say It Again: An Active Therapy Technique." In *The Handbook of Gestalt Therapy*, edited by Chris Hatcher and Philip Himelstein. New York: Jason Aronson, Inc., 1976.

Fort, C. *The Books of Charles Fort*. New York: Henry Holt & Company, 1941.

Freud, A. *The Ego and its Mechanisms of Defense*. Translated by Cecil Baines. 1936. New York: International Universities Press, 1946.

Freud, S. *The Standard Edition of The Complete Psychological Works of Sigmund Freud*. Vol. 2, *Studies on Hysteria by Joseph Breuer and Sigmund Freud*. Translated by J. Strachey. London: The Hogarth Press Limited, 1955.

————. *The Standard Edition of The Complete Psychological Works of Sigmund Freud*. Vol. 6, *The Psychopathology of Everyday Life*. Translated by J. Strachey. 1901. London: The Hogarth Press, 1955.

————. *The Standard Edition of The Complete Psychological Works of Sigmund Freud*. Vol. 7, *Three Essays on Sexuality*. Translated by J. Strachey. London: The Hogarth Press Limited, 1955.

Garrison, H. *An Introduction to the History of Medicine*. 4th ed. Philadelphia and London: W. B. Saunders & Co., 1929.

Haggard, E., and K. S. Isaacs. "Micromomentary Facial Expressions as Mechanisms in Psychotherapy." In *Methods of Research in Psychotherapy*, edited by L. A. Gottschalk and A. H. Auerbach, 154–65. New York: Meredith Publishing Co., 1966.

Harsanyi, Z., and R. Hutton. *Genetic Prophecy: Beyond the Double Helix*. New York: Rawson & Wade, Inc., 1981.

Hume, David. *A Treatise of Human Nature*. 1739. Oxford: Oxford University Press, 1888.

Isaacs. K. S. Relatability: A Proposed Construct and Approach to Its Validation." Unpublished doctoral dissertation, The University of Chicago, 1956.

————. "Crisis Intervention and Affect Theory." Paper presented at the midwinter meeting of the American Psychological Association, Division 29, San Antonio, Texas, February 1981.

————. "Feeling Bad and Feeling Badly." *Psyhchoanalytic Psychology* 1 (1984): 43–60.

————. "Affect and the Fundamental Nature of Neurosis: Logic and Reality." *Psychoanalytic Psychology* 7:2 (1990): 270.

Izard, C. *Human Emotions*. New York: Plenum Press, 1977.

Janov, A. *The Primal Scream*. New York: Putnam's Sons, 1970.

Kissen, M. *Affect, Object, and Character Structure*. Madison, Conn.: International Universities Press, 1995.

Klein, M. *Envy and Gratitude: A Study of Unconscious Sources*. London: Tavistock Publications Limited, 1957.

Kohut, H. *The Analysis of the Self*. New York: International Universities Press, 1971.

Krystal, H. "The Genetic Development of Affect and Affect Regression." *The Annual of Psychoanalysis* 2 (1974): 98–126.

————. "The Activating Aspect of Emotions." *Psychoanalysis & Contemporary Thought* 5 (1982): 605–42.

Kuhn, T. *The Structure of Scientific Revolutions*. 1962. Chicago: The University of Chicago Press, 1970.

Lee, H. D. "On Theoretic Interest in the Affects." Unpublished.

Lewis, M., and J. Haviland, eds. *The Handbook of Emotions*. New York: Guilford Press, 1993.

Loevinger, J. *Ego Development*. San Francisco: Jossey-Bass, 1976.

Marks, I. M. *Fears, Phobias, Rituals: Pain, Anxiety, and Their Disorders*. New York: Oxford University Press, 1987.

Mathews, A. W., M. G. Gelder, and D. W. Johnston. *Agoraphobia: Nature and Treatment*. New York: Guilford Press, 1981.

Maxmen, J. S. *Psychotropic Drugs: Fast Facts*. New York: W. W. Norton & Co., 1991.

Mill, John Stuart. *A System of Logic, Ratiocinative and Inductive: Being a Connected View of the Principles of Evidence and the Methods of Scientific Investigation*. 8th ed. 1843. London: Longmans, Green, Raeder, and Dyer, 1872.

Peck, M. Scott. *The Road Less Traveled*. New York: Simon & Schuster, 1978.

Piaget, Jean. *The Moral Judgement of the Child*. Glencoe, Ill.: The Free Press, 1948.

Sandler, J., with A. Freud. *The Analysis of Defense: The Ego and the Mechanisms of Defense Revisited*. New York: International Universities Press, 1985.

Shevrin, H. "Semblances of Feeling: The Imagery of Affect in Empathy, Dreams, and Unconscious Processes." In *The Human Mind Revisited*, edited by Sydney Smith, 263–94. New York: International Universities Press, 1978.

Smith, Adam. *Theory of the Moral Sentiments*. 1759. Oxford: Oxford University Press, 1976.

Socarides, C. W. *The World of Emotion: Clinical Studies of Affects and Their Expression*. New York: International Universities Press, 1977.

Solomon, Robert C. "The Philosophy of Emotions." In *The Handbook of Emotions*, edited by M. Lewis and J. Haviland. New York: Guilford Press, 1993.

Strongman, K. T. *The Psychology of Emotion*. 2d ed. Chichester, Eng.: John Wiley and Sons, 1978.

Tomkins, S. S. *Affect, Imagery, Consciousness*. Vol. 1, *The Positive Affects*. New York: Springer, 1962.

———. *Affect, Imagery, Consciousness*. Vol. 2, *The Negative Affects*. New York: Springer, 1963.

———. *Affect, Imagery, Consciousness*. Vol. 3, *The Negative Affects: Anger and Fear*. New York: Springer, 1991.

Weiss, E. *The Structure and Dynamics of the Human Mind*. New York: Grune and Stratton, 1960.

Wurmser, L. "Neurotic Depersonalization." In *Clinical Psychopathology*, edited by G. Balis, 309–25. Boston: Butterworth, 1978.

Suggested Readings

Because *Uses of Emotion* presents an innovative theory, there are few writings that directly offer a foundation for understanding its conceptual framework. The following writings were influential to this author by stimulating thought or suggesting ways of critiquing new or old ideas. In that aim it may be worthwhile to review literature about conscious and unconscious mental processes, the requirements of scientific logic when considering hypotheses, the meaning and use of emotion, developmental process in personality, and separation of psychological and genetic (physiological) elements.

The study of logic and philosophy of science has been an omission in most schools of psychology, social work, medicine, counseling psychology, and other such training centers. The skimpiness of offerings in many of the schools that include these studies has ill prepared mental health workers for thinking scientifically in their field. The typical courses in research design and those in statistics, because of narrow focus and time pressure, gloss over issues crucial for building a science, or even critiquing theories well enough to know which offerings are worthy of adoption.

The following list is a sampling of writings the author found meaningful over the years. (Full publishing information can be found in the Bibliography.) There are probably many books on the same subjects that are equivalent and could be substituted for some of these.

Alexander, J., and K. S. Isaacs. "The Function of Affect." This was one of our early tries at describing emotions as useful.

Benedek, Therese. "Adaptation to Reality in Early Infancy." An essay on the interworking of functions of relating to an "internalized object" or "other" as person.

Federn, Paul. *Ego Psychology and the Psychoses*. These are some of the best writings describing issues of varieties of experiencing and the meaning and usefulness of these.

Freud, S. *The Psychopathology of Everyday Life*. Vol. 6 in *The Standard Edition of The Complete Psychological Works of Sigmund Freud*. This is the easiest to understand of Freud's descriptions of the dynamic unconscious. Freud's discovery of the organization and meaningfulness of unconscious processes is likely to be a permanent part of human knowledge. This is where anyone who has not read anything by Freud could best start. Once one internalizes the general conception of subjective processes, one is unlikely to be satisfied with peripheral or tangential approaches to the human mind.

Harsanyi, Z., and R. Hutton. *Genetic Prophecy: Beyond the Double Helix*. This is an easy to read discussion of implications of genetic versus psychological basis of health and illness.

Hume, David. *A Treatise of Human Nature*. This is a clear argument for the significance of emotion in human life. Far ahead of its time, it fell on deaf ears.

Klein, Melanie. *Envy and Gratitude*. One of the first writings that distinguished interrelation of different emotions with consideration of their unconscious sources.

Kuhn, T. *The Structure of Scientific Revolutions*. An excellent reading for gaining a perspective of how the endeavor of science works.

Mill, John Stuart. *A System of Logic, Ratiocinative and Inductive*. Any readings in *A System of Logic* will be worth the effort. This gives a glimpse of one of the greatest minds at work describing how one can examine how close to reality any particular truth might be.

Piaget, Jean. *The Moral Judgement of the Child*. Piaget can be read to comprehend the architecture of his presentation of developmental process of personality. While details of content in his outline may not endure, the concept of developmental sequence is of even greater importance than the content he describes. It also presents the concept of awareness of internal process that is so useful in understanding health and illness.

Smith, Adam. *Theory of the Moral Sentiments*. This is an excellent try by a great mind struggling to present a new truth he perceived, in a world not yet ready for it, and handicapped in an attempt to support it without the later information brought by additional scientific knowledge.

Solomon, Robert C. "The Philosophy of Emotions." This is the most up-to-date description of the current quandary in thinking out problems about emotion. It is clearly written and easy to read.

Weiss, Edoardo. *The Structure and Dynamics of the Human Mind*. A clear description of the differences between reality testing and reality sensing.

Index

About the Author

KENNETH S. ISAACS was the first chief psychologist of the State of Illinois outpatient clinic system—Mental Health Centers. Later he was a faculty member at the University of Illinois Medical School. Dr. Isaacs is known in the profession as one of the founders and officers of several psychoanalytic psychology organizations. Currently he is chairman of the American Board of Psychoanalysis in Psychology and a member of the board of trustees of the American Board of Professional Psychology.

ISBN 0-275-96236-9

90000>

EAN

9 780275 962364

HARDCOVER BAR CODE